Social Justice and Development

Behrooz Morvaridi
Centre for International Development
University of Bradford

First published in 2008 by
PALGRAVE MACMILLAN
Houndmills, Basingstoke, Hampshire RG21 6XS and
175 Fifth Avenue, New York, N.Y. 10010
Companies and representatives throughout the world.

PALGRAVE MACMILLAN is the global academic imprint of the Palgrave
Macmillan division of St. Martin's Press, LLC and of Palgrave Macmillan Ltd.
Macmillan® is a registered trademark in the United States, United Kingdom
and other countries. Palgrave is a registered trademark in the European
Union and other countries.

ISBN-13: 978–1–4039–9239–0 hardback
ISBN-10: 1–4039–9239–8 hardback

This book is printed on paper suitable for recycling and made from fully
managed and sustained forest sources. Logging, pulping and manufacturing
processes are expected to conform to the environmental regulations of
the country of origin.

A catalogue record for this book is available from the British Library.

A catalog record for this book is available from the Library of Congress.

10 9 8 7 6 5 4 3 2 1
17 16 15 14 13 12 11 10 09 08

Printed and bound in Great Britain by
CPI Antony Rowe, Chippenham and Eastbourne

Contents

Acknowledgements

In preparation of this book I received many helpful comments both directly and indirectly. I started with the initial idea that the right to development is a means to achieve social justice and explored my ideas with colleagues and associates at various workshops, for example at the European University Institute in Florence and at the American University in Cairo. I have also been stimulated by many interesting debates with my students, in particular those who read the MA in Development Studies at Bradford University.

There are also some individuals who I need to personally thank for their helpful comments. I am particularly grateful to Shirley Parks and David Seddon for the time they dedicated to this project on my behalf and their scrupulous suggestions on each chapter, which made me critically reflect and make considerable revisions. Judy Wall was invaluable in helping me to sort out the references and ensure that the details for sources in each chapter were correct. My thanks go to others who have commented on individual chapters, including Kurt Hull, Margaret Sikwese, Jacob Azumi and Michael Pugh. I would also like to thank the editors at Palgrave and Vidhya Jayaprakash who have worked with me in the preparation of the publication. Finally I am indebted to my sons Alex and Jasper for their support and patience while I was writing this book.

1
Introduction: Social Justice and Development

The question I address in this book is whether a social justice approach to development could be achieved so long as 'hegemonic states' dominate institutions of global governance. Showing how development and social justice are intrinsically linked, this book analyses the legitimacy of power relations that perpetuate social, political and economic injustices and inequalities between nation states, groups and individuals.

Social justice has a heritage that lies in the early social scientists , who defined inequality as unjust social relations. The principle of equality that underpins social justice entails material distribution such as income and (as well as) 'the distributive paradigm' that encompasses power and domination. At the global level this means nation states and individuals are treated equally in terms of resources, opportunity and capacity. The current tendency, however, is to align social justice with development through the notion of modernity and the rise and practice of global capitalism. As such this fulfils a political function, being underpinned by two significant global shifts, the first being the rise of modern markets and secular states, and the second being the political claim to equality or rights which accompanied the development of capitalism.

The focus of this book is how the emergence of the right to development seeks to address social injustices that result in inequality and poverty, and why it struggles to succeed given that a whole host of economic and political forces contrive to undermine it. The pertinent question is why mainstream development theory and institutions of global governance continue to couch poverty reduction itself as an analytical category and a policy objective, rather than focus on inequality. This is despite the fact that ample evidence supports the

1

claim that poverty is grounded in inequalities within and between countries. According to the United Nations Development Programme (UNDP) the world's richest 500 individuals, almost all of whom are from northern countries, have a combined income greater than that of the poorest 416 million people (UNDP, 2005: 37). Extreme inequality between nation states has increased over the past four decades. Between 1960 and 1990 global per capita income trebled. However, per capita income has declined in more than 100 countries in the south since this period (Robinson, 2004: 139). Only 16 per cent of foreign investment is spent in the south or middle-income countries, while the bulk – $636 billion or 76 per cent – is spent in the north. Sub-Saharan Africa receives virtually no foreign investment. The ways in which multinational companies dominate trade in the most important primary commodities, controlling and dictating prices, are felt most acutely amongst producers in the south. Whether inequality is within a country (between groups or social classes) or between countries, the greater it is, the more dysfunctional and violent relations are likely to be. When people are unable to participate fairly in economic or social relations, they are more likely to live an undignified life of fear and hostility. Economic globalisation has not benefited all countries and patterns of uneven development are well documented. Sub-Saharan Africa and Latin America have perhaps fared the worst of all regions. What is often left unsaid, however, is how the asymmetric pattern of development testifies to the way that economic globalisation is manipulated by powerful nation states and their restrictive and protectionist strategies. Inequality is not simply, as the media and the mainstream development institutions would have us believe, a product of the incompetent management of natural resource wealth by nation states with weak and corrupt institutions of governance that make bad policy decisions. The question is not whether *globalisation* is good or bad or should be supported or not. It is whether *economic globalisation* that emanates from neo-liberal theory engenders specific difficulties for the achievement of social justice. Economic globalisation means closer capitalist integration between countries characterised by openness, trade, increased flow of goods and services, labour and capital. All states have to do, it would seem, is play by the rules of the global market and if they do not they remain isolated or are deemed to be so by default. In 'Reclaiming Development', Chang and Grabel, explore a number of 'myths' which dominate the current approach to development. In an interesting exposé of globalisation, they conclude that it is not globalisation itself that is the cause of social and economic problems experienced in the south but 'the aggressive promotion of a neo-liberal form of globalisation that is chiefly responsible for poor economic performance and the deterioration of living standards in so many countries' (2004: 25).

The salient feature of globalisation that is directly relevant to social justice imperatives is how neo-liberal economic globalisation undermines and weakens states' potential to provide the institutional and structural capacity needed for services essential for the basic needs and livelihood protection of individuals and groups. Some authors have gone so far as to suggest that state capacity has been eroded by economic globalisation (Griffin, 2003). Whatever the degree of impact, given the current situation, it is hard to see how the nation state can act as the regulatory agent or primary agent of justice and development as defined by the Universal Declaration of Human Rights 1948 and the Right to Development (1986). The claim that individuals and groups have 'rights to' development implies strong normative concerns and moral force. In other words the noun 'right' as in 'rights to' development denotes entitlements on an equal basis for both individuals, and the collective. Rights do not only benefit the rights' holders but more importantly they empower them. In view of this, 'rights' are a legitimate political demand expressed in terms of claims and entitlement that the state has a duty to deliver or protect. Protection is the social contract through which the state provides goods and services to citizens to meet basic rights' entitlements and to support livelihood survival. In essence, the state provides the institutional structure to promote social justice and to forge the links between civil and political rights and social and economic and cultural rights, with the authority for example to distribute resources as appropriate to those in need (poor, unemployed etc.). However, in practice not all nation states are capable of fulfilling their responsibility as the protector of rights or have the choice to do so and the chapters that follow explore the raft of reasons for this. Some states, for example, do not act as a vehicle for social justice, or lack the necessary human, material or organisational resources. Others comply with the pressures of neo-liberal economic liberalisation to disentangle development policy from state values, with the consequence of undermining human rights delivery.

Global justice

Cosmopolitanism: a paradigm for social justice and development?

A new paradigm for global justice is emerging from social justice scholars in response to the increasing interconnectedness of the world in which we live. Many issues of development are considered to be global concerns that cannot be handled by nation states alone because the risks of failure cross national boundaries (Pogge, 2002; Griffin, 2003; Held, 2004; Beck, 2006; Nussbaum, 2006a; O'Neil, 2005; Stiglitz, 2006).

There is also a perception that involving non-state actors such as private corporations, civil society organisations and global governance institutions in development issues will lead to more effective outcomes, through a redistribution or sharing of responsibilities. Thus 'people and their governments around the world need global institutions to solve collective problems that can only be addressed on a global scale' (Slaughter, 2004: 8). These developmental problems include, to name just a few, global poverty; climate change; conflicts, genocide, and failing states; migration; diseases without borders; access to education; debt sustainability and relief; biodiversity; management of the world's resources and trade. Scholars, who invoke a responsibility approach to human rights for global social justice, have argued for the need to reconsider the conceptualisation of the state as the deliverer and enforcer of rights.

There are several reasons why they no longer consider it to be workable. The gradual ravaging of state capacity in the south over the past 30 years or so from different directions is considered to have left states incapable of fulfilling their obligation to protect the human rights of individuals and groups. A growing proliferation of non-state actors, promoted by neo-liberal approaches to government, represents an effective shift in the balance of power between state and non-state actors in a world that is politically and economically interconnected. Changes in the form of government and the exercise of state power are taken to suggest that protection of rights and the delivery of development are no longer solely the responsibility of the state, but are effectively devolved to other non-state actors and agents, such as civil society, the private sector, and global institutions of governance.

One variant of cosmopolitanism hinges on the view that social justice and the distribution or transfer of resources to achieve development and address inequality do not necessarily have to be between the state and civil society or bilaterally from state to state, or between inter-state organisations and states. Instead there is a need to link the rich person to the poor person, and to link institutions of global governance directly to individuals regardless of the location in which they live. In other words, this approach 'involves three steps: raise money from the global rich, do not deal with governments of either rich or poor nations and transfer funds in cash to the poor' (Milanovic , 2005). For cosmopolitanism the principles of social justice are universal and apply to all human

must change Int'll Arbitral tribunal system

beings regardless of locale and cultural identity. Indeed 'the ultimate unit of moral concern is the individual, not states or other particular forms of human association' (Held, 2004: 172). The idea of shifting focus to the individual and away from the state as the unit of analysis to realise the protection of rights within the global human community is dependent upon effective global institutions, treaties and international laws. This means adopting 'universal criterion of justice' (Pogge, 2002: 34) and accepting that a plurality of agents of justice may be needed to institutionalise cosmopolitan principles of justice (O'Neil, 2006: 38). Griffin and Pogge have argued that the current form of global governance (World Bank (WB), International Monetary Fund (IMF), United Nations (UN), World Trade Organisation (WTO)) is not transparent and effective, and that radical change of these institutions is required.

However, global justice theory pays little attention to power relations that sustain inequality within and between nations. Reforming the structure of global institutions of governance, in isolation, will not be sufficient to achieve step change, unless it chips away at the disproportionate power and influence that hegemonic states and transnational corporations have over these institutions and through which they basically promote their own agenda. The increasingly complex interface between global, national and non-state organisations raises questions about organisational arrangements in terms of who is responsible for what and how power is mediated, for example 'shared', 'divided' and 'devolved'. Most importantly we need to think about why the current system operates to produce winners and losers and not net gains for all. The capacity to contest the legitimacy of actions varies in relation to the relative power of the different actors. The most powerful however can and do seek to enforce a different outcome when the prevailing view is not to their liking.

One of the main arguments of this book is that powerful states dominate global trade in such a way that they encumber the south from achieving the Right to Development. A prime route for the United States and the main European countries' influence is through global governance institutions, which concentrates power in their hands. It is worth referring to the widely used examples of the President of the World Bank, who has been from the United States since its inception and the President of the IMF who is always either American or European. To date none of the poorer countries of Africa or Asia has been represented in the presidency of either institution, irrespective of qualifications or background. Similar asymmetries within the Security Council of the United Nations give the most powerful nations – the United States of America, China, France,

Russia and Britain – domination over crucial decisions as permanent members of the Council. Despite recurrent protests, the fundamental inequality of this governing structure is unlikely to change. Essentially the current global order demonstrates that nation states are not equals.

I do not necessarily reject the proposition that the whole notion of obligation and responsibility needs to be rethought, given that the range of actors involved in development means that it is no longer clear who the agents of justice are and who therefore has effective responsibility to protect the rights of the individual and groups, and, perhaps most importantly, who represents the poor. However, the global justice theory glosses over the fundamental question of how non-state actors such as private corporations, civil society organisations and global governance institutions (World Bank, IMF, WTO etc.) could fill the human rights responsibility gap, when they do not fit within a robust accountability framework. More importantly, like neo-liberalism the focus on individual human beings tends to ignore groups and collective rights and how human rights norms can relate to specific locales and cultures, and community and social relationships. The capability of non-state actors is itself problematic, and many have neither the capacity nor the political will to protect the rights of individuals and groups. Moreover they are not recognised as duty bearers in treaties, such as Human Rights Declaration and the Right to Development Declaration, or international human rights laws. In fact non-state actors are beyond the direct reach of international human rights law and are only bound to Human Rights treaties 'to the extent that obligations accepted by States can be applied to them by governments' (Alston, 2006: 2). In social justice theory, the contract is between the individual and the state. This is enshrined in Human Right treaties and laws, which consider the state to be the primary agent of justice and development with the responsibility to regulate, deliver and enforce rights for the dignity of human beings. The challenge is how this is achieved when there is such a complex matrix of interests.

Poverty, inequality and human rights

A plethora of data points to confirmation that access to basic human rights, such as an adequate standard of living, good health and access to basic needs including food and clothing, is not uniform and in some parts of the world has worsened in the last three decades. For example, current indicators primarily from countries in the south show that 1.2 billion people do not have access to safe water and sanitation.

Approximately two million children die from water borne diseases and 1.8 million die from diarrhoea each year caused by bad sanitation and inadequate access to safe drinking water. The UNDP calls for access to water to be recognised as a human right by governments around the world (UNDP, 2006a). In Sub-Saharan Africa 66 per cent of the population are very poor. Eighteen per cent of children die before their fifth birthday, compared with only 0.6 per cent of children within the Organisation for Economic Development and Cooperation (OECD). This is despite the fact that recent indicators show improvements in GDP in the region due to demand for primary commodities from emerging economies such as China and India. We live in a world with a 100-fold difference in child mortality and a 100-fold difference in income between nations and regions. Gender inequality in some countries has deteriorated in recent years and no country in the south has been able to reduce gender inequality in wealth, employment, mortality rate, political participation. The richest 20 nations have 74 per cent of the world's income and the richest 1 per cent of adults (99 per cent men) in the world own 40 per cent of the earth's wealth; more than a third of whom live in the United States (UNDP, 2003, 2005).

These social and economic rights or positive rights and inequality indicators are compounded by civil and political indicators of rights abuses (or negative rights) and give us a clear representation of the world in which we live. Empirical evidence suggests that some civil and political rights violations are increasing, and these include torture, ethnic conflict, human trafficking, and abuses against refugees' and asylum seekers' rights. The people who are abused have no access to legal means to challenge the unfairness of the system. More than three billion human beings do not have any access to judicial means for protection of their rights, nor do they even have a claim to protection. Simply put, if you cannot afford legal representation you are more likely to be treated unfairly. In a similar vein southern nation states are at a distinct disadvantage when fighting challenges to intellectual property rights, such as claims related to bio-piracy or attempts to get compulsory licenses for lifesaving medicines, because they cannot afford to employ the same large teams of highly trained and expensive attorneys as the rich nations and large transnational corporations (Stiglitz, 2006: 128). The World Bank has reported that there are now $1.8 billion of lawsuits against poor countries in the south for non-payment of debts. A number of big law firms in London, New York and Paris are representing 'Vulture Funds' that have bought up poor nations' sovereign debt at a fraction or knock down prices, and are seeking payment. For example the Zambian government had to face the high court in London and pay $15.5 million to private creditors. A US company, Donegal International, took the government of Zambia, one of the poorest countries in the world with a per capita income of $500 per annum, to court in London for debts with a face value of $29.8 million that they purchased for less than $4 million from the Romanian government in 1999. Eleven out of 24 highly indebted countries have paid up to $1 billion in similar situations, including Nicaragua, Cameroon and Ethiopia (World Bank, 2007).

Inequality of this kind has a negative impact on a country one way or another. It induces lower potential growth and uneven development, but more importantly encourages the continuation of extreme poverty, that in itself violates the rights of individuals and groups. Such inequality has been a powerful barrier to integration into the globalisation process. There is a negative correlation between inequality and growth and plenty of evidence can be drawn upon to show how inequality is harmful to growth. Even some neo-liberal economists admit that the current level of inequality is destructive (Birdsall, 2005). Effectively, as poverty and inequality grows in a country, the damage to society as a whole is greater. In some countries inequality reduces life expectancy of the poorest by as much as 25 per cent – a recent report from Zimbabwe, for example, indicated that life expectancy for women is as low as 35 years, and 1.3 million children were orphaned by 2003; 75 per cent due to Aids. The average life expectancy at birth for nine African countries such as Kenya, Malawi, Mozambique, South Africa, Botswana, Zambia, Namibia, Rwanda, by 2015 is estimated to be only 47 years (UNDP, 2006b). The effects are wide-reaching as low status and lack of control over one's life destroys human health, well-being and happiness and national confidence. The empirical evidence has invoked normative and political questions about levels of inequality and poverty. Proponents of human rights challenge the extent of poverty and inequality globally through a moral and ethical critique of the nature of market fundamentalism. Some have even suggested classifying extreme poverty as a violation of human rights (Pogge, 2002; Campbell, 2006). A good starting point is to ask why it seems necessary and legitimate to fit the idea of human rights and social justice into the lexicon of development discourse and practice. Before I embark on this question we must first look at what we mean by development.

What is development?

A working definition of development is the progressive improvement in the social, economic well-being of people so that they live longer, healthier and fuller lives within any given political entity. According to Chambers 'the eternal challenge of development is to do better' because 'the underlying meaning of development has been good change' (2005: 185). But does good change necessarily bring about 'a good society'? A good society has a long pedigree, but what actually constitutes a good society? These normative questions have permeated the development discourse in order to 'emancipate development' from the 'engineering tradition' and a narrow focus on economic growth that has ignored social justice for so long. Thus development is about our views and values of what a good society is; in other words development is analogous with Sayers conception of capitalism in that it is 'structured by moral-economic norms about rights, entitlements, responsibilities and appropriate behaviour ... what is of value, how to live, what is worth striving for and what is not.' (2004: 2–3). Development in this conception classifies good change as that which makes society more equal, based on a fairer income distribution, gender equality, and equality of individual opportunity to access services such as education and health. Development also means equality of opportunity for nation states within the global economy and polity. In short development requires the removal of major sources of suppression and inequality: poverty, tyranny, lack of economic opportunities, systematic social deprivation, neglect of public facilities, and intolerance or over-activity of repressive states. Not everyone, however, agrees with this conception of development.

The meaning of development has changed over time in response to changing circumstances within the economy, ideology and politics. In fact the whole idea of development and human rights emerged during the Enlightenment period in Europe as a means to improve, or manage the chaos and pandemonium induced by modernity or industrial capitalism. One implication of this understanding is that 'the modern idea of development is necessarily Eurocentric, because it was in Europe that development was first meant to create order out of the social disorder of rapid urbanization, poverty and unemployment' engineered by modernity and capitalist development (Cowen and Shenton, 1996: 5). The Enlightenment thinkers collectively believed in a rejection of tradition and religious teleology and a commitment to free inquiry, rationality, reason, power of knowledge and scientific innovation to engender progress from tradition to modernity and in so doing to bring about, an improvement in the well-being of the human living condition. It is important to point out that the concept of universal values, morality and freedom, are the driving force behind these ideas. Right from its foundation the development agenda, advocated by Adam Smith, John Stuart Mill, Karl Marx, Comets, Weber and others, was motivated by the need to improve human life for human dignity.

To sum up, first the meaning of development itself has always been contentious, mediated as it is by political, ideological and time-specific influences. Second, any definition involves values and judgments, which is why there is no one single fixed definition of development. Theorising about development is an open-ended process that evolves from any number of starting points. There is no one idea or theory of development, which means, therefore, that there is also more than one practice. I have therefore been sceptical to give a firm definition of development. As Thomas points out it is 'impossible to avoid the contradictions behind the idea of development by laying down a single, simple definition of one's own' (2000: 2). The current dominant idea of development is more concerned with policy and development as practice rather than theory or an explanatory framework (Pieterse, 2001).

Third, the core concepts in development are defined in particular contexts but are continuously undergoing historical redefinition, and, in the words of E.P. Thompson their structure is not pre-given but is protean, continually changing in form and articulation (1978: 83). Thus development is contextually defined. Some terms and concepts that were once mainstream are no longer widely used in the development discourse (see Diagram 1.1) – for instance how valid is the concept of the Third World given globalisation and changes in the division of labour? The 'Third World' is terminology that was widely employed during the Cold War to explain the division of labour in the world; it is still employed by those who strongly believe that it is a generic term for 'poverty', or nation states that are marginal and excluded from the global economy. But it no longer describes a geo-political division around which aid programmes and policy interventions are constructed. Other concepts and ideas such as social justice and human rights have been excluded from the lexicon of development theory and practice right until recently.

The 'early' development models

The idea of development descended on the 'new nations' more or less at the time of the United Nations Declaration of Human Rights 1948. However, no obvious links were made between social justice and development. From the 1950s to the early 1980s, development theory and policy 'models' were driven by the social sciences' epistemological and ontological commitment to the objectives of the natural sciences.[1] Social justice and human rights were, therefore, devoid of meaning in

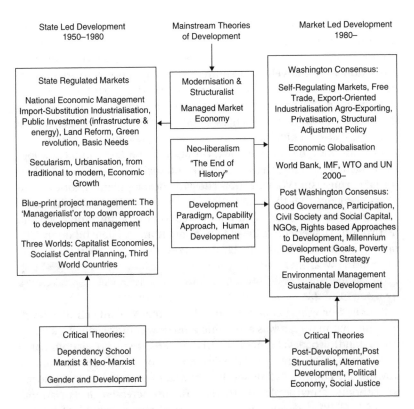

Diagram 1.1   The Development Discourse

the prevailing theory and policy of development. Mainstream development theory and policy claimed to be value-neutral, and did not set out to reflect normative principles that linked social facts and values. As such, few engaged in the hermeneutic tradition. Suggesting a clear dichotomy between objectivism and subjectivism, the core concern of analysis within development theory was economic growth and capital accumulation, or rather the lack of it. Within this paradigm, countries in the south were only considered to require the right conditions to move from a traditional economy towards modernity or from a state of 'underdevelopment' or poverty to that of developed.[2] Theories failed to take into account the specific social and economic characteristics of each nation and that most countries in the south lacked the necessary structural and institutional conditions to generate higher amounts of output.[3] The Harrod–Domar Model of modernisation was dominant among economists and policy-makers who maintained that capital accumulation in the south relied *only* on the right economic conditions or sufficient investment. In fact the early mainstream development theorists, such as Rostow, clearly believed that industrialisation or modernisation were the vehicles required to lift the poor countries out of poverty and to increase the living standards.[4] Reflecting this perspective, states were encouraged to invest in infrastructure that would facilitate faster economic growth, such as dams, roads and power generation projects. The evident failure of this strategy is probably the main reason industrialisation has shifted down the agenda of international development agencies, such as the World Bank and socialist states, despite their initial enthusiasm (Wade, 2002). The early development theories failed to acknowledge that the poor nations lacked not only the physical capital but also the human capital, and Weberian type bureaucracies and institutions that effective development programmes depend upon. The ratio of capital to labour was significantly different in poorer countries than in the wealthier nations. The new nation states also had little bargaining power over the international economy to attract necessary investment.

It took some years before the narrow view that the only kind of development that mattered was economic growth was replaced with a wider understanding of development. Until the 1980s, theories that dominated development policy reflected the vision that poor countries were simply low-income countries. This resulted in according some sort of priority to economic growth, placing the benefits of increased Gross National Product (GNP) per capita to wider 'society' above individual human needs. Essentially the running of economies excluded values and moral questions and paid little attention to the human agent as a purposeful and reasoning actor in the development process (Toye, 1987). The upshot was a form of development theory and practice that ignored normative issues relating to human rights, culture and the underlying causes of inequality and poverty, and in so doing perpetuated the continued marginalisation and exclusion of the most vulnerable. In fact development was habitually understood to be in conflict with social justice.

What is clear is the significant influence of Marx's ideas and liberalism of one sort or another in development theory and policy. While Marx promotes collective rights, liberalism reflects a commitment to individual rights, autonomy, equality, liberty, freedom; that is to say the idea that human beings are fundamentally equal and that individuals should be treated equally. We must not forget that equality for all is at the heart of any liberal political vision and the social justice discourse. However, liberalism is a contested concept.[5] The core issue of property rights provides a paradigm for variant liberal interpretations. Between 1945 and 1980, welfare liberalism dominated mainstream development theory and practice, securing a prominent role for the state in promoting development to stimulate growth. The more recent mainstream variation of liberalism, 'neo-liberalism', is less at ease with a liberal social justice and human rights perspective. For neo-liberalists, such as Hayek, social justice within a market economy is possible only so long as rights are institutionalised in particular around property rights and 'liberal trade' or a free market – 'the most important means for promoting freedom and individual welfare' (Hayek, 1976: 35). I shall return to this in Chapter 3.

In the 1980s, this dominant theory and paradigm came under considerable challenge. This was at a time when, on the geo-political stage, the collapse of state socialist economies was rampant with political and social crisis. Liberal economic ideas flourished once communism and socialism, the alternative paths of development that provided inspiration to radical forces in the Third World, lost credibility. The impact was a fundamental shift away from a bipolar system under the Cold War in terms of political and economic organisation and towards a more integrated one. The world arguably transformed through the 1970s and 1980s, with the differentiation of the so-called Third World, state socialism and state led developmentalism, replaced with new relations between capitalist powers, a new global structure and the new global context of development.

The abandonment of the Cold War and the *de facto* consolidation of the power of capitalism engendered the idea of an 'impasse' in development theory (Booth, 1985; Schuurman, 1993) or what Fukuyama, in outlining the new era of neo-liberalism and neo-conservatism, termed the 'end of history' thesis (Fukuyama, 1992). Increasing levels of poverty and a growing gap between the rich and the poor in terms of exclusion and inequality measured the onsetting crisis in the 'Third World'. There also seemed to be a widening gulf between development theory and development policy and practice (Booth, 1985). This shift has certainly had implications for our thinking about development issues within increasingly integrated global capitalism. Until the early 1980s, variant grand theories of Marxist persuasions offered explanatory concepts that challenged existing ideologies within a solid theoretical framework. However, the collapse of socialist models and the emergence of the East Asian model of the developmental state, left a gap in the explanation of social change that alternative theories of development, like dependency theory and structuralism, could not fill. Further fragmented attempts to fill the theoretical gap are denoted by the emergence of theories prefixed with 'post'-post modernism, post-development, and so forth, explicitly rejecting the rationalist tradition of the Enlightenment (Escobar, 1995; McMichael, 2000) and advocating enthusiastically the pursuance of alternatives to development rather than development alternatives (Watts, 1995: 44).

The normative questions

Attempts to integrate a normative approach into development theory and policy emerged from several different camps. These included variant liberals and proponents of some Marxist critical theories, what has come to be known as the 'advocacy group' and a group of Asian States proposing development led by 'Asian Values'. An identified urgent need for normative reflection in development theory was in reaction to the neo-liberal unregulated market of the 1980s and increases in poverty and inequality associated with economic globalisation (see Chapter 4). Moving away from a neutral stance, a normative approach involves judgments drawn on values and ethics on issues such as distribution, inequality, poverty and identity and it is, therefore, 'socially situated'. In questioning the traditional approach to development, focused on economic growth as the end-goal in itself, Sen (1999) made significant steps in shifting the ontological underpinning of development theory towards a normative commitment. He clearly articulated that development is about advancing human well-being and human freedom, and that increased income by itself cannot achieve these objectives; being only one contributing factor to poverty reduction.

There is always a need to question what occurs in a society and why, and to analyse who is responsible and accountable; in essence who determines who benefits and who does not (Young, 1990). Social movements that challenge hegemonic ideas and inequalities and the social relations that perpetuate them espouse normative principles. Feminists, for example, have argued that women's marginalisation and oppression requires a critical explanation, because without it, social theory is likely to reaffirm the given social reality. This is an interesting example given that women's needs still tend to be excluded from the human rights and development discourse. The critical issue here is that the Universal Declaration on Human Rights 1948, and subsequent declarations and treaties and human rights law (with the exception of the Declaration on the Right to Development 1986), give prominence to individual rights and not to group or collective rights, while ascribing to the liberal principle of equality and universality. Young argues that the main problem with this approach is that not all individuals are treated equally without bias or discrimination, because of underlying causes of oppression in a society. She identifies women as a distinctive social group that suffers systematic forms of injustice and argues convincingly for social justice to conceptualise group identity and associated rights as well as individual ones. Otherwise we risk a narrow conception of justice that has as its central goal the self-development of one's human capacities. Defining racial and gender justice in terms of the distribution of privileged positions among individuals, according to Young, fails to question decision-making power and structural power within institutional organisations and fails to acknowledge different causes of oppression, such as status, hierarchy, domination, exploitation, and cultural imperialism (Young, 1990: 193). Such unequal social relations generate, and are often thought to justify inequalities, in the distribution of freedoms, resources, and welfare. The challenge is how to empower both individuals and groups to articulate their rights, whether specific groups such as women, nations or nation states.

It is from the root of such normative criticism and group experiences of suffering and wretchedness, and consequent struggles to defend or realise dignity, that the concept of the Right to Development has emerged. It is not simply derived from abstract 'a priori moral principles'. In Chapter 2 the theoretical underpinning of the Right to Development is discussed – how it originated from these normative ideas and dependency theory, and moved towards arguments for the equality of people and nation states within the World System. The proponents of dependency theory discerned national independence that was both economic and political as the pre-requisite for development. The periphery, or the south, has been marginalised since the colonial period because of the perpetuation of unequal relations with the core or the north, based on unequal exchanges of commodities. Buoyant proponents of this school of thought have suggested that if the exploitative links between the core and the periphery, which are the catalyst of inequality, were eradicated it would be possible for poor countries to accumulate capital and develop. This would require the breaking of chains of unequal exchange, or 'delinking' states from the system (Wallerstein, 1976; Amin 1985). This is in effect what the Right to Development has the potential to achieve by challenging the unjust international division of labour which favours the countries of the centre to the disadvantage of those in the periphery, giving rise to a sense of an unjust international economic order (Marks, 2003: 2). These grand theories of dependency and neo-Marxism, have been identified with essentialism, structuralism and universalism (see Schuurman, 1993 and Leys, 1996). They have been criticised for ignoring key agendas including gender relations and gender inequality, environmental issues, culture, human rights and ethnicity. Although such critical reflections have validity, and may explain an 'impasse' in development theory that has not been overcome so far, there is a view that despite their shortcomings structuralist and dependency theories have contemporary relevance and that criticism is often misplaced, based on inadequate knowledge of theory (Robert and Kay, 1999: 4). The question of inequality between nation states was as relevant during the colonial period as it is now, but the form of relationships has changed.

The Declaration on the Right to Development adopted by the United Nations in 1986 was the result of many years of international campaigns centred on addressing inequalities between states and promoting the social, economic and political rights of the self governing state. The universal human rights agenda advocates the equal value of all rights and it is within this context that the Right to Development is framed. The demand for equal consideration of civil, political, economic, social and cultural rights is embodied in calls for both individual and collective rights, including the right of states to self-determination. This synthesis of rights implies that violation of one right equates to violation of the composite Right to Development. Similarly improvement in any one suggests moving closer to achieving the rest (Sengupta, 2002). The central contentious issue is the divergence between 'Western Values' and views of human rights as individual rights, with emphasis on civil and political rights, as opposed to the idea of collective rights and the right for self-determination that many countries campaign for. These include equal rights in trade and investment and the assistance of the richer nations to lift poor nations out of poverty while protecting democracy and cultural values.[6] It should come as no surprise therefore that tensions are inevitably created when, as evidence of both historical and current practice shows, civil and political rights are recurrently separated out from social and economic rights. A common genesis of such tension between the more powerful states and the south in recent years has been the tendency for the hegemonic states to promote civil and political rights over other rights.

Chapter 2 explores these contrasting perspectives. On the one hand, there has been vociferous opposition from hegemonic states to the Right to Development, and their prioritisation of civil and political rights. On the other, the ideas associated with Asian values and norms or Islam have been voiced by states to advocate social, economic and cultural rights and invoke a thesis of relativism, maintaining that their societies are fundamentally different in their social relations, traditions and values. Inevitably some states have integrated this argument into a political agenda that justifies undemocratic institutions and human rights abuses or to consolidate internal power structures. What is perhaps startling, however, is that Asian and Islamic states have felt the need to remind the rest of the world that the basis of their communities is different and that their cultural values are an important part of social relations. In some places they take precedence over the individual, which constitutes a fundamental difference from the Western notion of human rights that focuses on individual agency. Asian and Islamic values are not representative of ruling powers, although this is often misrepresented by the media for political purposes. As part of a mystification and representation of orient, Islam and democracy and human rights are often portrayed, in the words of Edward Said by the idea of a 'modern orient', which is incompatible with Muslim societies. It is not only the West however that seeks to cloud this relationship, as some Muslims reject the ideas of democracy and human rights as a Western construct that endorses Western cultural domination. As such they are 'incompatible' with God's sovereignty that requires moral codes, obligations and duties. Bayat argues elegantly that a new social movement, Post Islamism, has emerged to bring social justice and Islam together, maintaining the umma or community of Islam is inherently democratic because its values are based on 'pluralism, justice and human rights' (2007: 4). The concept of Post-Islamism accepts that there is a need to break down the idea of religious truth as acknowledgement of secular exigencies, and the need for freedom from rigidity. To some extent the recent struggle for social justice by post-Islamist social movements is an attempt to marry individual choice and freedom with democracy and modernity, and reinforces the idea and aspiration for an 'alternative modernity'.

interesting

Development without human rights

In retrospect we find that different models have been used to achieve development. And as we would expect, this has been noted by countries in the south, who object to the idea that there is only one perceived model for development – the neo-liberalist one. It is paradoxical that the north pursued a development model in the early period of its modernisation that violated both the rights of individuals and other countries (consider for example colonisation, and the use of slaves). During the period of initial industrialisation in Western European countries for

north – history of inequality (some of which continues today)

example, there were few laws to protect women workers and children, child labour was prevalent, workers had little security and there was no social protection or welfare system. Access to health facilities and education was also limited to those who could afford to pay. E.P. Thompson explains how the violation of civil and political rights was an historical reality: 'When Paine was driven into exile and his Right of Man banned as seditious libel, this was, in part, a matter of expediency. Paine's prosecution revealed limits of freedom permitted within the convention of constitutionalism. To deny altogether the appeal to our ancestors was actively dangerous' (1968: 95). We cannot forget that only in the first half of the twentieth century, after years of struggle for universal suffrage, were women granted equal citizenship rights. Basic rights inequalities between men and women continue today with women's wages on average lower than those of men in some of rich countries (the United States of America and the United Kingdom). More importantly the development model and policies that were adopted in the north to feed economic growth, were very different to those that International Financial Institutions such as the IMF and the World Bank impose on countries in the south today through conditionality. Chang (2002: 132) presents data that goes back 150 years which shows how the north, in particular the United States and the United Kingdom, promoted high protectionist measures and were highly interventionist. These are precisely, the polices that International Financial Institutions (IFIs), (as I discuss in Chapter 3) under the influence of powerful nations (Washington Censuses) over the past three decades, have prohibited the south from adopting on the grounds that they would impact negatively on their economic and social development.

Paradoxically, some Asian countries since the 1980s, in particular the newly industrialised countries of Singapore, South Korea, Malaysia, Taiwan, Hong Kong and more recently China, have experienced rapid economic growth and development, without following the World Bank and IMF development agenda or UN mantra on Human Rights. When economic development was criticised for being at the expense of civil and political rights, these states argued that it was because their social and economic stability was founded on Asian values, culture and traditions that emphasised community and duty rather than individualism. Within this context the Universal Rights agenda is branded as the 'cultural imperialism' of the West (for detail see Chapter 2). China has been relatively successful in terms of economic development and economic growth but the government continues to control major industries and owns most of the industrial assets. The implementation of any market

Question "Individualism" in U.S. as
Justification of corporate corruption

reform would have to support 'nation state interests' (Saul, 2005).
China's White Paper clearly specifies that

> on the international stage they (US and other western countries) take
> human rights as a means to compel developing countries to submit
> and a means to pursue hegemony and power politics, encouraging
> political confrontations in the human rights field. In view of this
> abnormal phenomenon in the international human rights field,
> China upholds principle and makes unremitting efforts to promote
> human rights, safeguard sovereignty and oppose hegemony, together
> with vast numbers of developing countries.

A clear case is made that the historical background, social relations,
culture and economic development of countries can mean that their
understanding and practice of human rights differs (People's Republic
of China to the United Nations, 1995).

We have to question whether for example, the Asian values thesis is ✗
in fact genuine or is used to justify authoritarianism and repressive
regimes. It may be that social and political struggles for rights in Asian
countries will ultimately define what 'Asian values' are (Cox, 2002: 62).
However it is important to point out that what some states fail to understand is that the demand for social justice, rights, the equality of opportunity to access basic resources and fairer distribution of goods were not
driven by Western states but arose out of social movements and principles that opposed states' actions.

Social justice for development – a turning point

The 1990s proved to be a turning point in development with the collapse
of central planning, the abandonment of the socialist model and the
dominance of a 'one world' vision of capitalist development. The reality of
uneven globalisation hit home as capitalist development on a world scale
took another leap forward under the political hegemony of the United
States. In response mainstream development theory and practice endorsed
a rights-based approach and a new agenda of poverty reduction strategy.
Sen's Capability Approach and Stiglitz' Post-Washington Consensus were
crucial in bringing forward considerably different but nevertheless new
perspectives. Sen and Stiglitz, both Nobel Laureates, were critical of orthodox neo-liberal scholars whose policies relied heavily on market forces,
deregulation and privatisation to achieve development in the south.
Stiglitz (2006) broadened the policy approach in Washington by drawing

attention to the inadequacies of the Washington Consensus, as elucidated in Chapter 3. By combining tools from economics and philosophy Sen restored normative and ethical dimensions to the discussion of vital development problems. Here, it suffices to say, that he articulates a vision of development that commits to the freedom, well-being and dignity of individuals; income being one of the factors that contributes to welfare and freedom, but not the only factor (Sen, 2004).

According to Sen, utilitarian analyses are limited, because in focusing on income they ignore 'non-labour resources' and other diversities, such as productive abilities or individual needs, which can also result in inequality (1992: 120). Social justice and human rights are, in the end, grounded in the importance of freedom (UNDP, 2000: 20). Thus, the denial of the opportunity to engage or participate fully in the social and economic life of a society represents individual failed capability, sufficient to establish the injustice of their situation and the society they live in. Development is now defined as 'equality of opportunity' for individuals to 'choose a life one has reason to value' (Sen, 1999: 74) Freedom, too, is often constrained by poverty. Sen's ideas have been influential in development thinking and policy, and have contributed to the shift from a public policy focus on poverty reduction at a local level to the universally adopted Millennium Development Declaration and Goals, and the concept of Human Development. The UN Vienna Declaration on Human Rights 1993 identified extreme poverty as being the rejection of human rights and UNDP Human Development Report (2000) to which Sen was a major contributor, maintains that human rights are grounded in the importance of freedom for a life of dignity (UNDP, 2000: 2). For Sen the idea of positive freedom necessitates the absence of coercion, and individual capability. Poverty is seen in terms of a short fall of 'basic capabilities' involving the inability to achieve certain minimally adequate levels of crucially important function such as being nourished or being sheltered. Thus the objective of development is to enlarge people's choices and to build enabling environment for people to live long healthy lives. Having said that Sen and other social justice theories have, to some extent, idealised what constitutes 'a good society' based on a welfare-oriented social democracy, while at the same time penetrating the 'sin of being insufficiently distributionist'.

The idea of addressing poverty and establishing equality is widely endorsed in global institutions and contemporary societies and is commonly referred to in legislation and constitutions, as well as in international documents such as the Universal Declaration of Human Rights, and the Declaration of the Right to Development. Recently the

World Bank's annual Development Report (2006) focused on 'equity and development' (see Chapter 5 for a detailed discussion), retreating from 'pro-poor growth' and replacing it with the concept of 'inclusive growth'. The concept of inclusive growth encompasses equality of opportunity that promotes sustainable economic growth, good governance and social development aligned with appropriate proposals for social expenditure. The policy thrust is that through a combination approach poverty could be reduced. Whether the World Bank is truly committed to the distributive justice or not is something to be seen, but Stiglitz reminds us that: 'The IMF...is like the Chinese Red Army – a tightly disciplined, regimented organisation where deviation from the orthodox ideology is not tolerated. The World Bank, on the other hand, is more like a university faculty...like a debating society' (Joseph Stiglitz, 2002).

The apparent consensus on the way forward obscures the fact that there are several interpretations or conceptions of equality, despite it being pivotal to social justice as a principle of rights. Miller suggests that there are two different kinds of equality – one is independent of the 'ideal' society and is socialist or Marxist, and relates to equality of status or social equality. From this perspective, injustice appears in the form of class-like inequalities, rooted in the economic structure of society. Injustice in this conception 'broadly encompasses income inequality, exploitation, deprivation, and marginalisation or exclusion from the labour market' (Miller, 1999: 230–234). The other kind of equality is subsumed under justice and sits within a distributive justice framework that promotes equal concern and respect and equality of opportunity. The Marxist class theory and analysis of income and asset distribution is in fact more or less anomalous with public policy, whereas the social justice conception of equality of opportunity has now become integral to public policy for some governments and international development institutions. It is this, in fact, that veers towards universal adoption of poverty reduction strategy. The World Bank (2006: 12) report remarks on the divergent positions of the 'equality of opportunities' as proposed by neo-liberals (and the Bank) and the 'equality of outcomes' as proposed by Marxists, maintaining the view that there is in fact trade-off between justice and economic efficiency in a sense that 'The pursuit of overall well-being requires some balance between the competing goals of equality and economic efficiency, as well as other individual freedoms and rights' (2006: 12).

To reiterate the question that I asked earlier, why is mainstream development about poverty reduction and not inequality? And why is $1-a-day used to define the global poverty line? Ann Krueger Vice President of the IMF provides some form of justification worthy of exploring further: 'Poor people are desperate to improve their material conditions in absolute terms rather than to march up the income distribution. Hence, it seems better to focus on impoverishment than on inequality' (2006: 14). Concentrating on inequality requires redistribution. This is obviously not in the interests of the rich nor necessarily the IMF or World Bank, all of which have a commitment to privatisation and market liberalisation policy and advocating less government and more governance. This seems to be in accordance with Cammack's (2004) argument that what the World Bank and other IFIs mean by poverty alleviation is the creation of a global proletarian army (a reserve pool of labour) who live just above subsistence ($1-a-day) and are as such amenable to exploitation from capitalist market forces. The focus is clearly not on getting people to have a wholesome livelihood but on allowing them to survive because extreme global poverty reflects badly on the institutions in question. However, without exploitation capitalism cannot exist as such there must remain those willing to accept unfair market terms.

A way of making the point more relevant to our discussion is embedded in neo-liberal thinking and the principle of private property rights or equal rights to the ownership of property, which is the crux of capitalism (see Chapter 4). That said, in 'practice the principle of the equal right to property does not translate into equal ownership of property' (Haugaard, 2002: 310). Basically the rich are content to be concerned with poverty so long as it sidetracks attention away from their own assets and income. In the words of Milanovic (2005: 5), concern with 'poverty is like as anesthetic to the bad conscience of the many'. As Friedman, one of the 'neo-liberal ideologues' and architects of free market ideals, puts it: 'The egalitarian...will defend taking from some to give to others, not as a more effective means, whereby the "some" can achieve an objective they want to achieve, but on grounds of "justice". At this point, equality comes sharply into conflict with freedom' (Friedman, 1962: 195).

Freedom by implication necessitates a role for other non-state actors as a check and balance on the power of the government. The suggestion is that only through private enterprise operating in a free market it is possible to establish 'a system of economic freedom and a necessary condition for political freedom' (Ibid.: 4). From this point of view freedom is not about distribution or welfare but it is about individual choice facilitated by a capitalist free market economy that gives individuals opportunity to work hard to earn income in order to improve their living standard and participate fully in social and political life. Individual agency is equal – so people are poor or face deprivation, they are 'free' to work hard and long hours to lift themselves out of poverty. This rational choice approach underpins neo-liberalism and therefore the dominant mainstream development theory and practice pursued closely by global institutions. In a nutshell neo-liberalism means less government and more liberalisation of the market through privatisation and trade and expropriation of the individual theme of liberalism (see Chapter 3 for a more detailed discussion). In this conception the unit of analysis is an individual who is a rational actor that can interact in the market for self-interest and utility maximisation. Collective action and community are displaced with the notion of individual agency, placing responsibility for poverty on the individuals who experience it. According to Laderchi et al., 'for economists, the appeal of the monetary approach [and there-fore its success] lies in its being compatible with the utility maximizing behaviour assumption that underpins microeconomics (Laderchi et al., 2003: 247). Thus socioeconomic inequalities are not in any way respon-sible for poverty and addressing them will not alleviate poverty. Instead, the correct approach is to allow the poor to learn to spend what little income they have '*wisely*' and become immersed in the market (particu-larly the labour market) as this is their route to higher incomes and sus-tainable livelihoods. The apparent solution to poverty is therefore economic growth. In capitalism the main aspiration is to eradicate or reduce poverty, not to address inequality, because in capitalism whether we like it or not inequality is inevitable. Bernstein (2006) argues that this commitment to 'win-win' policy solutions demonstrates that economic growth and poverty are considered the continuing problems. A steady depoliticisation of development has shifted emphasis onto individual agency within the market, dispossessing community or collective action. Ferguson (1990: quoted in Bernstein, 2006) captures this well in his analysis of main stream development as an 'anti-politics machine', which minimises any attempt to understand the sources, dynamics and effects of extreme social inequality in the south, and power relations within the international economic and political system.

The moral imperative of eliminating conspicuous poverty has become the key tenet of mainstream development theory and practice in the twenty-first century. The contemporary focus on poverty reduc-tion strategy and the core objective of the Millennium Development Goal to halve poverty by 2015, revolves around facilitating access to the resources that the poor do not have 'and gaps in service delivery rather than the unequal social relations that mediate the allocation of resources and the delivery of services' (Greig, Hulme and Turner, 2007). This can also explain the phenomenal growth of microfinance in recent years, as part of a strategy commodifying or 'marketising' the poor. This strategy includes so-called labour-intensive growth and microfinance as central planks. Under the mantra of microfinance policy-makers and development practitioners can legitimately place the responsibility for poverty eradication on poor individuals. Provide the poor with loans and they should be able to work their way out of poverty and there is no need to address the structural problems in society. The responsibility for redressing the massive loss of jobs that results from continual economic restructuring occasioned by neo-liberal policies is placed on the poor.

The complexities and problems associated with micro-loans are not explored (Hanak, 2000). High repayment rates are taken as evidence of success, although Hanak and others point to numerous problems in this conceptualisation. These include peer pressure to sacrifice feeding family to repay loans and self-exploitation and the use of unpaid labour of family members. Perhaps the most important problem with microfinance as packaged is the fact that it excludes the poorest from access to its resources as they are universally adjudged to be unable to pay. Another major effect of the dollar a day imperative must be considered. If the aim is to reduce the number of people living on less than $1-a-day (as poverty is frequently defined) and the commodification or 'marketisation' policies of the IFIs are neglecting the poorest, then the result is a shift from focus on the 'deserving poor' to the equally detrimental category of 'easy to assist poor' (Hulme and Shepherd, 2003: 404) or the 'entrepreneurial poor' as noted in the Voices of the Poor publication of the World Bank (Narayan et al., 1999). Those that the market cannot assist are left behind or as a very last resort with only minimal safety nets put in place to ensure they 'survive'.

The current approach defines poverty as a 'state' of being, and in absolute terms one of deprivation of basic materials needed to support a minimally acceptable way of life. So it is that unacceptable levels of diet, accommodation, and health translate into malnutrition, homelessness, ill health and premature death. The literature on poverty is vast. Lister in *Poverty* (2004) provides a robust examination of different conceptions of poverty. Her concern with poverty in the north, leads her to see poverty in 'relative terms, as having insufficient resources to meet socially recognised needs and to participate in the wider society' (Lister, 2004: 4). Poverty reduction has to be about addressing the individual's need. Poverty reduction strategies are however only able to capture what appear to be characteristics of poverty universally rather than the social relations that produce it. This explains why studies of 'poverty' across different geographical and economic areas reveal virtually identical clusters of associated phenomena in relation to characteristics of the 'poor' and the households so classified, ranging from poor health, malnutrition, shortages of cash and food to the inevitable figures on dependency ratios, educational levels, and literacy (Green and Hulme, 2005: 874).

Inequality, on the other hand, is clearly about social relations or relationships between those that have and those that have not – between rich and poor, between different classes and between men and women. When poverty exists it is because individuals and groups are drawn into unequal relations with others who are more powerful or have a more privileged position through which they have advantage. Analyses of conflicting positions challenge the major institutions to consider distribution. In critical social justice theory the real analytical issue is inequality, which is structural in origin and relates closely to unequal power relations. Inequality leaves individuals, groups and nation states with no control over the major decisions that affect their lives. Structure and agency here are conceptualised as mutually inclusive. Fraser reminds us that, it is important to bear in mind that social justice is no longer restricted to the question of material or income distribution, but includes issues of representation, identity and difference including gender, race, ethnicity, nationality (Fraser, 1997) and power relations.

Such is the epistemological break from the liberal tradition of equality of opportunity and social justice. Unless inequality is reduced at both national and global level poverty could not be effectively tackled. Poverty and inequality are intricately interwoven but an important question that can be asked here is whether an end to inequality will necessarily translate into an end to poverty. Is poverty then solely the result of unequal relations? Also quite important is the question of what forms of inequality can be feasibly ended. Age inequalities are part of all societies (parents and children) but can lead to suffering even where there is no apparent lack of resources. The same is true of other socially legitimate forms of inequalities such as teacher and student, employer and employee, or even old and young. Not all forms of inequality can be ended but all forms have the potential to cause human suffering. As inequality is irreducibly complex there must be careful consideration of the ways in which we can approach its harmful dimensions and effects. However, poverty and inequality are quintessentially issues of social justice, not only within the nation state but between nation states.

Law, morality and the right to development

In response to this, Cosmopolitans argue that to reduce poverty and protect individual rights global institutions of governance (IMF, WB, WTO, UN) need to be reformed and strengthened. Rights protection has to be structured to ensure that the treatment of human rights and laws protect the rights of individuals wherever they are, regardless of space and time. Chapter 5 exposes the inconsistencies of current institutions of global governance and teases out the feasibility of multi-managing globalisation to include a role for non-state actors, such as transnational corporations. As explained in Chapter 4, despite its useful challenge to the forces of economic globalisation that underpin uneven benefits and have intensified inequality and poverty, cosmopolitanism misses the point that international treaties and laws are often flawed. Some, including human rights lawyers, have argued however that since the Right to Development has no legal status from a legal positivist position, it is not possible to effect or implement its articles and they cannot therefore be considered as human rights (Campbell, 2006). A key legal distinction is made between 'ought' to be and 'is' in that laws are empirically observable and can be used to prevent individuals and nations from doing harm to others, because they are integral to the judicial system or an act of parliament or and enshrined in national and international human rights law. In this sense, this standard is contrasted with natural law theory, which holds that what counts as law is determined by moral values that lie beyond the opinions of any particular human beings. In short legal positivism considers that citizens 'and courts should be able to know what the law that binds them is without having to make moral judgments in order to do so' (Campbell, 2006).

This was the starting point of the critique of natural rights and it seems that we have come full circle for how some would like the Right to Development to be interpreted. Bentham, the father of utilitarianism forcefully argued that there is no such thing as a natural right when it comes to private property, for example, as it cannot be defended on the basis of moral obligation. Property is entirely the creation of the law and therefore has credibility because it is through legal institutions that people buy, sell and protect property. According to Bentham's utilitarian approach, from real law comes real rights but from imaginary laws, from 'the law of nature' can come only 'imaginary rights' (Quoted in Sen, 2004: 11). Private property cannot be defended on the basis of moral obligation or freedom, but it might be an institution demanded by justice. However for Sen rights are derived both from law and from moral values or the concept of human dignity. Human rights can be fulfilled in different ways depending on the acceptability of the ethical base of claims. As Cohen explains, the 'language of natural right (or moral) is the language of justice, and whoever takes justice seriously must accept that there are natural rights' (1995: 12). It is morally unacceptable that some people live in extreme poverty and inequality, while others revel in the ownership of private property with annual income that amounts to millions of dollars – it is simply unjust.

Underpinned by universally recognised moral values and reinforced by legal obligations, international human rights provide therefore a normative framework for the formulation of national and global development policies. Sen (1999) suggests that the general idea of freedom is particularly relevant to normative social choice theory, in general, and to the theory of justice, in particular. Not only can freedom figure powerfully in the normative foundations of human rights, but, in relation to development, it is particularly relevant as poverty-related deprivation tends to be caused by a lack of freedom to avoid it. Cosmopolitans are right to point out the fact that many countries have endorsed UN binding and nonbinding rights' declarations, and that a number of global institutions are involved in reinforcing these treaties. However, in a globalising world the articulation of rights is not straightforward, despite what may be set down in international laws, treaties and conventions and the assertion that they effectively blur national boundaries. True that there has been a proliferation of international laws and institutions that support global justice, such as the International Criminal Court and laws and Treaties that establish positive rights for individuals and groups and positive duties for states to protect them. Similar frameworks exist to secure the social and economic rights of nation states. However, in reality none of these have much of a bearing when hegemonic states decide a course of action, whatever the cost in terms of systematic human rights violations.

For example, the United States has been holding prisoners from 35 countries at Guantanamo Bay, for more than four years against international law. These detainees, who were captured from various countries, have been held on the grounds of crimes against humanity and acts of terrorism – 'combatants' that have waged a 'war' against Western civilisation and the United States. Civil society organisations and UN agencies, including the inter-American Commission on Human Rights and others, have objected to this violation of human rights and disregard for the Geneva Convention and laws of war, detention without trial and so forth. Though not 'at war', the US government planned to try detainees as War criminals before a military commission. Why does the United States continue to detain these so called 'terrorists' somewhere outside US territory in a purpose-built offshore prison on a military Naval base? The important point is that if they were in the United States the detainees would be subject to the country's constitutional civil rights laws or international human rights law such as the Geneva Convention which the United States signed in 1949. In 1996 the supreme US court rejected the government's argument that Article 3 of the Geneva convention did not apply to Al Quaida, because the Geneva Convention only applied to 'international' armed conflict between two or more states and with 'non-international' armed conflict between a state and non-state actors and therefore could not apply to the phenomenon of global terrorism.

The United States has international obligations to several Human Rights treaties including the International Covenant on Civil and Political Rights, Convention against Torture and the International Convention on the Elimination of All Forms of Racial Discrimination. Additionally the United States has adopted several binding and non binding international humanitarian law treaties related closely to the circumstances of prisoners in Guantanamo Bay. They are the Geneva Convention relative to the Treatment of Prisoners of War (Third Convention) and the Geneva Convention (United Nations Economic and Social Council, 2006: 7). In this context the United States has not only respected international laws but basically ignored them. The current debate around national and global security and the war against terror has effectively revamped the notion of law, morality and the right to development.

'Benign hegemony' and the right to development

Once upon a time President Harry Truman stated that:

> We must embark on a bold new programme for making the benefits of scientific advances and industrial progress available for improvement and growth of underdeveloped areas. The old imperialism is dead – exploitation for foreign profit – has no place in our plans. What we envisage is a programme of development based on the concepts of democratic fair dealing. (Truman, 1950)

This widely quoted proclamation from his inaugural address to the US Congress in 1949 was a critical moment in not only acknowledging poverty in 'underdeveloped' countries but also, in the words of Kofi Anan (2006: 2), proposing a programme of 'development assistance' through multilateral instructions such as the UN. Even though his resolution was questioned at the time, in Sachs' view (1999) such an observation was in a way the starting point of 'development planning' and the development agenda. The interpretation is a rather poor analysis of development assistance and what has turned out to be a far wider agenda, focused on the instrument of foreign policy and the domination of liberal and neo-liberal paradigms. The basic assumption that has continued to this day is that liberal 'free market democracy' is one of the by-products of the modernisation process, and something that becomes a universal aspiration only in the course of time, as many countries in the south adopt models of development that enable them to catch up with the rest.

Truman's legacy was embodied in the move more than 50 years later, at the dawn of the twenty-first century and post 9/11, to revive imperial power control with the invasion of Iraq and Afghanistan. The cosmic military power of the United States of America is justified by the fact that it is deemed to represent global law in the fight against 'global terror' in order to bring about peaceful global change through 'humanitarian' intervention. Beck (2006) calls the threat to change the world order through force 'military enlightenment' – it conveniently disregards cosmopolitan laws and human rights to bring about regime change while maintaining its own hegemony. The 'imperialism of human rights' that require cross-border armed intervention in order to establish human rights has become legitimised and something necessary for the advocates of growing global violence and disorder (Hobsbawm, 2005). This imperial grand strategy basically 'dismisses international law and institutions as of "little value", promoting military action in its place' (Chomsky, 2003: 11). Human rights and development are now employed as the ultimate trade-off for security activity for the fight against terrorism both domestically and globally. This testifies to the fact that powerful states use and abuse human rights talk as, almost exclusively, an instrument of foreign policy. The President of the United States, George Bush, now makes the most of human rights, poverty and development talk to legitimise concern over security issues:

> We fight against poverty because hope is an answer against terror...This is the commitment of the United States to bring hope and opportunity to the world's poorest people, and to call for a new compact for development defined by greater accountability for rich and

poor nations, alike ... developed nations have a duty not only to share our wealth, but also encourage sources that produce wealth: economic freedom, political liberty, the rule of law and human rights ... We will challenge the poverty and hopelessness and lack of education and failed governments that too often allow conditions that terrorists can seize and try to turn to their advantage. (Bush, 2002: 2)

The idea of rights and its associated worth has been hijacked by political forces that are ideologically oriented and responsible for many of the injustices that we find within specific nation states and across the world. People in the south increasingly view the idea of rights and development with suspicion. As Mary Robinson the former United Nations High Commissioner for Human Rights points out 'In the countries in Africa which I concentrate on, if I mention international human rights to a grass-root groups, they do not see it as an ally, they look at me with suspicion' (2007: 9). The 'global war on terror' or 'political Islam' has muddied the foreign policy of powerful states directed at nation building and establishing universal 'democracy and freedom' along Western lines, occurring as it has against the backdrop of attempts to consolidate the UN and the universalism of rights regimes based on the sovereignty of nation states. In some ways recent events are a pivotal point in global social relations, related as they are to political and military domination of hegemonic states and a transnationalism that reproduces inequality between the rich and poor and the north and the south (Castle, 2003).

Neo-conservatism, the dominant ideology of the Bush Administration's foreign policy, forcefully promotes the idea that there is a moral rationale for the United States using its power to create a benign, peaceful democratic global order (Fukuyama, 2006: 41). Free market democracy, nation building and securing civil and political rights are nourished under the banner of human rights with scant regard for the wider interpretation of rights that encapsulates social and economic rights.[7] The strategy of 'benevolent hegemony' supports the justification of any form of intervention in the affairs of other nations on the grounds that the US peacekeeping agenda is humanitarian. What actually justifies this assumption? The Americans believe that they have a moral duty or obligation to enforce the law of nature as conceived under Kantian rationality, which rather ironically embraces a cosmopolitan view that peaceful communities can establish effective relations with one another. So military intervention is a means to peace and global stability. The

Kantian perfect duty demands 'that serious consideration be given by anyone in a position to provide reasonable help to the person whose human right is threatened'[8] (Sen, 2004). Does this justify the moral nature of the role that the United States plays globally? Can any intervention in the affairs of other nations be regarded as humanitarian intervention and part of the peacekeeping agenda? The source, then, of police power is the right that the United States has to enforce the law of nature based on this obligation towards 'mutual love amongst men.' (Such a narrative is driven in the US military academy and is summarised in an essay by a US army cadet Dan Zupan, 2004).

Individuals have a certain value that is equal and worthy of respect; in virtue of which they have real rights, amongst them the exclusive rights to their person and property. Any violation of these fundamental rights constitutes a moral wrong. And since the sorts of rights that are in question are the rights that impose *perfect* duties on others, it cannot be the case that United States involvement in protecting others, in the absence of a designated police force, is an act of beneficence. Rather it is the performance of a *perfect* duty to protect the defenceless. This obligation in terms of perfect duties involves making a commitment to world peace and the United States believes it has a responsibility to further this aim even if doing so involves positive measures, such as adopting a so-called world police role. In the words of Bush 'History has called us to a titanic struggle, whose stakes could not be higher because we're fighting for freedom, itself. We're pursuing great and worthy goals to make the world safer, and as we do, to make it better' (2002).

So what is the merit of pursuing a social justice agenda given the constraints that exist? The point is that a right is never given but taken and in fact as Molyneaux and Razavi tell us 'the language of rights has considerable mobilising power; it reminds us that people have justified and urgent claims; rights confer agency' and enable the individual person and groups in particular to articulate strong claims for their space' (2002: 12).

It also poses enormous challenges, in particular in the context of market-dominated development. The practice and articulation of rights is easier said than done in countries where political regimes control the extent of individual agency – the degree of free will exercised by the individual. Added to this other factors, such as structural constraints like inequality, poverty and economic and physical vulnerability, reduce the individual's and group's agency. Even in settings where civil society mobilises to engage in securing rights, we find civil society organisations increasingly being co-opted by governments, which limits their potential to lobby for structural changes to address poverty and inequalities (Ibid.: 84–85). The relationship between social justice, human rights and development is complex and opaque; opaque because the language of rights has weakened from one that reflected its initial emancipatory power and principles to one that has become obscured by security and foreign policy rights talk. Rights and its associated worth has been hijacked by political forces that are ideologically oriented and responsible for many of the injustices that we find within specific nation states and between nation states across the world. As Cox points out: 'To remove the factor of dominant power as the author of rights, these rights to be fully legitimate, would have to be gained through struggle within each civilisation or each culture' (Cox and Schechter, 2002: 63). The struggle for social justice and equal opportunity means identifying agency in social movements as a potential source of counter-hegemony.

It is in this context that in Chapter 6, I discuss how new social movements and civil society organisations in response to hegemonic states and transnational corporation's operations and human rights violations have been actively involved in the quest to protect the rights of the individual and the collective. Poverty alleviation and securing the Right to Development encapsulates far more than the provision of opportunities for generating wealth; it requires careful consideration of, and thoughtful responses to, those factors which obstruct poor people's ability to access opportunities necessary for them to move out of poverty. This tends to be overlooked by enthusiasts of economic globalisation and transformation, resulting in injustices at the local level. Transnational social movements have made an active contribution to the rights to development agenda by drawing these to our attention.

2
The Right to Development

The beginning: natural rights and the challenge to power

The idea of justice is not new but can be found in the philosophies of many ancient civilisations and cultures from the Greeks and the Romans through to the Persians and Chinese. In pre-capitalist or pre-modern periods, social hierarchy and the differentiation that went with it allowed rights to be wrapped up in the privileges of status. Aristotle, for example, did not view justice as entailing equal rights, but he emphasised the notion of the 'right proportion', which only sometimes meant 'equality' as we understand it today (Russell, 1979: 186–187). Similarly the chain of command that existed during the Roman period ascribed rights through birth and citizenship. Some of these interpretations continue today in cultural or religious contexts, for example, the Indian caste system. During the Medieval era discrimination persisted between believers and non-believers and between the rulers and the ruled, despite the moral obligation within Christian and Islamic societies to treat all individuals equally. In all of these early contexts the behaviours of rulers were not questioned by the majority, as individuals or groups, because they did not have the natural right to question authority.

The ideas of rights that we are most familiar with today have been systematically formulated within Western political philosophy and normative economics. And, not surprisingly, it is within these paradigms that they are embedded. The liberal social contract theory of Locke, Rousseau, Mills and Kant is the foundation of the concept of rights as equality. These thinkers encapsulated the dynamism of the Enlightenment in Europe, which rejected the stronghold of tradition and religious teleology, by promoting a commitment to free inquiry, rationality, reason, power of knowledge and scientific innovation. This shift from tradition to the modernity of the early liberals represented the progress needed to improve the well being of the human condition. It is important to point out that universal values, morality and freedoms, are the driving force behind these ideas. In fact natural rights, derived from reason, self-evidence, or an empirical conception of 'nature', and based on the study of how humans actually behave, were a foundation of critiques of traditional society (Campbell, 2006: 7). More recently Nozick, Rawls, Dworkin, Cohen and Sen have extended the debate that the early theorists started to cover a spectrum of interpretations of social justice, as I will examine in the next Chapter.

The basic tenant of the early theorists on rights was that all individuals should be treated as equals. For Locke individuals 'are naturally in, ... a state of perfect freedom and equality. The equality of men by nature ... [is] the foundation of that obligation to mutual love amongst men.' (Locke, 1952: 4). This reflects a fundamental understanding of what is meant by 'natural' in contrast to an understanding of society based on theological beliefs and institutional explanation. The whole notion of the social contract is based on mutual advantage, in that rational people get together and decide to leave the state of nature and to govern themselves by law in civil society. The language of rights was used to challenge traditional forms of power relations wrapped up as divine rights or absolutist power, such as the ascendancy of hierarchy by rank, caste or birth. Most importantly Locke provides us with a framework for a 'social contract' that captures political relations, and challenges the Hobbesian understanding that competition and war between human beings are 'natural'. Locke's framework, which establishes that social contracts or agreement between individual human beings in the state of nature are rooted in mutual advantage, supports the establishment of a sovereign authority or supreme political and legal power for the protection of rights. This goes some way to overcoming the Hobbesian problem of how social and political order might be achieved. The idea of 'natural rights' defied the nature and legitimacy of existing paradigms of power in the seventeenth and eighteenth centuries and challenged the legitimacy of power relations that had existed for centuries. The concept of absolutist states and the divine right of the king were undermined by the notion, for example, that sovereignty is derived from the people and not God. Suggestions that everyone had a right to private property questioned the prevailing belief that all property was ultimately vested in the crown. Stammers (1993: 448) suggests, however, that rights as perceived by the early liberal theorists, in fact, both challenged and sustained power relations. While the dichotomy of the private and public realm evolved into a concept of rights that recognised the threat of the state, the concept of civil society and natural rights that developed on the threshold of capitalist development also fulfilled an ideological role of reinforcing prevailing relations of power. The idea of 'rights' that Locke initiated soon lost out to government and the rule of law or to the sovereignty of parliament. In the words of Foucault,

> It was life more than the law that became the issue of political struggles, even if the latter were formulated through affirmations concerning rights. The 'right' to life, to one's body, to health, to happiness, to the satisfaction of basic needs, and beyond all the oppressions or 'alienations,' to rediscover what one is and all that one can be, this 'right' – which the classical juridical system was utterly incapable of comprehending – was the political response to all these new procedures of power. (Foucault, 1976: 145)

The first generation – civil and political rights

It was through the discourse on natural rights of the Enlightenment period that the first generation of rights' activists was born. Their activities were manifested mostly in the promotion of civil and political rights. This was first reflected through the US Declaration of Independence in 1776, and the enshrining of natural rights in the text of the Constitution. In a very different historical and cultural context in France, the whole notion of rights instigated a new discourse that justified the transition from a feudal society of patronage and hierarchy to one of bourgeois social relations based on property rights. Under the influence of Jean-Jacques Rousseau, the Social Contract (that was adopted in 1789 as the French declaration of 'the Rights of Man') promoted the liberal mantra that 'men are born and remain free and have equal rights', as a fairly direct response to Rousseau's famous remark 'Man is born free, but is everywhere in chains' (Rousseau, 1973). The idea of the Rights of Man was not without its critics from the emerging capitalist class that, through economic liberalism, justified a utilitarian approach to society. Bentham, for example, rejected the idea of the rights of man as ethical 'nonsense' that had no relevance to the freedom of the individual within capitalism in his critique of the French declaration; he claimed that a right has to be substantive and that individual rights and freedoms could only be

✳ *Sad & Beautiful*

protected through laws, justifying the concept of property rights in a market economy:

> All men are free? Absurd and miserable nonsense!...The professed object of the whole composition i.e. the Declaration, is to tie the hands of the law, by declaring pretended rights over which the law is never to have any power, – liberty, the right of enjoying liberty: here this very liberty is left at the mercy and good pleasure of the law. (Bentham, 2000: 426)

Although the early liberal theory of social contract advocated that civil society involved the rule of majority, it was in itself incomplete in that, as Russell points out, it excluded women, the poor, children and indigenous people from the rights of citizenship, as well as those who did not own property mainly the working class and the peasants (1979: 607). In short the earlier classical liberals were preoccupied with civil and political rights and the objective of giving individuals freedom from abuses of the state. They were less concerned with economic, social and cultural rights or how poverty could be addressed. To some extent this continues to be how rights are perceived today, particularly in 'successful' states such as the United States. The desire to separate civil and political rights from social, economic, and cultural rights remains one of the main challenges of the implementation of the right to development, as we shall see later.

The idea of natural rights, that underpins liberalism and liberalist rights theory, was developed on the threshold of capitalist development. Liberalist rights theory reflects a commitment to individual autonomy, equality, liberty and freedom – all concepts that were defined and constructed in a society based on a market economy and the ownership of private property. The problems that we might seek to address today through the human rights discourse were not considered to be social problems before the creation of capitalist market economies and modern nation states. To some extent this view has been carried forward into the contemporary liberal tradition where we find that the legitimacy of the institution of private property is considered to be a necessary condition for individual self-preservation; frequently argued to be core to social justice (Cohen, 1995: 56). These values form the basic principle of liberalism, that is to say the idea that human beings are fundamentally equal and that individuals should be treated equally. The core issue of property rights however provides a paradigm for variant liberal interpretations (Lukes, 1985: 179) and is pivotal to why liberalism is a contested concept.

So how has the rights debate evolved from these early liberal ideas to a wider approach that synthesises how civil and political rights intersect with other rights, including social, economic, and cultural rights? Social and economic rights do not have their origin in the early liberal theorists, but tend to be referred to as the second generation of rights, linked to contemporary egalitarian liberals and to a great extent to Marx's ideas and the early struggles for social justice. So it is that in the late nineteenth and early twentieth centuries workers' movements grew across Europe, resulting in constitutional amendments such as the abolition of child labour and the right to vote. Marx established how rights could function as a tool to address power imbalances within capitalist society. Some may argue that this claim is somewhat exaggerated, but there can be no doubt that his examination of the relationship between capital and labour demonstrated that the injustices of the capitalist market economy was, at the time, anchored in exploitation – long working hours for workers, the use of child labour, insecure contracts, appalling working conditions and other similar violations of rights.

The challenge of the second generation of rights

The question that preoccupied Marx, and continues to this day to preoccupy philosophers and political economists, is whether capitalism can promote freedom, liberty and equality. Like the early liberals, Marx challenged power relations. But, taking a very different approach, Marx vehemently believed that capitalism and the market economy were founded on social injustice. Marx's early writing reflects his view that the notion of the individual's natural right to private property effectively protected the market economy, and allowed 'an individual *to be* withdrawn behind his private interests and whims and separated from the community...The only bond that holds them together is natural necessity, need and private interest, the conservation of their property and egoistic person' (Marx on the Jewish Question, 2000: 58). Instead he believed passionately that the so-called 'natural rights' or the 'rights of man' could only be realised through the abolition of private property.

Marx observed from his experience in Western Europe that the working class was not a beneficiary but the victim of capitalist development. Only the owners of the means of production benefited from industrialisation, at the expense of the majority who were deprived of access to productive resources and whose only commodity in the capitalist market was their labour power. The minority capitalist class not only had sole control of resources, they also had the power to manipulate the state and control the majority of working people. Marx used this concept of exploitation in the context of value theory. The surplus that labour produces is realised in the form of profit for the rich bourgeois class, as the owners of the means of production, while the working class, the proletariat, has to rely on wages kept to a minimum, despite working for long hours and in degrading conditions. Workers' wages were barely sufficient for family survival. Long working hours, the use of child labour, insecure contracts and other similar violations of rights were directly linked by Marx to the economic power of the capitalist class. Under capitalism the worker has no right to the full value created by his (or her) labour (Lukes, 1985). For Marxists, this amounts to capitalist appropriation and exploitation, based on an unfair distribution of rights and social injustice directly linked to the unequal distribution of productive resources (Cohen, 1995: 119). Thus there is seen to be an inbuilt contradiction in individuals having rights under the market economy given that capitalism is by its very nature unjust, based as it is on exploitative relations of production. This clearly suggests that capitalism is not oriented to satisfying human needs and rights.

At the time Marx was writing, there were few laws to protect workers. Child labour was prevalent, workers had little security, and there was no social protection or welfare system. Access to health facilities and education was also limited to those who could afford to pay for them. Marx not only challenged the power relations of capitalism, that underpinned this inequality, but also the whole notion of capitalism as a mode of production. Thus he ascertained that the only way to restore 'natural rights' and equality was to change capitalist social relations and replace them with socialist relations based on the rule of the majority; that is the working people. In such social relations, the notion of rights and social justice are redundant. For if there is no private property as such, and workers own the means of production themselves, society operates 'from each according to his ability, to each according to his needs' (Marx and Engels, 1963). Marx focused his concern for individual rights into the concept of collective rights, .arguing that agency for social change lies with the whole society or the collective given how it is 'structurally determined', and not with the individual. However implicit to his whole approach to rights is the need to address the lives of individuals and to determine conditions that allow the 'freedom of action' of individuals. Hence to change history and the world individuals were called to act collectively – workers of the world unite, you have nothing to lose but your chains. However, Marx clearly perceived an individual's obligation and duty to the collective, which in organisational terms means a society governed by the rule of the majority. In post-capitalist civil society where there is no private property and capitalist modes of production, Marx conceptualised a transition from socialism to communism in which there is no need for human rights laws to protect from or mediate the actions of coercive state institutions because all would truly be equal. If in a communist society each individual makes a contribution and receives according to their needs, conflict would not exist. In this alternative society there would be equal power relations and therefore no abuses of civil and political rights. Social justice and freedom would be truly based on equality between individuals. At best, the Marxist concept of agency focused on whether the working class carried out, or not, its historical potential to secure emancipation from the injustices of the market economy.

Marx was critical of the liberalist concept of natural rights because its narrow focus ignored economic and social rights.[1] Subsequent Marxist theorists have advocated that rights claims challenge power relations and they have, therefore, extended the concept to include social and economic rights. Marx's ideas were bound by both implicit and explicit moral judgements, presenting a moral critique of capitalism, together with the vision of a better world. In other words, Marxists have treated moral discourses and systems concerned with rights and obligations and with justice and injustices as historically critical. This reflects the position of political philosophers, such as Cohen,[2] who argue that the majority are deprived of rights over what ought to be held in common by the free market (Geras, 1991: 6). The key question is whether capitalist property is defensible. Cohen considers private property to be the unjust foundation of capitalism, for private property restricts general freedom, as the majority (workers, peasants etc.) are property-less, while at the same time it supports bourgeois freedom (Cohen, 1994: 8). Some Marxists reject normative concerns around ethics, culture and law and have regarded them as irrelevant, focusing on the perpetuated inequality of capitalism. For other Marxists rights represent a set of ideological formulations inextricably linked to capitalism, which function as an ideological mask at home and are a form of cultural imperialism abroad (Lukes, 1985: 57). In practice, Marxists have been actively involved in social movements fighting against civil and political rights' violations and in favour of securing the social and economic rights of labourers and nations.

Marxism or Liberalism – who got it right?

So far I have discussed what I consider to be the two key perspectives on rights and justice most relevant to discussions of the right to development – liberal egalitarianism and the materialism of Marx. The egalitarian liberals believed that it was possible to achieve social justice within a market economy, so long as rights were institutionalised, in particular around the ownership of property (Hayek, 1944; Bentham, 2000). Although some Marxists acknowledge the existence of natural rights on moral grounds, Marx promoted the idea that only through abolishing private property could social justice be established. Other critiques of capitalism have adopted a wider approach, based on the view that issues of social injustice arise when benefits and responsibilities are not fairly shared or where decisions affect the distribution of benefits and burdens between individuals and groups. What is important to bear in mind is that the crux of Marx's criticism of capitalism was belief in the distribution of resources on an equal basis. This requires moral and ethical judgements, in other words a commitment to normative principles. As Sen rightly points out, it was the connection of poverty with a lack of freedom that led Marx to argue passionately for the need to replace 'the domination of circumstances and chance over individuals by the domination of individuals over chance and circumstances' (2004: 318).

At the same time as liberals were concerned with protecting civil and political rights, Marx believed that, for as long as inequality persisted, liberty was a shallow concept. Marxists have made a number of enduring contributions to human rights: promoting the need for a secular and historical approach to human rights; supporting the struggle for universal suffrage, economic equity and other social rights; challenging the state and free market as a central vehicle to promote human rights, and rights to self determination; and arguing for a broadening of the human rights agenda.

In the nineteenth century this was evidenced in laws that responded to concerns about the social and economic impacts of industrialisation. In England, for example, a Poor Law in 1834 resulted in public relief; The 1833 Factory Act banned the employment of children under the age of nine years old in textile mills; and in 1842 women and children under ten were prohibited from working in coal mines. In 1901 the data from a study in York by Rowntree, found alarming evidence of poverty with 28 per cent of the population living well below the poverty line, along with a high level of unemployment and child mortality (Rowntree, 1941). In response Lloyd-George, the Chancellor of the Exchequer of a Liberal government, introduced reforms to relieve the deprivation that the old, the children and unemployed suffered from, that in a sense were the foundation of state welfare. A number of laws were introduced by the government to prevent further unrest in response to a strengthening labour movement that through collective action, such as the emerging trade unions, demanded changes in working and living conditions. Demands for welfare reform also came with the newly formed Labour Party. Elicited responses from the government included the 1908 Children and Young Persons Act, the Old Age Act which introduced pensions for the over 70s and the 1911 National Insurance Act which allowed workers free medical treatment and paid sick leave. The political rights of workers were also asserted through the Chartist movement and socialist movements for parliamentary reform, later to be known as modern labour movements, culminating in the granting of universal suffrage in 1918 (Ishay, 2004).

To summarise, I think it is entirely reasonable to suggest that conceptually civil and political rights are closely identified with liberalism, whereas economic and social rights are derived from Marx and Marxists. As a source of collective identity, the latter provided the framework for challenging post-colonial inequality between nations and the credibility of the right for national independence and determination.

The trajectory of human rights

Following the Second World War the rights discourse flourished on the global stage with the formation of the United Nations. The UN was to take a leading role in addressing the inhumanities and abuses of war, and the construction in 1948 of the Human Rights Declaration clearly set a framework for its operation. The epistemological underpinning of this declaration originates in the concept of 'natural rights' and the 'rights of man' and it clearly reflects the notion that all individuals, by virtue of being human, are equal and should receive fundamental freedoms without distinction of any kind such as race, colour, sex, language, religion, political or other opinion, national or social origin, property, birth, or other status (Article 2). Within this conception the very concept of 'right' denotes equal worth of human beings and equal entitlement and is, in a sense, individualistic. All the rights in the Declaration of Human Rights are attributed to the rights of individuals, based on a common standard for all nations.

Rights are entitlements that require correlated duties. If person A has a right to X, then there has to be an agency that has a duty to provide it (Sen, 1999). To say that an individual has a 'right' to something suggests entitlement and that something is owed. Rights do not only *benefit* the right holders but more importantly they *empower* them. In this sense, 'rights' is a legitimate political demand expressed in terms of claims and entitlement and the state has a duty to deliver or protect them. Social protection at the national level is the social contract through which the state provides goods and services to citizens to meet basic rights' entitlements. In this capacity, it reflects the role of the state as the deliverer and enforcer of access to rights, which are practical entitlement that, potentially, makes a difference to the people who hold them.

The articulation of human rights

Human rights are articulated in four different ways. The first route to articulate rights, which Sen refers to as the 'recognition route' (2004: 10), is through global obligations and inducements to secure rights, framed by the UN Universal Declaration of Human Rights of 1948 (and by later declarations such as the Declaration of the Right to Development, 1986). They are non-binding route establishes fundamental human rights for individuals and groups and suggests an ethical dimension to rights rather than a purely legislative institutionalisation. Subsequently, there has been a sequence of other international declarations and conventions often through the United Nations, again giving recognition, rather than a legal and coercive status, to various general demands.[3] This approach is motivated by the idea that the ethical force of human rights is made more powerful in practice through giving it social recognition and an acknowledged status, even when no enforcement is instituted (Sen, 2004).

Common to all claims is the universality of human rights that are equal, inalienable and apply to all human beings regardles of location. Universalism has been the main contentious issue of the credo of human rights. Human rights are implemented and protected through the state and its institutions. Often, even though states may sign the standard declarations, some do not ratify them within their own legal systems and as such claim them to be non-binding. International Conventions provide a clear benchmark against which how governments pursue the establishment of a set of universal standards and principles can be measured as a means to ensuring that they are progressed. They cannot however be forced upon states. Examples of such conventions include the Convention of the Rights of the Child, the Convention on Climate Change, Convention on Corruption, or the first Convention of the twenty-first century adopted by the UN on the Rights of People with a Disability in 2006. The United States, for example, has signed up to the Convention of the Elimination of Discrimination Against Women but it has never been ratified. Unlike these Conventions, human rights laws are based on rules that are enforceable and can be executed and, if laws are violated, the violator can be punished. This is similar to Bentham's commitment (as I discussed earlier) to positive rights that promotes the idea of rights as 'a child of the law', and rights that are not, as nonsense.

The second route to articulate rights is through the legislation route and the application of human rights laws that give legal force to certain rights as basic human rights, as detailed in the UN declarations. These have either been enacted by individual states or through associations of states such as the Convention on the Status of Refugees (1951) and its 1967 protocol that defined refugee rights and the legal obligation to protect them. The principle of non-refoulement has made such conventions a fundamental part of international law. However, the tension between international human rights law and individual state law has had a considerable impact on the protection of the poor and marginal people such as forced migrants (see Chapter 1 on hegemonic states and the war on terror). Post- 9/11, for example, support measures that offer temporary protection for refugees rather than integration into the host society has been actively promoted in a political climate of 'containment' and increasingly restrictive protection. (see Chapter 5 for more discussion on this).

The case of refugees is particularly interesting given that international law protects the refugee, but does not protect Internally Displaced People (IDP) who come under local national jurisdiction. The United Nations document 'Guiding Principles on Internal Displacement' contains only recommendations (Deng and Cohen, 1998) in respect of the protection of the rights and entitlements of internal displacees. Ultimately the state is responsible for the protection of IDP as their own citizens,[4] and this is clearly documented in international human rights law and international humanitarian law. The obvious oversight in this approach is when the state is itself the cause of the civil conflict that IDPs seek protection from. The experiences of internal displacement occur in situations of armed conflict and civil war or where there is social injustice and unequal political freedoms. In Darfur in West Sudan, systematic persecution and discrimination by the state and militia forces against civilians (including sexual violence, destruction of property and violent forced displacement) has resulted in more than one million IDP and 11,000 refugees fleeing to neighbouring countries (United Nations Economic and Social Council, 2005). The question that is frequently asked and raised by The International Criminal Court is when the UN or individual states should take steps to protect people against their own governments. The UN Charter does not permit the UN to intervene in matters that are essentially within the domestic jurisdiction of any State, other than in special circumstances when the UN resolves to place peacekeepers or peace enforcers in a state. Thus, the protection offered to IDPs by way of the international community is limited to what might more commonly be termed humanitarian 'assistance', which does not constitute 'intervention', and this again tends to be short-term. Recent examples of such intervention by the UN include Rwanda, after the mass genocide between the Tutsi and Hutu tribes in 2004–2005, and the former Yugoslavia, where conflict, and ethnic cleansing of Muslim by Serbs led to UN intervention on the grounds of human rights violation.

It is important that the International Criminal Court is mentioned here, as it represents the trend to do away with the principle of the absolute subjection of individuals to the state and to develop the status of individuals under international law. Other insitutions such as The European Court of Human Rights established by the 1950 European Convention, considers individual cases involving the violation of human rights within signatory states. This allows individuals and groups to use appeals, after exhausting all possible avenues at national level, at the European Court on Human Rights in Strasbourg. For example the Kurdish rebel leader Abdullah Ocalan was given a death sentence by the Turkish court, but the European Court of Human Rights overruled this decision on the basis that the Turkish authorities had breached international treaties by denying Ocalan the right to a fair and independent trial, and by barring his legal representative from contacting him after he was detained.

The sovereignty question and tensions between European laws, the Convention of Human Rights, and individual state national law and legislation on human rights have developed into a fairly raucous political debate in the United Kingdom in recent years. One Conservative MP in the United Kingdom demanded a cut back in the 'cancer of litigation' caused by the Human Rights Act, and the need to distance the idea of rights from inherited English liberties. In response to the 7 July 2005 bombings in London, the media has campaigned against the Act which is seen to undermine the protection of national security, and to favour the rights of terrorists or suspects (Daily Express, Monday 1 August 2005 headline). The Human Rights Act, which was adopted in the United Kingdom in 1998 and re-enforced in 2000 focuses on the right to life, prohibition of torture, right to fair trial, right to respect for privacy and family, freedom of thought, conscience and religion, freedom of expression, right to marry and prohibition of discrimination. The biggest issue seems to be Article Three of the European Convention on Human Rights which has been incorporated into United Kingdom Law by the Act, which states that individuals have the legitimate right to stay in this country and not to return to the country of origin where they may face degrading or inhuman treatment. Other critiques coming from a different perspective suggest that tensions are inevitable as a result of slotting the European Convention on Human Rights into UK law, because the government has effectively endorsed the prioritisation of civil and political rights over social and economic rights (Robinson et al., 2007: 35). In other words the government has not committed to fully supporting the European Social Charter. The fundamental question is whether legal entitlement to access to healthcare and education, food and clean water, housing and social security should be established? Some states have approached human rights in this social justice context, such as South Africa where social and economic rights are endorsed in the country's constitution.

The third route to articulate rights is through the advocacy or 'agitation route'. The active involvement of individuals and groups and civil society organisations to ensure the protection of rights has sometimes been necessary, and this frequently takes the form of protest and social movements (see Chapter 6). The fourth context through which rights are articulated is the relationship between the sovereign state and the individual. The most important actor in the provision of rights and social protection is the state and the welfare rights and protection of individuals and groups remain within the jurisdiction and political power of the nation state. However, since the 1980s states, ostensibly at least, do not operate independently (see Chapter 3). This suggests that the state is not the sole agent of justice and development and the concept of the state as the 'primary agent of justice' referred to in Human Rights Declaration 1948 and Article 3.1 of the Declaration of Right to Development (1986) requires explanation (see Chapter 4).

The international framework of protection through laws, conventions and institutions has made a contribution to human rights advancement in the classic manner. Nevertheless, states retain responsibility for their own policy formation and implementation. In spite of comparatively robust international laws, conventions, principles, norms and rules, sovereign states exert considerable discretion in how they are interpreted and executed. This varying interpretation of the definitions of rights alluded to in the declaration is the source of considerable tension. There are many examples where rights are not considered to be 'natural' and have not therefore been equally granted, conceived in some states for example as only applying to men or in some case only to white men. For example, the United States did not apply the same freedoms to the black population as the white population in their constitution and similarly colonial powers did not always grant indigenous people their full rights. This persists today despite the fact that modern constitutional law has become the dominant basis of justice, and tends to be the main route through which rights are articulated. An additional difficulty that some national states face is how modern constitutions recognise and accommodate customary law and cultural diversity (Tully, 1995). In countries such as the United Kingdom, United States, and Australia, Tully argues that

> These constitutions formed over the past three hundred years or so since the emergence of capitalism and modernity and has not changed to incorporate the full mutual recognition of different culture of its citizens...The age of multiculturalism has seen a kind of extension of the last three centuries of multi nationalism with no fundamental change to constitutions. (Ibid.: 8)

This is complicated further by the question of whether there is or could ever be a widely accepted universal rights standard, given relativism or cultural specificity.

Even though the UN Human Rights Declaration was non-binding and many states adopted the common normative framework that it represented, some states reacted on ideological grounds. In reality a whole range of complicating factors challenge the articulation of rights and individual agency. Mostly advocated by Western liberal states, the institutionalising and mediating of rights tend to focus on civil and political rights, based on the principles that states exist to protect civil society and to defend and uphold property rights. This liberalism has, nonetheless, been considered to represent 'false universalisms', promoting an equality that is merely formal rather than substantive and one that prioritises the individual's civil and political rights over social and economic rights. In some ways this accommodates the position of Western countries. During the 1960s, the Socialist State of the Soviet Union also demanded recognition of collective social and economic rights, as opposed to only those of the individual and then only civil and political rights. In response the UN emphasised the division between social and economic rights on the one hand and civil and political rights on the other by dividing the common normative framework of the Declaration on Human Rights into two international covenants in 1966 – one on Social and Economic and Cultural Rights and the second on Civil and Political Rights.

Dependency theory and the right to development

States from the south have been instrumental in encouraging the UN to adopt a broader and more 'multidimensional' understanding of rights specifically in relation to social and economic development. This was clearly aimed at the elimination of obstacles to development in the newly emerging countries that gained independence in the 1950s and 1960s following decolonisation. These nation states aspired, somewhat ambitiously, to 'catch up' with western modernisation. They maintained that political independence required equality with other nations in economic terms and saw the UN treaties as important recognition of this.

Countries from the south formed a forum within the United Nations to raise apprehensions over their marginalisation in the global economy, and these concerns were reinforced by dependency theory, a variant of Marxism. Critical of mainstream development theory and practice of the time, in particular modernisation theory that promoted the traditional pathway of economic development, the aim of dependency theory was to show that for as long as poor or undeveloped countries were dependent on wealthier nations in the north and there were unequal relations between nations, development and the elimination of poverty and inequality based on the capitalist market economy, economic growth or capital accumulation would fail. The state, as the facilitator between the world market and national economy, was criticised for operating to protect the interests of both the rich in the metropolis and its satellites. It is within the Marxist discourse that dependency theory sought an explanation for inequality between nation states. The central concern was not liberal rights issues based on individual and civil liberty, but normative arguments for collective rights and opposition to the exploitation and oppression of weaker nations by the more powerful ones.[5] This reflected Marx's perspective that without economic equality liberty is meaningless.

The demand for rights of nations to self-determination and recognition of collective rights is a key driver of the right to development and the linking of development with human rights. The idea that social and economic development would only be achieved if new nations were in an equal relationship with other nation states and not while relations between states were based on an unequal exchange of commodities was fundamental to the dependency school of thought (Frank, 1967; Wallerstien, 1976). In dependency theory, the human rights agenda focuses not only on political independence but also on the rights of new states to be independent economically for development to take place. This is the framework within which individual human rights could then be developed – in other words, rights for states first (the collective) and individual rights afterwards. Change the structural conditions and real individuals will be 'set free' as governments are able to establish the autonomy of their national economy and society. Inequality between nation states effectively constitutes a violation of social and economic rights.

Dependency theory failed to explain why some countries from the periphery, such as Newly Industrialised Countries (NICs) 'developed'. In some senses it was ultimately overtaken by events.[6] However, it was highly influential in the 1970s and its legacy continues even today in that at the global level the development community felt obliged to accommodate some of its perspectives. For instance, it influenced both the International Labour Office to call, in 1972, for 'redistribution with growth', and the World Bank's adoption, in 1973, of the principle of meeting 'basic needs' (Leys, 1996: 12). Dependency theory also influenced states under pressure from social movements to reconsider their dependency on the powerful countries to achieve economic growth.

However, in the late 1970s and early 1980s Franks' idea that development was not possible in periphery countries was 'abandoned', in the acknowledgement that development was difficult and dependent on external forces (and was at times distorted by them). But as Cardoso (1972) points out, the form of development in these countries was likely to be 'dependent development'. Some Dependency theorists, such as Samir Amine and Raúl Prebisch, were resentful at the unjust international division of labour, which favoured the prosperous countries at the expense of those in the periphery. They argued that the unjust international economic order could be redressed if the right to development was respected through the promotion of South-South trade and investment relations (Marks, 2004). This of course requires a pro-active state, which encourages development for its own national interest and for its own people's benefit, while strengthening its position at the international level. It is in this context, and under pressure from organised civil society movements from within the south, that forums were established to challenge the hegemony of the more powerful nations, and to promote the right to development as an agenda to put all nations into a position of equal status. However, one should be cautious here as some states pursued the right to development agenda to safeguard their own power and others were ideologically motivated.

Rights to development as a means
to social justice

Countries from the south articulated a clear view that a rights-based claim to development would be a major step forward in addressing imbalanced relations between countries, linking their claim to years of colonial exploitation and domination of their resources that left them socially and economically excluded in the global order. A fundamental plank of their argument was that richer nations had an obligation to support their right to self-determination. The African Charter of Human Rights and People's Rights stipulates self-determination, the right to existence and development and minority rights (Organisation of African Unity, 1981). Article 22 of the African Charter points out that:

> (1) All peoples shall have the right to their economic, social and cultural development with due regard to their freedom and identity and in the equal enjoyment of the common heritage of mankind. (2) States shall have the duty, individually or collectively, to ensure the exercise of the right to development.

Their focal point on social and economic rights and equal rights on all aspects of trade, investment, aid and economic co-operation was encapsulated to some degree in the UN Declaration on the Right to Development (1986), ratified by over 100 countries. It promotes a new international economic order based on equality between nations, interdependence, mutual interest and co-operation among all states (Article 3). It also presents an attempt to synthesise how civil and political rights intersect with other rights, including social, economic, and cultural rights and how national self-determination and collective rights also promote individual human rights. The Right to Development adopts a normative understanding of international human rights, as framed in the UN Declaration of Human Rights 1948. Although the right to development has no legal status on its own, its reference to the two international Covenants on Human Rights is considered to give legal force to the obligation to respect civil and political rights and social, economic and cultural rights (Sengupta, Negi, Basu, 2005: 77). Some have argued however that since the right to development has no legal status from a legal positivist position, it is not possible to effect or implement its articles and they cannot therefore be considered as human rights (Campbell, 2006). A key legal distinction is made between 'ought' to be and 'is' in that laws are empirically observable and can be used to prevent individuals from doing harm to others, because they are integral to the judicial system or an act of parliament or are enshrined in national international human rights law. In this sense, this standard is contrasted with natural law theory, which holds that what counts as law is determined by moral values that lie beyond the opinions of any particular human beings. This was the starting point of the critique of natural rights and it seems that we have come full circle for how some would like the right to development to be interpreted.

The practical application of the Right to Development has been difficult, not least because its language is at times imprecise and vague and because it is not legally binding and does not require legislation or institutional enforcement.[7] In fact 'the challenge right from the start has been to translate the hopeful but ambiguous language of the Right to Development into concepts that are meaningful for economists and useful for the rethinking of the development process' (Marks, 2005: 37). Nevertheless, a wide body of literature advocates the fostering of human rights as a means to address social injustice, poverty and inequality, with the articulation of rights facilitating access to development. This is not a new discourse as we have already discovered, but the notion of rights carries with it an eclectic mixture of conceptual thinking and practices (Gaventa, 2002; Morvaridi, 2004). Essentially, the right to development approach integrates the norms, standards and principles of the universal human rights agenda into processes of development. For the UN, the Right to Development is a conceptual framework for the process of human development that is normatively based on international human rights standards, and is operationally directed at promoting and protecting the individuals' agency. Article 1 of the Right to Development declaration states that 'the right to development is an inalienable human right by virtue of which every human person and all peoples are entitled to participate in, contribute to, and enjoy economic, social, cultural and political development, in which all human rights and fundamental freedoms can be fully realised'. In 1993 the Vienna Declaration and Programme of Action stated that the Right to Development constituted 'a Universal and inalienable right and an integral part of fundamental human rights' and a High Commissioner for Human Rights within the UN was established to promote the right to development. This subscribes to the view that the right to development is a synthesis of many human rights and is about empowering governments to meet their obligations to promote universal human rights that enable all members of society to reach their full potential. Underpinned by universally recognised moral values and reinforced by legal obligations, international human rights provide therefore a normative framework for the formulation of national and global development policies. Sen (1999) suggests that the general idea of freedom is particularly relevant to normative social choice theory, in general, and to the theory of justice, in particular. Not only can freedom figure powerfully in the normative foundations of human rights, but, in relation to development, it is particularly relevant as poverty-related deprivation tends to be caused by a lack of freedom to avoid it (see Chapter 3). Although the crux of the Declaration of the Right to Development is that the nation state is the primary agent of development, as the duty bearer responsible for protection of individual rights, it is also clear that the international community and therefore global institutions of governance should support states in carrying out these responsibilities, but this has not been the case (see Chapters 4 and 5).

Opposition to the right to development

The more powerful nations have been reluctant to accept the Declaration of the Right to Development, in particular the United States which perceives the Right to Development principle as a challenge to its neo-liberal priorities. The United States has voiced concerns about the Declaration of The Right to Development from its inception in 1981, when a draft was submitted to the Council of the UN. The United States opposition was such that it voted against a legally binding declaration on the Right to Development, conceding only later when it was agreed that it would be non-binding. Effectively the United States opposed the UN Commission using the human rights agenda to address issues that the United States was already engaged in tackling through the major development institutions (the World Trade Organization (WTO), the World Bank (WB), the International Monetary Fund (IMF), regional development banks, the Organization for Economic Cooperation and Development (OECD), and regional settings such as the Asia-Pacific Economic Cooperation (APEC) summit). More importantly the focal point of the Right to Development is the state as the primary agent of development, which is at variance with the neo-liberalism market economy model that has dominated development practises in many countries since 1980 (see Chapter 3). Three ideological reasons underpin the US position. The first is concern that as the initiator of the right to development, the UN would be used to shape or influence sovereign decisions about aid and the transfer of resources under the banner of human rights, effectively allowing the UN to regulate state behaviour (Marks, 2004: 143). Secondly, the declaration promotes development that gives equal attention and consideration to the implementation and protection of civil, political, economic, social and cultural rights, as specified in Article 6 (2) of the declaration. This provoked major opposition, as voiced by Novak the then UN US representative, who refused to accept that civil and political rights could not be fully accorded until an ideal economic order was established (Ibid.: 135). Novak asserted that an ideological commitment to freedom and democracy also encourages nation states and individuals to use their own initiative in the market and gives all an equal right to compete. The third reason for US opposition to the Right to Development centred on its own use of the human rights agenda as a pragmatic instrument for US foreign and security policies. Simply put, the United States did not want to encourage this to be subject to UN scrutiny. The rhetoric of human rights has long been integrated into US foreign policy as Madeleine Albright, the Secretary of State in the 1990s, made clear:

> Support for human rights is not just some kind of international social work. It is vital to our security and well being; for governments that disregard the rights of their own citizens are not likely to respect the rights of anyone else. In this century, virtually every major act of international aggression has been perpetuated by a regime that represents political rights. Such regimes are also more likely to spark unrest by persecuting minorities, sheltering terrorists, running drugs, or secretly building weapons of mass destruction. (Albright, M, 1998)

In general, the north has made little attempt to take steps to support the implementation of the Right to Development even though, on paper and conceptually, progress has been noted at several UN forums (Commission for the Right to Development Report, 2005). The result is a widening gap between the rich and the poor. The Right to Development challenges the current economic order by supporting equality between nations and, as Toye (1987) argues, already rich nations do not welcome late developers. In a capitalist world economy, it seems that the system functions by virtue of states not developing simultaneously and the perpetuation of an unequal core and peripheral regions (Wallerstien, 1976). The success of late developer countries is often cited as the cause of economic disruption (through lost markets and lost access to cheap food and raw materials) to the established states. The rapidly growing economy of China for example has been partly blamed for increases in oil prices in recent years and concern has been expressed that if this process continues with a population of nearly 1.2 billion increasing demand for more energy resources will within a decade have even more far-reaching global impact. And so it seems to many, such as Chang (2002), that the north continue to 'kick the ladder of development away' from 'developing countries' and in so doing they ignore the historical events that resulted in the development of their own countries.

Here goes another limitation; a persistent imbalance in the articulation of economic and social rights can be evidenced that reflects inequalities and tensions not only between the powerless and the powerful or rich and poor individuals within states, but also between states themselves. These differences are rooted in the complex historical development of states and their interrelationships. However, challenges around the delivery of rights tend to focus on the capacity of national institutional frameworks to deliver rights benchmarked against the universal rights standard that is prescribed in UN rights frameworks. This is despite the fact that many states question the acceptance of a universal rights standard. Islamic and Asian states have joined together, for example, to criticise Western policy for its 'double standards', its violation of sovereignty and neglect of rights though its imposition of 'Western values'. Is the philosophical underpinning of the Universal Islamic Declaration of Human Rights[8] different to that of the UN declarations? Why have some states invoked a thesis of relativism, maintaining that their societies are fundamentally different in their social relations, tradition and values? Is there an operational gap between the universalism of the rights agenda and particularism that is a local interpretation based on concepts of sovereignty or locally entrenched politics and culture? Or are such arguments presented in order to justify human rights abuses or to consolidate internal power structures in particular states? These are some of the questions that the next section will consider.

Is there an alternative to the concept of universal rights?

As I have already examined, the rights that underpin the UN declarations are derived from Western political philosophy. Is this because there are no alternative philosophical, economic and political approaches to those developed in the West or an insufficient body of knowledge about them? Even though we associate the term 'rights' with the European Enlightenment, its component ideas have deep roots in many other traditions (Nussbaum, 1999: 8). It is also evident that how rights and obligations are discharged in Western and non-Western settings can vary, and that notions of rights and social justice are historically and culturally shaped. Values and rights often reflect traditions that for centuries are passed on from one generation to the next through unwritten rules.[9] This continues today despite the fact that modern constitutional law has become the dominant basis of justice. Some critiques suggest that the current basis of justice embodies a 'false universalism', as it presumes a modernist and modernising frame of reference, and thereby fails to mediate between the pre-modern and modern to offer protection for traditional values. Falk suggests this has to be 'linked to an enquiry into how to overcome a circumstance of inter-civilisation inequality when the claimant is neither individual, minority group, nor state entity, but rather civilization itself'[10] (Falk, 2001: 89). Others who support the thesis of universalism, on the other hand reject the concept of inter-civilisation rights and collective human rights, arguing that human rights, by their very definition, belong only to individual human beings (Donnelly, 2003). Donnelly assesses the human rights listed in the Universal Declaration of Human Rights and the two International Covenants on human rights to be based on a moral vision of human nature that views human beings as equal and autonomous individuals who are entitled to equal concern and respect. These are not necessarily distinct to Western culture and therefore they should have wider international recognition and endorsement.

The UN Declaration (1986) reinforces this position in its expectation that states will take steps to realise the right to development by delivering equality of access to basic resources, education, health services, food, housing and employment, as well as carrying out economic and social reforms to eradicate social injustice and ensure the fair distribution of income (see Article 8). This concept of universal equality is nevertheless a considerable challenge given that there are a number of cases where customary rights and practice treat individuals within the community differentially. How can states ensure 'that women have an active role in the development process' (Article 8) when in many settings customary law discriminates against them? In most countries from the south it is social custom for women not to have formal rights to land, despite their input in terms of labour. In many settings traditional inheritance laws do not allow widows to inherit land from their deceased husband or daughters are prohibited from inheriting any family or clan land and so forth. This was evidenced recently in Sub Saharan Africa, where in the context of HIV/AIDS the number of destitute widows and orphans has greatly increased. Modernity has shaped traditional social relations so that the regulation of inheritance is particularly problematic (Magoke-Mhoja, 2005: 256). Similar problems exist when there is displacement as a result of large development projects. Women are rarely granted compensation for loss of resources such as land that they should be entitled to receive because customary law regards them as 'housewives' and not the owners of resources. We have archives of rich resources provided by feminists that empirical data from different countries clearly shows persistent inequality between men and women in relation to assets, and access to education and health.

Some argue that a universal standard exists, but that many states simply fail to live up to it (Booth, 1999; Dunne and Wheeler, 1999). Donnelly in defence of universality defines human rights as 'a social practice that aims to realise a particular vision of human dignity and potential by institutionalising basic rights' (2003: 25). Even when different societies 'sign up' to the idea of universal rights, they disagree over the meaning and priority accorded to these rights, implying an operational gap exists between the universalism of the rights agenda and particularism. In the Middle East, and Muslim societies in particular, there has been both caution and resistance to universal conceptualisations of rights, in particular when universality is perceived to be an attack on Islam and a threat to sovereignty (Soysal, 1994). This tends to be based on the perception that rights are derived, on the one hand, from Western epistemological critiques and codes, which are considered irrelevant to non-Western cultures, and on the other from secular law that is non-Islamic and does not apply to Muslim countries (Afshari, 2001).

Through the forum of the United Nations, developing countries have signed up to the Declaration of Universal Human Rights and to the ideal of the right to development, but overall there has been resistance to the whole notion of universality (civil and political rights) for basically three reasons. First, states are wary of the whole idea of universal rights framed around conventions, international laws, and legislative frameworks, out of concern that this could constitute an infringement of their sovereignty and thus impose accountability on state-civil society relations. Second, a significant debate that has ensued around human rights and Asian and Islamic values boils down to the fact that the idea of universal human rights is considered to be of Western origin and therefore not compatible with other cultures or customary practices. This has culminated in the thesis of cultural relativism, which rejects the whole notion of universal civil and political human rights. Third, we find ourselves in territory that would place some kind of hierarchy on rights, with civil and political rights having priority over social, economic and cultural rights. These points were raised at various UN forums throughout the 1990s, most vociferously by 'Asian States' at the Right to Development Conference in 1993 in Vienna and more recently by numerous social movements.

Asian values: social, economic and cultural rights

For some Asian leaders, the West conception of rights is considered to glorify a 'destructive' and 'gross individualism' which is not compatible with Asian culture and values. Instead limits on personal freedom under strong state leadership are considered to be acceptable to 'secure public order, greater economic growth and preservation of religious and social values' (Chang and Grabel, 2004). Although cultures may differentially conceptualise duties and responsibilities, critiques of this version of Asian position have argued that States employ the concept of individual 'duty' to the wider community for political ends to maintain their powerbase, brush aside their human rights violation, and silence the opposition (Sen, 1999; Cox, 2002). Those in power use the concept of individual duty to the state and/or society, almost universally, to control and suppress human rights. In fact Asian leaders have rejected the use of human rights as an instrument of political and economic conditionality and legitimate humanitarian intervention, stressing the importance of national sovereignty and the principles of non-intervention in domestic affairs.

In the middle of this unconventional development period both China and India experienced high economic growth. Between 1993 and 2004 China's average GDP growth rate averaged 9.7 per cent and India's 6.5 per cent per annum. This was achieved behind very protective walls, without following the orthodoxy of international development institutions nor pretending to secure civil and political rights or individual rights. Some of the development policies that arguably were promoted as a precondition for China's growth were in fact quite repugnant to mainstream development parameters and paradigms. Policies such as absence of private property rights (only granted in February 2007);[11] restrictive movement of labour from rural to urban areas which essentially arrested rural-urban migration; land reform; nationally owned industries; and the abolishment of large landholdings, are all typical of a state-led development that barely reflects the preferred neo-liberal economic policy prescriptions for a developing country.

Amnesty International's report on China's widespread violation of civil and political rights states:

> Tens of thousands of people continued to be detained or imprisoned in violation of their fundamental human rights and were at high risk of torture or ill treatment. Thousands of people were sentenced to death or executed, many after unfair trials. Public protests increased

against forcible evictions and land requisition without adequate compensation. China continued to use the global 'war on terrorism' to justify its crackdown on the Uighur community in Xinjiang. Freedom of expression and religion continued to be severely restricted in Tibet and other Tibetan areas of China. (2005: 1)

China has seen concerns about violations of human rights as an infringement of its Right to Development and its sovereignty. It believes international criticism of its environmental record is part of a conspiracy to contain its economic development. China's rapid economic growth has been linked to environmental degradation and increased pollution. China believes that criticism of its environment record is unjust and reflects an unwillingness of the rich nations to see China progress, given that the rich nations are responsible for emitting 75 per cent of carbon monoxide in the atmosphere (*The Guardian*, Saturday 4 January 1997. 14).

It is a state's capacity to be inclusive and to effect social justice and equal rights to development, not merely its capacity to stride towards economic growth, that is under question at this point. Understandings of diversity tend to be oversimplified into generalisations about 'Western Civilisation', 'Asian Values', 'African Cultures', and they are often associated with the state and those who govern, whether religious leaders, elected members or military junta. Sen draws our attention to the fact that these 'leaders' who represent their countries in international gatherings and organisations (such as World Bank, IMF, WTO) do not necessarily have a monopoly in their country, so that 'an adequate approach to development cannot really be so centred only on those in power' (Sen, 1999: 247).

The Asian examples feed the debate about whether there is or could ever be a widely accepted universal rights standard. Most criticisms are derived from the religious values of mainly Islamic and Confucius scholars and focus on concerns that conceptions of human rights are inappropriately individualistic and as such disregard other cultures and philosophies that balance the rights of the individual against duties to families and communities. Following the Universal Islamic Declaration of Human Rights in 1981 and the Cairo Declaration on Human Rights in Islam, 1990, Islamic states joined with Asian states in criticising UN and Western policy for its double standards, its violation of sovereignty, its neglect of economic rights and imposition of 'Western' values.

Islam, modernity and human rights

In order to reject external criticism of their human rights records, Halliday argues that Islamic countries and states have 'found it necessary to invoke a thesis based on particularism – the cultural and historical specificity of their society' (1995: 137), maintaining that their societies are fundamentally different in their social relations, tradition, values and development. In reality many of the issues are dressed up as being Islamic or traditional to support existing authoritarian and patriarchal social and political contexts. Thus we find some states in the Middle East constructing a discourse of cultural relativism 'based' on Islamic values but which is really embedded in sovereign space and consolidating internal power structures. This implies, as Booth argues, that culturalism produces, or more accurately re-produces, traditionalism, and this can have several regressive consequences for the theory and practice of human rights (1999: 25). If principles or codes of conduct were in fact derived from Islam, they would construct a divergent form of universalism, since the religion itself is without particularism. Closer scrutiny of the Islamic Declaration of Human Rights (1990) reveals that the Articles are comparatively consistent with the UN Human Rights declaration, although on the face of it the declaration appears to support the idea of cultural relativism (see Article 1 of both declarations on race). In many respects the wording is similar to that of UN documents, although it is based strongly on Sharia Law and is derived from divine revelation that presents the equality of humanity before God:

> Believing that fundamental rights and freedoms according to Islam are an integral part of the Islamic religion and that no one shall have the right as a matter of principle to abolish them either in whole or in part or to violate or ignore them in as much as they are binding divine commands, which are contained in the Revealed Books of Allah and which were sent through the last of His Prophets to complete the preceding divine messages and that safeguarding those fundamental rights and freedoms is an act of worship whereas the neglect or violation thereof is an abominable sin, and that the safeguarding of those fundamental rights and freedom is an individual responsibility of every person and a collective responsibility of the entire Ummah. (Islamic Declaration of Human Rights, 1990)

Halliday suggests that many of the issues sanctioned as being Islamic or traditional are actually 'a set of discourses and interpretations that are created by contemporary forces for contemporary needs' (Halliday, 1995: 147). In a sense traditions are reinvented to perpetuate the structure of power relations pertaining to the values of patriarchy, class and religious authority. Afshari (2001) provides us with the prototype of the ruling clerics of Iran, who argue that their rejection of Western universal human rights is a defence of Islamic religion. Iran, Saudi Arabia, Pakistan and Sudan, along with other nations, have made much of the West's 'double standards', where tolerance of civil and political rights abuse is seen as selective and driven by power relations and economic interest. Anyone who is critical of the modus operandi of the state and its culture is considered de facto to be a supporter of Western culture. When Iranian Human Rights activist Shirin Ebadi was awarded the Nobel Peace Prize in 2003 for her efforts to promote democracy and human rights, the Iranian media accused her of being an 'agent' of Western cultural imperialism and part of a plot by enemies of Islam to undermine the Islamic republic. For two decades she used the UN Convention on the Rights of Children and other declarations to argue against a civil law that allowed children to marry at the age of puberty – specified as 15 for boys and 9 for girls (Note 1 of Article 210). Ebadi, presents a different view of Islamic rights to that of the ruling authoritarian state of Iran:

> Human rights are compatible with Islam. The problem is that if some Islamic countries don't implement human rights law, it's because of their misinterpretation of Islam;…you can be a good Muslim and follow the human rights charter. It's all about the right interpretation. (Ebadi, 2003)

Ebadi cites her own dismissal as a judge after the Islamic Revolution, on the basis that the Ulema or religious authorities in Iran ruled that Islam forbids women to be judges, as an example of misinterpretation. This judgement has now been overturned.

Civil society in Islam and community development

Emerging critiques highlight a range of problematic assumptions when the influence of local traditions, institutions and practices, including faith on civil society are insufficiently recognised within the development discourse (Hann and Dunn, 1996). There are two areas that are worthy of further consideration in relation to Islamic interpretations of human rights – firstly how states perceive civil society and Islam to fit together, and secondly how Islam as a religion places expectations on its congregations. Some states (e.g. Saudi Arabia) that pursue conservative Islam reject the whole notion of civil rights and civil society, as a Western import. In such states the only acceptable civil society associations are those that promote the spreading of religious sentiments and further religious activities, such as mosques (Kamrava, 2001: 181). Paradoxically Islamic social movements, local civil society organisations and opposition to the authoritarian state use the language of rights to critique the state. There are a number of political Islamic movements and parties that have attempted to incorporate modernity/development and human rights standards into their agenda – examples are Janaa al-Islamiyya and Al-Wassal in Egypt (which were both radical Islamic organisations in the 1970s) and Turkey's Justice and Development Party. Currently in power, the Justice and Development Party has endorsed the principles of human rights, democratisation and sound economic growth, stressing that they do not compromise Islamic values. In essence the government is seeking a balance between tradition and modernity, between the forces of Islam and the forces of secularism: 'A modernity that does not exclude tradition; A universality that accepts locality; A rationality that does not reject the meaning; A change that is not radical.' (Prime Minister Erdogan cited in Dinc, 2005: 148.) Nevertheless, popular critics of the Justice and Development party suggest that it has a very clear Islamic agenda within the machinery of a secular state, echoed recently by the election of a party member as Turkish president. It is criticised for popularising modernism, nationalism, tolerance, and democracy while cherishing religious precepts. Similar movements are observed in Tunisia in the al-Da'wa Islamic Party led by Rashed Al Ghannoushi and in Egypt where the the Al-Wasat Party represents an alternative to both Militant Islamists and the Muslim Brotherhoods. In India the discursive shift of Jami at-i Islam towards more inclusive and pluralist politics and the emergence of new social movements in Saudi Arabia in the late 1990s, point to an 'Islamo-liberal' trend that seeks a compromise between Islam and democracy (Bayat, 2007).

Bayat asserts that there is trend in some Muslim countries towards what he entitles post-Islamism that corresponds closely to democratic ideals and attempts to 'fuse religiosity and rights, faith and freedom, Islam and liberty' (Bayat, 2007: 11). This new social movement re-interprets the underlying principles of Islamism by emphasising rights instead of duties and plurality in place of a singular authoritative voice. Some scholars have even suggested that this could be an 'alternative modernity', which by marrying Islam with individual choice and freedom, and democracy with modernity, acknowledges secular exigencies and breaks down the monopoly of religious truth: 'In short, whereas Islamism is defined by the fusion of religion and responsibility, post Islamism emphasises religiosity and rights'. (Ibid.: 11) The post-Islamists' acknowledgement of civil society, but endorsement of its Islamic structure around the notion of community (Umma), distinguishes it from Western approaches. This is because the notion that Islam is not essentially about the state, market or individual, but about a community (Umma) based on shared faith and the active participation of citizens to support all members of the community, including the poor. Gellner considers that as 'theocracies', Islamic societies are defined by their faith – thus 'the boundary of the acceptance of doctrine becomes the boundary of community. Society is then a shadow of faith; and we have an Umma' (Gellner, 1994: 195). Islam fails to endorse a separation between religion and politics, unlike Christianity. According to Gellner, a free and open civil society cannot operate in such situations. Gellner associates Islam with the state and in so doing ignores the contribution of the Islamist movement for social justice and Islamic scholars who argue that Islam is not essentially about the state, but about community (Ramadan, 2004).

Huntington strongly believes that liberal capitalism is a predominantly western vision, and that many of its values, for example individualism, human rights and free markets, have little resonance with other civilisations throughout the world (1993). Conceivably this is verified by Islamists who promote the Islamisation of civil society to distinguish it from its counterpart in the West. This reflects on the notion that Islam is essentially about a shared faith community (Umma) in which individuals and groups actively participate to support all members, including the poor, and that this shapes interaction with the state and the market. The concept of 'Umma', which is at the crux of the Islamic conception of human rights, has ethnographical particularities. However in general it has a bearing on how the Right to Development might be conceived and delivered in Muslim societies. As Keddie (1969) points out Umma is an Islamic concept of community through which poverty is reduced and social injustice in society is achieved. The Islamic perception of community may conflict with the idea of a 'world community', as it fortifies regional and religious identities and in a sense presents a case for the Islamic world's opposition to the West. To Huntington this represents a clash of civilisation and cultures that threatens to undermine the idea of a 'liberal capitalist world' (Huntington, 1996). It is the conflict between different civilisations, mainly Islam and the Christian west, that Huntington in his book, claims to be the underlying problem that needs to be addressed and not issues of inequality between nation states and social classes.

> The underlying problem for the West ... is Islam, a different civilization whose people are convinced of the Superiority of their culture and are obsessed with the inferiority of their power. The problem for Islam is not the CIA or the U.S. Department of Defence. It is the West, a different civilization whose people are convinced of the universality of their culture and believe that their superior, if declining, power imposes on them the obligation to extend that culture throughout the world. (Huntington, 1996: 2)

The impact of economic globalisation and the ways that market forces undermine the principle of social justice and, as such access to life-chances, has in fact nothing to do with countries being Islamic or Christian. Adverse impacts on the fundamental areas that cut across human rights and development, such as health, education, housing and the supply of adequate food, brought about by neo-liberalism and macro-economic reform and structural adjustment have been felt, in the Middle East, Latin America and Africa and in some countries in the north too. What is distinguishable is the response of civil society and its underlying influences. In Muslim societies, for example, a growing number of Islamic NGOs are involved in service delivery and community development in order to fill the vacuum left by the shrinking involvement of the state in delivering social services to the poor. This might be the reason why organisations such as the Department for International Development (DIFD) and the World Bank prefer to engage with Faith based organisations working at the grassroots level for community development, rather than encouraging them to enter the political scene.

Faith-based civil society organisations by and large work with local communities across a range of issues including peace building, promotion of sustainable and long-term development, education improvement, overcoming of emergencies and disaster, capacity building, helping with urban and rural development and health improvement. They often focus on fighting poverty inequalities, the realisation of human rights and justice, supporting developing countries to speak out against the impact on poor communities of issues such as globalisation, free trade, debt or global institutions exigencies. As a result, Faith based organisations are reputed to be effective in reaching the most marginalised populations, as well as efficient in using a participatory approach to development, so as to enhance the continuity of their initiatives. They are competent in empowering people from the grassroots level, thereby promoting change in behaviours. They are hence seen as an essential component for the promotion of neighbourhood cohesion and development of local communities.

Within the Islamic community, poverty is approached through the prism of charity, with charitable actions and donations fulfilling a religious obligation. This is known as Zakat, the need to assist the needy and less fortunate with donors furnished with a corresponding spiritual award. Zakat is one of the five pillars of Islam. It is obligatory for Muslims who have a relatively high income to contribute two and a half per cent of their income annually to charitable causes. Vakif refers to the gift of money; property or other items to charity and the Western equivalent are charitable trusts or endowments. Such payments, although not enforced by any regular system of collection, tend to be considerable (Keddie, 1969). Zakat is paid annually to religious leaders or NGOs who use this income for local foundations, such as Madrasse or schools, and health centres, and to assist orphans or other religious activities and charities they control. Several NGOs have recently used the internet to raise funding through Zakat and Vakif and find projects that aim to alleviate poverty in Muslim communities. There are now a number of international Islamic NGOs involved in poverty reduction and the human rights movement. Islamic Relief and the Agha Khan Foundations, for example, are actively involved in development projects. Islamic NGOs operate the institutions of Zakat and also Vakif or religiously sanctioned charitable donations within the principles of Islamic Sharia. Some NGOs use Zakat to specifically raise funds for the poor, as a targeted intervention to transfer benefits directly to the poor. These transfers are needed to help those who would not otherwise benefit from growth; the destitute, the unemployed, the sick, and the aged. However, the extent of benefits to the poor from the NGOs' activity and targeted programmes is no replacement for the social contract that should exist with the state. An active civil society is no replacement for the state as the protector of rights, but governments and international development agencies, have all to some degree neglected their social and moral responsibilities in the south and in some areas, more than others. Ray Bush argues that this neglect relates to the dominance of a neo-liberalist conception of development that assumes all markets can be accessed equally, and one that assumes that there is no subordination or exclusion of workers and peasants, be it from markets, sources of production or international economic relationships. The neo-liberalist view of the need to reduce the 'exclusion' of the poor tends to obscure the crucial issue of how poverty is created and reproduced and demonstrates a fundamental lack of understanding of the fact that poverty does not emerge because of exclusion but because of poor people's 'differential incorporation' into economic and political processes (2004).

An inalienable right to development

Like other religions, there are different interpretations and underlying connotations of Islam as a way of life. Islamists, who are committed to the establishment of Islam as a fundamental framework for the political and social ordering of state, are those mostly identified with radical Jihad and rejection of Western modernity. Other Islamists do not reject all aspects of modernity but believe that it should be adjusted to reflect Islamic principles. In general, this represents a consensus that the modernity of Muslim societies is defined as progress in science, technology and industrialisation. This does not mean 'secularisation and secular understanding of the nation, universal human rights and democracy which is often either delegitimised or re-defined in a way incompatible with certain tenets of liberal democracy' (Dinc, 2005: 152). Historically, there is an understanding that Islam must be free from non-Islamic and foreign influences. It was in this context that the Islamic Republic of Iran quoted Article 1 of the Right to Development to support its inalienable rights to technology and as justification for Iran's questioning of the legitimacy of Western hegemony over the right to nuclear energy:

> How can one talk about human rights and at the same time blatantly deny many the inalienable right to have access to science and technology with applications in medicine, industry and energy and through force and intimidation hinder their progress and development? Can nations be deprived of scientific and technological progress through the threat of use of force and based on mere allegations of possibility of military diversion? We believe that all countries and nations are entitled to technological and scientific advancement in all fields... Such access cannot be restricted to a few, depriving most nations and by establishing economic monopolies, use them as an instrument to expand their domination... The UN must be the symbol of democracy and the equal rights of nations. If we talk about the equal rights of nations in political forums, we must talk of the same concept in this forum as well. Similarly, if we talk about the right of sovereignty, then all nations must be allowed to exercise their rights on an equal footing and in a democratic process.[12]

(Mahmoud Ahmadinejad Speech in the sixtieth session of the United Nations General Assembly, 21 September 2005)

Although Muslim states accept the opportunity to develop in technical terms, they tend to reject the imposition of social relations and cultures derived from modern western societies. In other words they accept modernity but without the institutions of secularism. At the thirty-sixth session of the UN General Assembly, an Iranian representative suggested that the Declaration of Human Rights represents a secular interpretation of the Judeo-Christian tradition, and as such was not relevant to Muslim societies. What is important for Muslims is 'the divine law of the country', based on Islamic Law (Littman, 1999). Justice, rights and equality are conceived as extensions of religious thought. This is a diversion from the 'natural rights' of the Enlightenment and seems to basically reject Western notions of civil and political rights. For this reason, the incorporation of normative ideas of morality or 'spirituality' into global institutions and international relations for global justice has been requested, as this would allow for acceptance of Islamic Law. The concepts of justice, rights and equality are integral to the idea of sovereignty, culture and spirituality, effectively encapsulating internal relations between state and society. However, all rights are socially constructed and reconstructed, whether by reference to a holy book or some other document (such as the UN Declaration). Who defines rights and in whose interests is a political and ideological matter?. Those who argue for cultural particularism and local identities tend to view rights as being territorially bounded, in contrast to universality or some form of abstractedness defined at a global level. If we take any region of the world we are likely to find numerous examples of where the interpretation and mediation of rights occurs through local institutions, economies and political structures, which act to reinforce structural inequalities that are social and/or economic. For, as Edward Said reminds us, notions such as modernity, enlightenment and democracy are by no means simple and universally agreed-upon concepts (Said, 2003: 2).

Conclusion

Normative pressures for a more equitable international economic order and the need to address the perceived grievances of disadvantaged nations in relation to the existing global order have driven the idea of the Right to Development. The concept of the Right to Development reflects far more than the contrivances of weaker nations to seek protection against the strong states, embedding a fundamental respect for the equality of every individual. In theory the concept has broadened from that of a restrictive liberal perspective, which centres on civil and political rights, to reflect a more 'multidimensional' understanding of how civil and political rights intersect with other rights, including social, economic rights. However, as I have sought to demonstrate in this Chapter, the interface of development and human rights is subject to both enormous challenges and constraints, some of which are fairly fundamental, such as a perceived conflict between the idea of universal rights and relativism or cultural specificity, and the dichotomy between social and economic rights and civil and political rights. It is perhaps understandable in the modern pluralistic world that we live in that there is some questioning of whether there is or could ever be a widely accepted universal rights standard.

The framing of the Right to Development requires careful consideration. As I will show in the next Chapter, the neo-liberal development strategy has contributed to set-backs in achieving equality through subordinating human rights of an economic and social character and the Right to Development to fiscal criteria. Neo-liberalism has never been entirely at ease with the liberal social justice and human rights perspective, and the promotion of equality across areas such as gender relations, and environmental issues. This is evidenced, in Chapter 3, in the continued efforts to shift development away from the state and towards market-oriented individualism and private sector activity.

3
Neoliberalism and Social Justice

Capitalism can make a society rich and keep it free. Don't ask it to make you happy as well. Capitalism can make you well off. And it also leaves you free to be as unhappy as you choose. To ask any more of it would be asking too much.

(*The Economist*, 23 December 2006, Editorial: 1)

About 400 farmers in India's most prosperous state, Maharashtra, have committed suicide this year as a result of failed crops, import competition and crippling interest payments, a farm lobby group Shetkari Sangathana, said yesterday. Farmers suicides have been on the rise due to poor harvests and trade liberalisation.

(*The Guardian*, Saturday 3 December 2005)

Introduction

This Chapter begins with a discussion of neo-liberal scholars who have engendered a new vision of economic development that undermines the Rights to Development agenda. Since the 1980s, almost all nation states have followed a development path that has neo-liberalism as its theoretical underpinning and which promotes market-led development through measures such as free trade, privatisation and minimal state intervention. This does not necessarily sit comfortably with the role of the state to deliver and enforce access to rights in line with Article 3 of the Right to Development, and Article 25.1 of the Universal Declaration of Human Rights that specify that

Everyone has the right to a standard of living adequate for the health and well being of himself and his family, including food, clothing,

housing and medical and necessary social services, and the rights to
security in the event of unemployment, sickness, disability, widow-
hood, old age or other lack of livelihood in circumstances beyond his
control. (UN, 1948: 9)

There is a direct interface between the concepts of rights as encapsulated here and social protection. In policy terms this generates a need
for states to intervene to address poverty and inequality through social
protection measures that provide income and consumption transfer,
employment opportunity for the poor and the associated enhanced
social status. The predominance of neo-liberal policy has, however,
politically and ideologically constructed human rights around the protection of individual rights in defence of property rights. The more
encompassing economic, social and cultural rights have tended to
elapse in theory and practice, because the neo-liberal economic paradigm that governments are encouraged to adopt glosses over the underlying causes of inequality and poverty. In so doing it perpetuates
unequal development.

This Chapter, then, examines critical responses to the neo-liberal
economic paradigm from the egalitarian liberal point of view. In
Chapter 6 a comparable examination is conducted from the critical
theory perspective. Social justice theory critiques neo-liberal ideas by
focussing on the injustices of market fundamentalism and the persistent poverty and inequality that is associated with the downside of capitalism. By putting rights issues at the centre of their critique, they have
inspired vocal resistance to prevailing development thinking. This
reflects a shift towards the overarching aim of incorporating human
rights and social justice into a framework of development, based on the
view that issues of social injustice arise when the benefits of growth are
not fairly shared or where decisions distort the distribution of benefits
and burdens between individuals and groups. Development theory and
policy faces the challenge of bringing development and social justice
together. But how? What can be done to synergise development outcomes and social justice? Is it possible to combine economic growth
with social justice? How can the need for high levels of social protection
to ensure equality be squared with market drivers?

The neo-liberal counter-revolution

The theoretical foundations of neo-liberalism are attributed to contemporary neoclassical economists, such as Hayek (1976), Friedman (1962)

and development economists, such as Lal (1983), Little (1982) and others, who consistently argue that unwise government interventions failed to achieve their prime objective of poverty alleviation through economic growth. State activity in the development process tends to take the form of expansion of the public sector and investment in physical capital formation.[1] This has been criticised as inefficient for the reason that it can lead to price distortion and monopoly of the market. The failure of states to avoid structural crises and economic recession and to reduce poverty by stimulating economic growth engendered what appears to be a neo-liberal counter-revolution (Toye, 1987) that promised to solve the problem of poverty through economic growth stimulated by market liberalisation, privatisation and free trade. This is basically what neo-liberalism is all about – disentangling development theory and policy from values attached to the state and replacing it with the invisible hand of the market, privatisation and formal democracy.[2] In a nutshell neo-liberalism means less government and in doing so it expropriates the individual theme of liberalism. Let's be clear, the shift of development thinking towards neo-liberalism has not been out of concern for social justice or rights. Hayek, one of the main intellectual contributors to the theory of neo-liberalism, argues that the whole idea of social justice is meaningless, primarily because it has to be directed by governments that frame economic activity to realise distributive justice. In fact he considers any form of state intervention to be nothing but 'an invasion of freedom' (Hayek, 1976: 97).

Rational choice, agency and rights

The rights' discourse, which is embodied in the various UN declarations, recognises the agency of rights-bearers, and the role of states to protect individual rights. Neo-liberals are apprehensive about this, as it seems to contradict the idea that individuals are 'rational' economic actors, who operate in the market for utility maximisation and are motivated by self-interest. This stand leads the neo-liberals to suggest that we could do away with the idea of public goods and community, replacing it with the notion of 'individual responsibility'. Agency, in this sense, places the individual as the agent responsible for his/her own poverty. In other words, 'the poor' are perceived to be 'rational actors, rather than victims' (Lister, 2004: 127). This neo-liberal conception of agency largely ignores constraints as a result of cultural and social structures that operate to limit individual ability to access the opportunities that the market may present. Such a reductionist approach does not work when it is applied to customary law, traditions and local norms, which are complex and often historically rooted, and which in some cases induce constraint on individuals' agency to express free will.

The neo-liberal paradigm fails in adopting a too individualistic stance and treating human agency as essentially linked to the individual person's cognitive, emotional and strategic capacities, without appreciating the context within which they are situated. This is well captured by the current president of South Africa who asserts that the neo-liberal economic paradigm in its purest form does not fit into the reality of African people because there is too much emphasis 'on the private, as opposed to public, the individual as opposed to collective, the individual versus the state' (Mbeki, 2003: 1). His concern is that when people are only connected because they interact with each other to achieve their competing objectives, then society as a whole loses out as the individual lives only for personal gain. In Mbeki's view it is impossible to solve the problem of global poverty solely through reliance on the market forces alone because the poor are not an appropriate object of the market, with an inner logic to maximise profit: 'Billions across the world, including in Africa, are too poor to achieve beneficial integration into the global market, even if they do create the macro conditions attractive to capital' (Mbeki, 2003: 1). To some extent this explains why in 1996 South Africa was the only country that provided a constitutional right to water, specified in the South African Constitution's Bill of Rights that everyone has the right to an environment that is not harmful to their health or well being…everyone has the right to have access to sufficient food and water. The legislative framework confers responsibility on the government to provide 25 litres of water per person per day as a minimum free basic supply (United Nations Development Programme (UNDP), 2006a). Other countries in contrast have commodified water by giving it an economic value and charging people irrespective of income. Effectively the poor have to pay for their livelihoods (see later), while the World Bank suggests it is about 'getting prices right'. Water privatisation has been adopted in many countries from the more affluent to the poorest justified by incentives of private sector investment and addressing public sector under performance. The World Bank and the International Monetary Fund actively supports privatisation within the overall objective of reducing poverty and achieving the Millennium Development Goals objectives. However, opposition and resistance to water privatisation have been widespread, documented in countries such as Argentina, Bolivia, Brazil, Thailand, Sri Lanka and South Africa. In Ghana water charges of 30p to 40p a day have spurred resistance from civil society organisations representing the poor. Some governments have also opposed privatising key public sector operations that are vital to secure livelihoods. In Tanzania, a private company, Biwater, built a new pipeline to Dar el Salaam as part of a $140 million World Bank funded and Department for International Development (DFID) supported (British government aid) privatisation project. The government of Tanzania had little choice but to agree to the privatisation of water as part of the conditionality package that was imposed by the global institutions as part of debt forgiveness. However, the company did not succeed at improving infrastructure and services for the people as their profit margin was too low, and the ten year water privatisation contract was terminated by the government of Tanzania after two years, with a possible court case to resolve outstanding issues (Vidal, J, 2005; *The Guardian*, 25 May).

The idea of success or failure determined by the market is fine as far as the rich and the more powerful people are concerned. But how can the poor and vulnerable be held responsible for their own poverty and exclusion in circumstances where there are little resources and no protection? There are many valid concerns that rights are being technically packaged in ways that ignore power and structural inequalities, which in reality have a very real impact on agency and choice. In addition valuable lessons are being ignored from the 'lost innovations' of earlier rights and empowerment strategies (Miller, 2005).

In defence of market liberalisation, promoters of neo-liberalism in the wider media, such as *The Economist*, are at pains to point out that the individual knows best what serves his/her interests and that choice will therefore produce socially good results. Market power ensures that factors of production are paid what they are worth, and this supposedly removes the need for institutions of social protection and institutions that regulate fairness, such as trade unions. Successful development sets its stall against 'dirigiste dogma', on the grounds that 'getting prices right' is probably the single most important means of reducing poverty (Lal, 1983: 102); while the market and private property are the most important guarantors of freedom. This is simply because the ownership of the means of production is divided among people who are independent and essentially not within the control of any institution, including the state. Individuals are, therefore, considered to have real freedom under neo-liberalism because they are treated equally in the market and their individual rights are not infringed upon by state interventions. In this paradigm, even taxation of personal income is considered to be an infringement of an individual's rights to keep what they earn. Neo-liberals do not ignore the issue of rights, but place clear emphasis on the protection of property rights and the legal rights of individuals within the market and democratic institutions. Development theory and policy is expected to promote this approach to rights through effective institutions like the rule of law and property rights. This has given rise to a 'new economic institutionalism' that encourages rational individuals to maximise their utilities within the market economy (North, 1990). In other words 'what makes for an efficient economy is a set of 'new institutions that permit individuals to benefit personally from doing what will also serve the interest of the society as a whole' (Leys, 1996: 73). By implication, this creates a tension between social and economic rights and civil and political rights – any direct action to secure the former is seen as a potential threat to the latter if it is perceived to undermine individualism and consolidate power.

There is some acknowledgement that neo-liberalism lays down no certainties about the requirements of social justice in terms of income redistribution or the extent of the role of the welfare state. In fact it is not difficult to recognise that markets have their limits in supplying public goods such as a clean environment, because the prime motivation of business will always be profit. Moral values tend to, therefore, be expelled from consideration under a market economy where we are obliged to work not in order to produce what is needed on moral grounds but to produce what is profitable (Sayer, 1998). In the words of Marx capital is about profit maximisation and has very little, and in some cases no, sagacity of social responsibility. This is clearly reflected in both the early neo-liberal development policy framework, which is commonly referred to as the Washington Consensus, and its later reconfiguration as the Post-Washington Consensus.

The Washington consensus

The initial neo-liberal development policy framework was constructed in Washington by the powerful global International Financial Institutions (IFIs) – The World Bank, IMF and US Treasury. The consensus of the IFIs on the broad ideas, objectives, means, and aims of neo-liberal development became known as the Washington Consensus (WC). The main components of development policy promoted by the Washington Consensus are fiscal discipline, the redirection of public expenditure, tax reform, interest rate liberalisation, a comprehensive exchange rate, trade liberalisation, liberalisation of inflows of foreign investment, deregulation, and securing property rights.[3] The IMF and the World Bank, institutions at the forefront of these ideas, used their influence to pressurise nation states to adopt institutional reform to deliver development through the neo-liberal paradigm. The modus operandi was to basically impose obligations and expectations on recipient governments in return for loans, grants or technical assistance, branded as conditionality. These conditionalities were attached to loan agreements to ensure that states appropriately redirected their macroeconomic policy in accordance with the interests of official and commercial creditors. There was, therefore, an increasingly close relationship between debt management policy and macro-economic reform.[4]

Since the 1980s, structural adjustment and stabilisation loans from the World Bank and the IMF have supported policy reforms intended to shift Third World economies from an inward-looking orientation to export-led growth. This was to be achieved through restrictive policy tools – a restrictive monetary and fiscal policy, cutbacks in Central Bank funding of the public sector, and the promotion of export commodities. Over the past three decades, several third world countries have been faced with pursuing policies that have been dictated to them through the constraints imposed upon them from outside institutions, undermining their ability to act independently. Even leading economists, such as Joseph Stiglitz, World Bank Chief Economist from February 1997 to February 2000, have acknowledged that conditionality effectively undermines domestic political institutions and this in turn undermines democracy as the electorate sees its government giving in to international institutions believed to be run by the United States (Stiglitz, 2006: 12). The number of conditions set for each debt tends to be so high that the heads of states from poor countries have been seen to campaign for re-negotiation at every opportunity.

A contravention of human rights

The 'market fundamentalism' of the Washington Consensus was rooted in the belief that markets by themselves would make people better off and that facilitating the pursuit of self-interest would lead to economic efficiency. However, we have yet to see a country from the south that has successfully implemented WC policies and reduced poverty and inequality. The argument usually put forward by the proponents of Structural Adjustment Policies (SAP) is that programmes have not worked because countries lack capacity or have not fully implemented them. However, this argument does not hold in Sub-Saharan Africa where only 21 of 241 programmes were abandoned or terminated before set deadlines and 75 per cent of all programmes met the conditions set by the World Bank (Lopes, 1999). Yet this region continues to have extremely high and increasing rates of absolute poverty. A UNDP report from the early days of this development policy points out that 70 per cent of countries in Latin America, the Middle East and Africa experienced a rapid decline in household incomes and/or government expenditure in the 1980s, resulting in setbacks in improvements in standards of child health, nutrition, and education. This decline reflects an essential lack of appropriate policies for social protection in general and for safeguarding children in particular (Giovanni, Jolly, and Stewart, 1987: 34–35). Empirical evidence from Abouharb and Cingranelli's (2006) analysis of 131 countries, between 1981–2004, shows that SAP has caused increasing destitution for the poor, greater civil conflict and domestic violence and an increasing likelihood of states using repression. Their research suggests that there is a close correlation between these indicators and a low rate of economic growth and development. They conclude that structural adjustment has led to less reverence for economic and social rights, and workers' rights, while at the same time creating a context for more interest in governance and democratic rights. The findings also provide enough evidence to support the view that World Bank SAPs worsen government respect for physical integrity rights, with governments abandoning their duty to protect citizens from abuses such as political imprisonment, torture and crime related endangerment.

It has not been all gloom and doom since the 1990s – in some countries we have witnessed improvements in life expectancy, child mortality and literacy rates. However, the World Bank and IMF are a little too eager to claim the benefits of the economic growth and either increasing or stable rates of GNP that occurred in some countries between 1980 and 1995. In Latin America and the Caribbean, for example, the measurement of such growth tends to mask extreme income inequality, aggravated and worsened by a lack of social development policy and political commitment to redistribution, legal reform, and the implementation of property rights and human rights for minorities. Indicators from World Bank economists point to levels of inequality in Latin America and the Caribbean region that are alarmingly high with regard to almost all development indicators. Forty-eight per cent of total income in this region rests with the richest tenth of the population, while the poorest tenth earn only 1.6 per cent. There are huge inequalities in Latin America in terms of income and access to fundamental services, including education, health, and utilities such as water and electricity. There are also huge disparities in relation to assets and opportunities, reflected in the fact that the poor have less voice. All these inequalities slow the pace of poverty reduction and undermine the development process. The World Bank study focused on seven countries – Brazil, Guyana, Guatemala, Bolivia, Chile, Mexico and Peru. Examples of the inequalities that it uncovered are that indigenous men earn 35–65 per cent less than white men (and a similar disparity exists between white women and non-white women), and men and women of African descent in Brazil earn about 45 per cent of the wages of white workers (Perry et al., 2006). The Organisation for Economic Co-operation and Development has reported that in Turkey 'income inequalities are increasing in a country that has the second widest (after Mexico) income dispersion among the OECD countries: the bottom 20 per cent of households account for only 5 per cent of disposable income. Thirty-six per cent of the population is unable to purchase the basic needs basket including non-food items' (OECD, 2001: 100). In Asia despite phenomenal economic growth and some reduction in poverty, inequality has been rising. In India and China for example income inequality has been rising. although there is a lack of reliable data to on which to base an assessment of by how much. Indicators from central rural areas in China and North West India show that the ratio of female to male is very low which is indicative of the fact that life opportunity depends on gender. More reliable data on inequality from Bangladesh, Nepal and Sri Lanka shows inequality in the late 1990s with a Gini of 0.30 to 0.40 between 1991–2000. However inequality is not just found in the south. In the United Kingdom for example inequality has been rising dramatically since 1980. Between 1980 and 1990 the Gini Coefficent in the United Kingdom rose by 10 percentage points which was an unprecedented increase over a short period of time. Lack of data makes it difficult to assess the level of inequality across regions, although the UNDP notes that 'extreme inequality between countries and within countries is identified as one of the main barriers to human development and as a powerful brake on accelerated progress towards the Millennium Development Goals' (see later) (UNDP, 2005: 21).

Poverty reduction

Hitherto, advocates of the Washington Consensus have claimed that inequality is not necessarily bad for economic growth, as it is an incentive for wealth creation. In this sense the concentration of wealth in the hands of a few is considered to be a positive way of ensuring that capital can be invested wisely in the economy with the effect of increasing productivity and consequently driving economic growth. In China the number of people living in poverty at the $1 a day standard has apparently fallen from 634 million to 212 million (World Bank 2006).

However, at the same time, inequality has increased significantly. Income inequality between rural and urban areas is considered to be unavoidable in the early stages of development as the economy shifts from one based on subsistence farming to a more labour intensive system with higher value produced in urban areas. Lal considers that there are two options for income growth within a capitalist economy. The first is that the income of all groups, including the poor, rises but with relatively larger increases for the rich. In this case the uneven distribution of income is worsened. In the second option, the poor do not experience income growth but there is reduction in the income of the rich. In this case, poverty remains unchanged even though the distribution of income improves – 'Those concerned with inequality would favour the second option; those with poverty first' (Lal, 1983: 89).

Neo-liberal economists, including the major institutions such as the World Bank, tend to focus on economic growth as the single most important driver of poverty reduction rather than of income distribution. According to Dollar and Kray (2002), 'Growth is good for the poor' because an increase in GDP of say 2 per cent per annum reduces the poverty rate from 1 per cent to 7 per cent per annum depending on the country. Thus poverty reduction achieved through economic growth is promoted as the focus of public policy. The World Bank has hyped evidence that supports poverty reduction achievement, in the south, as a result of economic growth. The data suggests that market led development has helped to reduce global poverty with the proportion of people living in extreme poverty (less than $1 a day) falling from 29 per cent in 1990 to 23 per cent in 1999 (World Bank, 2005a). Even within the World Bank, there is a deep intellectual rift on this issue. In 2000 Ravi Kanbur (appointed 1998 to act as the leading author of the World Development Report) resigned amid claims that the then US treasury secretary, Larry Summers, and other economists were seeking to rewrite the world development report he authored to make it less radical. Kanbur wanted to emphasise that economic growth alone would not be enough to reduce poverty and that it would also require at least equal emphasis to be placed on redistributive tax and spending policies. However, he was opposed by the more orthodox economists within the World Bank who believed that growth is paramount and should not be equated to other policies even in the face of overwhelming evidence. Kanbur's draft criticised free market reforms advocated by the Bank and the International Monetary Fund, for the harm they have done to poor people in some countries. It also blamed the rapid opening of financial markets for the crisis that swept Asia in 1997 (Wade, 2004). Most importantly the draft not only argued that growth was insufficient for poverty reduction (this was already accepted, although played down), but that growth alone had been and would continue to be detrimental to the poor unless issues of inequality and wealth distribution were addressed. The final version of the report omits most of the sections describing the downside of market reforms and concentrates on their benefits for economic growth.

$1 a day and human dignity

The World Bank claims that, in response to Poverty Reduction Strategy, the number of people living on less that $1 a day has dropped since the World Development Report of 2001. This estimated that 1.1 billion people living in extreme poverty had consumption levels below $1 a day and 2.7 billion lived on less than $2 a day (World Bank, 2001). Currently roughly 877 million people live in extreme poverty (on less that $1 a day), but the methodology used to generate these figures and their accuracy is subject to ferocious debate.

Universal convergence has now become a reality by constructing a global poverty line of individual consumption or income of $1 a day, based on Purchasing Power Parity terms (or $2/day PPP for a certain year). Academics, journalists, politicians and advocacy groups cite this as a shared standard that can be used to form a view of whether the income of the poor is rising or falling. The method of measurement is based on the income or consumption level of an individual; with the 'poverty line' determined as the minimum level that the individual requires to satisfy individual basic needs. An individual is considered, therefore, to be poor when his/her consumption level falls below the poverty line. Reddy and Pogge (2002) argue that such a methodology is flawed and has shaky foundations. The World Bank's 'money metric' approach based on consumption PPPs understates the extent of global poverty, because the PPP price indices are based on the prices of *all* commodities weighted by their share in international consumption and include services and goods that are very cheap in the south. They, therefore, overstate the purchasing power of the poor relative to the basic necessities on which they are compelled to concentrate their expenditure. By using PPPs that average out price differentials across all commodities, economists inflate the nominal incomes of the poor, as if their consumption mirrored that of the world at large (Reddy and Pogge, 2002: 7–10). A more relevant methodology to measure poverty would be to concentrate on the consumption bundle needed to avoid poverty. Food and shelter, for example, are relatively expensive and if they alone were included in the PPP indices, used to adjust the income of the poor, national poverty lines would go up (Wade, 2004). The current methodology clearly underestimates global poverty and produces unreliable estimations of levels, distribution and trends of global poverty.

Pogge makes the valid point that 'If you want to have an absolute income poverty line, you have to start out with some sort of idea about what the important needs or requirements or capabilities of human beings are,' (2002: 10). A fundamental contention with current estimations of poverty is that they are not based on what poor people are able to do in life. Income is an important factor, but by no means is it the only way to measure well being. Certainly it is one of the easiest, which is probably why utilitarian and neo-liberal economists favour it. It is quite possible to find situations where increased income is not a priority for the poor. In some rural areas for example, there may be little or no cost for food or water and shelter could be quite easily self-made (Satterthwaite, 2003: 5). In these cases the lack of access to land and resources is not a result of low or no income, but a result of extreme social inequality and/or social exclusion and as such the income measure is irrelevant. Jodha's findings in India present an even more convincing argument against the use of monetary measures – wherein he found that people whose income had decreased by 5 per cent reported themselves as being less poor. They had improved in gaining secure employment, being less dependent on others etc. and, in their estimation their condition was improving even though they were earning less money. Income poverty is only one aspect of poverty. Other estimates of poverty based on nutrition, infant mortality, access to health services, and other human rights indicators, are very important determinants of well being (see later discussion of Sen and social justice theory). Monetary measures of poverty are often meaningless to the poor; not only because of their very abstract conception (and complexity in calculation), but more importantly these measures neglect what the poor think about their situation (Chambers, 1998). Despite the evidence that clearly indicates that income on its own cannot capture the potential of what a person can do or what the community allows people to do, the main global institutions continue to insist on measuring poverty in isolation from many of the inequalities that impact on life experience and which are the main sources of social injustice. A new methodology is clearly required.

The continued focus of development policy on the benefits of economic growth for the greater good ignores social contextual issues and structures of inequality and the fundamental question of justice. These tend to be sidelined by macroeconomic policies that, in both their design and implementation, in the words of Elson embody 'a profoundly unjust social content giving the financial rights of creditors priority over the human rights of the people' (2002: 82). To sum up, deregulated markets have played some part in generating social problems and have threatened social cohesion in several countries. We now have ample data and evidence that the market fundamentalism of the Washington Consensus has delivered more harm than good and has aggravated poverty in many countries.

Deconstruction of the Washington consensus

During the 1980s, the hegemony of the Washington Consensus was challenged by egalitarian liberals and critical theorists on the one hand and from within the neo-liberal camp on the other. Various reports, such as the report of the World Commission on Environment and Development Report sponsored by the United Nations (the Bruntland report), challenged the principle of market fundamentalism and raised ethical concerns on North/South inequality. The Bruntland Report launched the concept of sustainable development and both popularised the idea and set the terms of the debate on environment and development at the UN conference in Rio 1992. The Commission called for 'sustainable development' defined as development that meets the needs of the present without compromising the ability of future generations to meet their own needs (WCED, 1987). The concept of sustainability broadly acknowledges that the relationship between society and environment is intrinsically intertwined. The Bruntland report pointed out that not only does the environment currently endure indiscriminate growth, but a degraded environment can undermine the foundations for growth. The issue was no longer one of growth or no growth, but what type of growth. The economic activities of the 1980s and early 1990s played a major role in making the question of environment and development the focus of policy initiatives. There is general agreement in the vast literature that sustainable development is a means to achieving resource conservation and environmental integrity, but it is also a means of ensuring some accountability for social justice. Dealing with the problem of poverty is a goal in itself as well as a means to protecting the environment and increasing economic output. There is not sufficient space here to go into the debate in detail, but for our purpose it suffices to say that the concept of sustainable development has remained vague as a statement of intent, rather than a framework for compromise between the natural environment and the pursuit of economic growth

(Redclift, 1987: 199). The causes of environmental crisis are structural and historical with roots in social and economic institutions as well as social relations.

Another challenge to the Washington consensus emanated from the UNICEF report on 'Adjustment with Human Face'. Giovanni et al. present empirical data from a number of countries such as Ghana, Brazil, Jamaica, Philippines, Sri Lanka and Chile, that show the negative effects of structural adjustment programmes on child health, education and nutrition (Giovanni, Jolly and Stewart, 1987). Reductions in public expenditure have limited the chance of vulnerable children going to school and child mortality has increased as cut backs in health have reduced the chances of survival for infants. The 1990s saw the early foundations of human development that identified the need for a joint focus on addressing low incomes by increasing growth and social protection policies that directed public expenditure on essential services, in particular health, education and nutrition (see later in this Chapter).

Other critiques of the Washington Consensus included Stiglitz, during his time as Chief Economist of the World Bank, who argued that the limitations of the market were evidenced by the failure of market fundamentalism to fulfil its promise to resolve development problems. Evidence from regions as diverse as Sub-Saharan Africa and parts of Latin America supported his arguments. The market has frequently failed to produce efficient outcomes, which have contributed to high levels of poverty as well as high levels of pollution and environmental degradation. Excessive reliance on the market has gone hand in glove with increasing social frailty, and consequential social conflict, often associated with violence (Stiglitz, 2002, 2006). In launching the Post-Washington Consensus, Stiglitz declared that it provided for a wider view of development, in a paradigm that is more open, transparent, and participatory than its predecessor. In particular participatory processes were considered to be an important ingredient of development transformation – important both for sustainable economic development and for social development, which was considered to be an end in itself, as well as a means to more rapid economic growth. The Post Washington Consensus (PWC) was the neo-liberalist response to a mounting critique of its market fundamentalism. Stiglitz' analysis 'Asymmetric Information and Market Imperfection' focuses on poor institutions and market problems, making both of them the target of economic social policy that operates with less austerity, and less extreme dominance of the state by external institutions, than under the Washington Consensus.

There is another reason for deconstruction of the WC. Stiglitz argues that the state could play an important role 'in both promoting development and protecting the poor', but the state is only a facilitator (2006: 27). The state and its institutions are framed in the PWC as regulators of the market, taking steps where necessary in order to avoid market failure and financial crisis and to promote just competition. This means selectively facilitating privatisation by creating adequate basic conditions, including investing in human capital and better access to education and health. Stiglitz carves out a clear need for acknowledgement of 'non-economic values' or social justice through the engagement of civil society in decision-making processes (Stiglitz, 2006: xiv). In establishing state regulation and intervention to ensure that markets lead to both economic efficiency and greater equity, the PWC has added new concepts such as social capital and participation to its predecessor policy instruments, as shown in diagram 3.1. These comprise the policy of development as currently promoted by the World Bank.

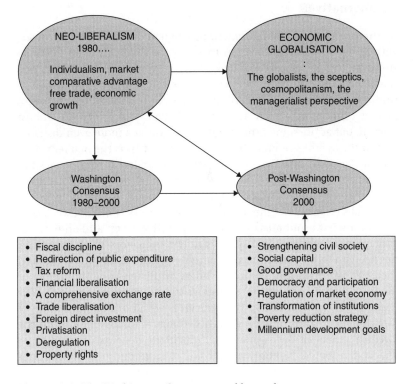

Diagram 3.1   The Washington Consensus and beyond

It is perhaps too early for us to make a judgement on its success or failure. The important question that we can consider now is how radical is the PWC? The PWC's ideological commitment remains faithful to the principle of the centrality of the market and its determination. But is this approach out-modish? Fine (2002) maintains that the PWC is 'flawed' in that the idea of new microeconomics is about how best non-economic, or non-market agencies, such as social capital can make the market 'work or work better' for capital. An understanding of social categories and institutions are appended to an economistic framework for a limited purpose. Like previous mainstream development theories, PWC is in fact silent over the power, conflicts and meanings of social relations that have traditionally been the preoccupation of the social sciences. Concepts such as social capital, participation and civil society may assist in attacking the symptoms of development, but they do not address the causes of the problem.

An alternative?

By the late 1990s the development debate had declared the WC 'dead', with its replacement in the mainstream by the PWC (Maxwell, 2005: 3). However, the neo-liberal agenda and the universal consensus that 'one size fits all' continued to be seriously contested and the challenge to find the best alternative began. There are, for instance, other forms of market economies – such as that of Sweden, which sustains robust growth, but at the same time sustains equity and a more even distribution of the benefits of growth. In other words, this is the market with a human face and one that promotes less inequality through measures such as accessible health and education for all. The main explanation for the success and distinctiveness of this model is that policies are designed to narrow the inequality of conditions between social classes, based on what economists would call 'punitive taxes' and an extravagant programme of public spending. The indicators show that there has been an improvement in productivity which has in turn 'enhanced the country's economic competitiveness, while ensuring that the poor obtain a higher proportion of total national income (Monbiot, *The Guardian*, Tuesday 11 2005). WC policies have led to a concentration of wealth in the hands of a few and this compares unfavourably with the Swedish model of development in which the benefits of growth are widely distributed. Not only has the rate of economic growth been consistently high in Sweden, but also social indicators on life expectancy, health, education, equality between men and women, and child poverty reflect a more just society. Only 6.3 per cent of the total population live below absolute poverty. Economic success requires getting the balance right between the government and the market and between private and public sectors and changing the balance as and when required. Miller argues that what distinguishes social democratic parties and movements from the neo-liberalists and Marxists is the conception of social justice that is integral to their policies. The commitment is to the principle of fairness and the belief that a society can be reshaped by its major social and political institutions to ensure that every individual not only gets a fair share of the benefits, but also carries a fare share of the responsibilities of living together in a community (Miller, 2005: 3). The Labour Party has used the concept of the Third Way to promote the ideas of equality of opportunity, that rights come with responsibilities, the protection of the more vulnerable people in society and the idea that freedom is autonomy but there is no autonomy without democracy. Delivery is underpinned by the principle of involvement of the third sector or NGO's, and civil society and government partnerships with the private sector (Giddens, 1998). These principles are more or less in line with PWC, but unlike the countries in the south that are subject to external intervention there is no conditionality imposed by external forces in the north as such.

When does conditionality end?

The PWC continues to promote conditional adjustment policies that are difficult to reconcile with human rights standards. Of course every bank imposes conditionality on customers, but they do not dictate what the individuals or private companies have to do or how they should behave. The International Financial institutions tend to disproportionately hurt the most vulnerable, such as the poor and women, by impacting directly on their rights to development and the capacity of states to protect them. Most simplistically, when states are encouraged to restructure the economy in the direction of a reduction in state intervention, their ability to secure rights is undermined. When conditionality that encourages this is built into lending agreements, it is difficult for governments to consider expansion of active intervention in rights delivery and this becomes most apparent when governments need to redirect economic resources into social protection programmes in order to achieve rights outcomes. This is one of the reasons why an increasing role is being carved out for the voluntary and private sectors in protection programmes. In a number of different contexts, Pogge (2002) raises concerns about the influence of

IFIs in this respect. For example, the economic platforms designed by political parties in poor countries, and upon which they were often elected, tend to be utterly disregarded by the economic restrictions placed on the state by the IFI driven SAP policies. In this, the IFI has backed violations of constitutional rights validated and legitimised in the service of the 'international community's' highest law, that is the law of the market. Moreover, the fact that countries are locked into these agreements by penalty of exclusion from the international community means that the avenues for economic change in future governments are non-existent. To ensure citizens stay in line with IMF and World Bank policy, these institutions often openly support the political parties that they want to be in power using finances as a threat to the electorate, (a prominent example is Jamaica in the 1980s). The policies and activities of the IFIs in this sense actively violate democratic principles and the people's right to elect governments without coercion. Here, the hypocrisy of these institutions becomes apparent – they demand democratic and good governance practices from recipient countries while they directly abuse the civil as well as the social and economic rights of whole populations.

A response to the neo-liberal counter revolution

The neo-liberal paradigm has been criticised from a number of quarters, out of increasing concern about poverty, inequality, cultural identity and environmental issues. Social justice theory, on the one hand, and an advocacy and civil society responsibility framework, on the other (in the form of new social movements and emancipatory politics) has been an obvious response to its hegemony (see Chapter 6). The more robust critiques of neo-liberal scholars come from egalitarian liberals, amongst whom are the prominent contemporary political philosophers, normative development economists and social theorists – Sen, Nussbaum, O'Neill, Piggot, Cohen and Giddens, to name a few. While acknowledging issues that exist with failed states, they clearly frame poverty and inequality as injustices of capitalist development, unjust global institutions and market fundamentalism. Contemporary political philosophers, in a conscious attempt to avoid abstraction, are becoming directly engaged in the public policy debate around poverty, inequality and human rights issues. Sen, for example, argues that a conception of justice can be determined that overcomes the blindness of the earlier classical liberals and even the Rawlsian standard, that can be applied to a range of inequalities based on difference and diversity. Sen's (1992) pertinent question posed in his earlier writings 'Equality of What?' sets the context for his alternative conceptualisation of social justice which moves away from income, class and wealth to incorporate normative ethical concerns.

Before discussing this in more detail, it is important to understand the heritage of the concept of social justice. The concept of social justice is derived from the view that if you were to set aside individual preferences and capacities, people would agree to certain general principles of justice. The challenge, according to Rawls, is to consider how 'a just and stable society of free and equal citizens' can be achieved, even when people are segregated by religious and cultural divides (Rawls, 1993: 3–4). For Rawls the issue is political – how can the main social and political institutions of society and the way in which they distribute fundamental rights and duties be reshaped so that benefits and responsibilities can be fairly distributed and shared? This presupposes that society can be changed to offer a shared institutional order, which maintains genuinely equal treatment of individuals (Miller, 2005: 1–3). It also suggests that social change is possible in liberal capitalist societies without major transition or fundamental political change.

Rawls turned to the liberal and democratic traditions of Locke, Rousseau and Kant in developing his alternative approach, which focuses on the unfairness of capitalism. In his view the basic institutions of capitalist society are regulated by two principles of justice. The first is the 'liberty principle', the equal rights for each individual to political liberty; and the second is the 'difference principle', that the socio-economics of opportunity can benefit all citizens, in particular the marginal and worse-off in society. Making no reference to diversity, Rawls defines justice in terms of the distribution to individuals of 'primary goods', essentially the resources needed by human beings in general. These include 'rights, liberties and opportunities, income and wealth, as the social basis of self-respect' (Rawls, 1993: 60). The social contract that arises is based on these two principles of justice that Rawls believes govern our lives and apply to the basic structure of society and its institutions, thus ensuring equality for all. According to the doctrine of social contract, laws are just when they are agreed to by free persons from a position of equal right. Therefore, to be just, laws must promote the common good and not just benefit a majority. Rawls suggests that inequality is justified only to the extent that it benefits the worse off in society; this is what he describes as the *difference principle*. So long as constitutional, legal arrangements and institutions provide fair equality of opportunity in education, health and employment, it is not unreasonable for systems of property, taxation, and public spending to prioritise the interests of the least advantaged in society. Social justice in this framework is concerned with fair distribution across society, giving citizenship and civil and political rights on equal basis and thus also personal security. It may require access to resources, which are essential not only for the livelihoods of citizens but to ensure equal opportunity. Hence, we would expect people to have access to education and jobs, for example, without prejudice on basis of gender or ethnicity (Miller, 2005: 5–9).

In fact, it is the very relevance of the 'difference principle' in relation to 'primary goods', which is of the greatest interest to Sen, contributing to the evolution of his thought on capability rights and poverty issues in poor countries. Rawls' difference principle draws attention to the welfare of the least well-off people in liberal capitalist society. Inequality of income and differential pay rewards, for example, can be tolerated in a market economy as long as they optimise the position of the disadvantaged or the poor. For Sen, this implies that development policies ought to be structured so as to have the largest possible effect on raising the welfare of the poor in those societies. However, Rawls' theory tends to assume the levels of wealth most associated with Western economies and, therefore, distributive justice is only applicable to 'decent societies', and only at the national level, where there is high income per capita and mature democracy based on individual rights within a cohesive community. The difference principle is not appropriate at an international level or to poor countries because, Rawls believes, 'circumstances of justice' do not emerge until rather late in the process of economic development. Cohen argues that the shortcoming of Rawls' principles of justice is that they are only applied to the basic 'structure of society' and not to anything outside of this structure (1994). However in the following pages we shall see that the broadening of the difference principle within the context of global injustices (Pogge, 2002) and in relation to the south, in particular, has engendered new questions (Sen, 1981, 1992, 1999).

Capability approach and social justice

Sen, who was profoundly influenced by Rawls, draws our attention to the epistemic inadequacy of Rawls' conception of social justice in the context of poverty and hunger in poor countries. However, using the concept of inequality to show the degree of diversity in a given society, he has developed what is commonly referred to as a capabilities approach.

This identifies deprivation and the degree of inequality through analysis of capability. A person's well-being depends not only on his/her own endowment of resources or abilities but also on circumstances and the environment in which the individual lives (1999: 61). Concerned with advancing human well-being and human freedom, Sen sees income (GNP) as only one factor among the many that contribute to welfare and freedom. As such, economic growth is considered to be a rather poor criterion for judging the progress of a country.

Sen's approach to the criterion of social justice considers how institutions can be assessed and reformed in the name of justice (Piggot, 2002). According to Sen, a utilitarian approach is limited by its income-based analysis of rights, because it ignores non-labour resources and other diversities, such as productive abilities or individual needs, which can result in inequality (1992: 120). The central argument of Sen's critique of Rawls' theory is that it converts 'primary goods', such as income and resources, into the freedom to be, to do and to live the way one chooses, and ignores the fact that access to 'primary goods' is also affected by what an individual is able to do. In focusing on reciprocity between people, Rawls fails to adequately acknowledge that we are not equal. Variation means that individuals can need different kinds and amounts of goods to reach the same levels of well-being or advantage.

This approach builds on the very concept of diversity and difference. Of course, the material basis of well-being, such as income and commodities, is acknowledged, but the use of these resources depends on variation in social and personal situations. Sen presents us with five distinctive sources of variation that influence relations between income and well-being. The first is personal heterogeneity – age, sex, physical and mental abilities. The second is environmental diversity and the influence this has on human beings. The third variation is social climate, and the different opportunities and constraints that societies place on individuals. The fourth element of variation is relational and established patterns of behaviour, which can vary between communities, depending on conventions and customs. The last element of variation is distribution within the family. These five sources of variation 'make opulence – in the sense of high real income – a limited guide to welfare and the quality of life (Sen, 1992: 71). This advocates that individual shares should be defined so as to take account of personal quality that governs the conversion of primary goods into the person's ability to promote her ends. It is important that measurement of inequality takes into account 'conversion factors' – for example able-bodied and disabled people would not have the same substantive opportunities even if they had the same set of means (such as income and wealth and other primary goods). Similarly someone may have high income or be wealthy, but be restricted by the burden of caring for elderly relatives. Under a just institutional order, therefore, some people would receive more resources than others, to enable them to reach the same level of opportunities to promote human ends, in so far as this is reasonably possible. This suggests that the capability approach features elements of rights theory or, in Pogge's (2002) words, criteria of social justice that take account of the specific ends that different persons are pursuing.

The two core concepts in Sen's explanation of how variation influences relations between income and well-being are 'functioning' and 'capability'. Living is a set of interrelated 'functionings', which denote a person's achievements or what an individual manages to do or to be, such as basic things like being adequately nourished or in good health, or more complex achievements like being happy or taking part in community life (Sen 1992). Functioning is measurable, for example, by life expectancy, infant mortality, literacy rates, political participation etc. The other core concept of capability is assessed by the freedom that a person actually enjoys to choose the life that they have reason to value, not just whether they have access to goods (income) or not – 'It is actual freedom that is represented by the person's "capability" to achieve various alternative combinations of functionings' (Sen, 1992: 81). Freedom might represent living in a disease free environment or the enabling opportunity of access to education, the economic means to move freely or the social freedom to participate in community and political life. For Sen, poverty is not merely a reflection of low income, but equates to deprivation of elementary capabilities, that is, a lack of the capability to function. When poverty prevents a person from functioning or exercising the capability to achieve well-being, we find failures such as premature mortality, significant under nourishment (especially of children), persistent morbidity, and widespread illiteracy and so forth. It is here that I find Sen most critical of the utilitarian definition of well-being based on income, which can never be an end in itself but only has value if it leads to poverty reduction and improvements in well-being. Development, therefore, should be viewed in relation to the effective freedom a person has to achieve status of being and doing, or as a vector of 'functionings'. Prendergast points out the similarity between Sen's emphasis on basic capabilities and Marx's view that unless people have their basic needs met, they cannot be liberated. However, he criticises Sen's treatment of capability for having 'a whiff of voluntarism' (2005: 1164).

Sen is reluctant to offer a set of human capabilities that he considers fundamental for human functioning. However, Nussbaum provides us with 'a list of central human functioning capabilities necessary for living a proper life with the stated goal of wantin g to help shape public policy for development goals' (1999, 2006a). This elaborates a partial account of social justice by suggesting that there is a basic list of entitlements that any civilised and just society should secure for all its citizens as a prerequisite for human dignity. The key capabilities listed are life, bodily health, bodily integrity, senses, imagination, thought, emotions, practical reason, affiliation, other species, play, control over one's environment, political well-being and material. Human rights principles are embedded in this list, which supplies 'a moral and humanly rich set of goals' for development and cover both the so-called first generation rights (political and civil liberties) and second generation rights (economic and social rights) (Nussbaum, 2002: 5). In her most recent work, she has moved further towards establishing a threshold for global justice. As she points out, her approach 'defends some basic political principles that can provide material for constitution making for nations, and also for thinking about the goals of international co-operation toward the creation of a decent world order' (see Chapter 4) (Nussbaum, 2006a: 29). Sen acknowledges that a list is useful in particular for the contention of human rights, but considers it important that any list is contingent upon public discussion and should be changeable with context and circumstances[5] (Sen, 2004).

According to Nussbaum, capability theory provides a framework for assessing the articulation of rights, in particular on gender equality. For example, if people's rights to political participation are secured they have the capabilities to function in the political arena. If in a particular area people do not have the relevant capabilities to function, then their rights are not secured. If we use rights to define social justice, a society cannot be considered to be just, unless capabilities have been effectively accomplished. Nussbaum looks at how traditional liberalism (of Mill, Rousseau, Rawls) approaches gender equality, and concludes that it ignores the issues of equal concern and respect to women and to relations between women and men. The crux of the feminist critique of Rawls' liberal theory of social justice is that it ignores an unjust division of labour and unjust power relations in relation to gender.

Nussbaum specifically uses capabilities in analysis of gender inequality, recognising women's rights as central to social justice (1999: 54): In her criticism of neo-liberalism's ineffectiveness to support universal rights for women, we are reminded of the distinctions of (neo) liberalism, and that while current mainstream thinking represents bad universalism that fails to respect differences, the traditional liberalism of Mill supported positive rights and state action to secure human well-being and to develop individual and group capabilities. Nussbaum considers this to be the only sort of liberalism worth defending. This version of liberalism departs from traditional liberalism by focusing on social justice and, crucially for feminists, places women's rights as central human rights: 'Women, unlike rocks and plants and even horses, have the potential to become capable of these human functions, given sufficient nutrition, education, and other support. That is why their unequal failure in capability is a problem of justice' (Ibid.: 56). A state that wants to guarantee people's rights has to be prepared to rethink how rights are distributed, whether they are property rights, legal or social. If you apply a capabilities' approach to development and quality-of-life, the state needs to consider what people, groups or the country in question are actually able to do and to be.

Public policy for development

Within the capability approach, the central goal of public planning and public policy interventions is to support an expansion in the capabilities of individuals to perform various functions. This could involve material or institutional support measures, such as providing free education to all, or access to health care, depending on local context. If rights are used to define social justice, only if capabilities have been effectively achieved can a society be defined as just. It is not enough for rights to exist in theory or written in a constitution, measures have to be put in place to make people capable of exercising their rights and they have to be effective (Nussbaum, 1999: 42).

However, it is not only through public policy that rights and capabilities can be enhanced but also through individual agency, and engendering a belief in individuals that they can make a difference. Both Sen and Nussbaum use the concept of agency to express the degree of free will that is exercised by the individual in their social action. In other words 'as someone who acts and brings about change, and whose achievements can be judged in terms of her own values and objectives, whether or not we assess them in terms of some external criteria as well' (Sen, 1999: 19). A key issue for development is the capacity of the poor to reconstruct their livelihoods. The poor are not passive agents, but individuals who proactively aspire to transform their lives and to use their own agency to be productive. However, the poor have fewer agencies than others because of lack of material resources and structural constraints like poverty, and some circumstances that create less agency for all, like an oppressive political state. So, how far can the poor be the authors of their own biography? The answer lies in the extent to which they are able to exercise 'generative power to control their own lives despite their subordinate position in wider hierarchical political, economic and social power relationships' (Kabeer, 2002: 59). By and large, poor people can exert very little agency over decision-making processes. Often decision-making structures exclude them or where they attempt to be inclusive, such as through consultation processes, these are formulated as a means of providing information rather than encouraging participation. This is particularly the case when major agencies are involved in delivering development projects that will impact on local populations. On a more local level, the poor may not feel able to participate in the civic realm due to a lack of capabilities due to constraints arising from factors such as ill-health, domestic responsibilities and low levels of education; and in being poor. They are often passive recipients of decisions taken at higher levels such as the compulsion to undertake communal labour. However comparative empirical study of different locales shows that poor people do resist impositions from above through different mechanisms, such as the non payment of contributions for village projects, through non-attendance at communal meetings, or ignoring the recommendations of institutions such as village leaders (Toner, 2007). Poor people exercise personal agency everyday within their family and neighbourhood networks, but they are largely excluded from significantly influencing the collective actions or the decisions of authorities that impact upon them.

The capability approach has eroded the credibility of economic growth-led development and has enlarged our understanding of poverty and its relationship to human rights. Sen's social justice theory that links poverty to the rights of the individual has influenced the theory and practice of development and multilateral organisations. Although it may not address inequality directly, its strength lies in the way that it accommodates the structural constraints and opportunities, faced by the individual (Lister, 2004). Social justice theories have, to some extent, idealised what constitutes 'a good life' based on a welfare-oriented social democracy, while at the same time penetrating 'the sin of being insufficiently distributionist'. The core concepts of the capability approach are equality of opportunity and symptomatic, unbalanced poverty. The real analytical issue is that of inequality, which is structural in origin and relates closely to power relations. Inequality leaves many with no control over the major decisions that affect their lives. This is not adequately captured in social justice theory, which pays little attention to power relations that sustain inequality within and between nations. Nevertheless, it does capture the most important feature of a human rights framework for development, which is the moral imperative of eliminating conspicuous poverty within societies. This has become the key tenet of mainstream development theory and practice in the twenty first century, as I discuss in the following section.

How do we achieve social justice?

The greatest question to preoccupy social justice theory scholars is how social justice can be integral to development or how the two can be brought closer together. Is it possible to combine economic growth with social justice that is dependent upon high levels of social protection? As I discussed earlier, social justice philosophers, such as Rawls, pursued an inward looking idea of justice that applied to the institutions of a nation state and had most resonance in respect of rich countries and less relevance to poor countries because they had not reached the necessary level of 'maturity'. Sen, in a critique of this position, explains how the criteria of social justice can be applied equally to the south and also to global institutions such as the UN. The prominence given to Sen's capabilities approach in the human development discourse has been deeply rooted in the United Nations Human Development Report, which harnesses development to the realisation of rights. Development is now defined as 'the enlargement of people's choices' and it is viewed as a means to advancing human well-being and individual freedom.[6] Human development is conceptualised as the achievement of equality of opportunity or capabilities for individuals to pursue a life of their choosing by removing some of the structural constraints they face. Increasingly, the degree of poverty is being assessed by the capability failures of individuals and groups, with the degree of failure defined in relation to local environmental factors. Capability has become a decisive factor to look at when judging how well a country or a person's life is going, not just income per se. Human Development Index is made up of composite measures that uses three dimensions of human development reflected in the form of indicators: living longer and healthier (life expectancy), education and living standard (income) to arrive at an indexed value of the average level of human development in a given country (UNDP, 2006a). It is in this context that Nussbaum sharply points out that 'to the extent that rights are used in defining social justice, we should not grant that the society is just unless the capabilities have been effectively achieved' (1999: 6).

Basic capabilities include access to adequate food, shelter, primary health care, basic education, equitable access to justice and employment, and being able to earn sufficient income for sustainable livelihoods and to participate in the life of the community. These are all basic human rights (see Articles, 23, 25, and 26 on table 1 Chapter 2). The UNDP builds on Sen's approach to link rights and poverty. This is reflected in the United Nations Human Development Report (2000), which asserts that: 'a decent standard of living, adequate nutrition, health care, education and decent work and protection against calamities are not just development goals – they are also human rights' (UNDP 2000: 8). The United Nations High Commission on Human Rights': confirms that 'Poverty is the principle cause of human rights violation in the world. It also prevents people from assuming not only their duties as individuals, but also their collective duties as citizens, parents, workers and electors' (United Nations Commission for Human Rights, 2000: paragraph 9).

In the early part of this decade, the UN predominantly adopted a human rights based approach to development. In a meeting in 2003 of all UN agencies, the core values assigned in the 'Common Understanding on the Human Rights Based Approach to Development Cooperation'[7] were accepted. This was followed by the publication of *Poverty and Human Rights: A conceptual framework* (2004) by The Office of the High Commissioner for Human Rights, which was the foundation of the 'Guidelines on Human Rights Approach to Poverty Reduction Strategies' proclaiming that responsibility for poverty reduction becomes a universal obligation that all states have to adopt and, as duty bearers, have to implement.

Rights based approaches to development

The basic assumption of rights based approaches to development is that poverty reduction is no longer simply a matter of charity, but it is an individual's rights claim. This accordingly necessitates legal and moral obligations on the part of others. In fact most of the salient features of the human rights normative framework are geared to empower the poor in one way or another. This relies upon accountability, the principles of universality, non-discrimination and equality, the principle of participatory decision-making processes, and recognition of the interdependence of rights, as the essential characteristics of a human rights approach to poverty reduction (UN 2004). Empowerment of the poor is a prerequisite of development in practice as it enables the poor and excluded persons to participate fully in society and enhances the capabilities and confidence. These enable people to change their lives, improve their communities, and influence their destinies. In the context of the rights agenda and access to development, participation itself has become a fundamental human right and one that is essential for articulating other legitimate rights. UN guidelines specify that essentially a human rights approach to development 'requires active and informed participation by the poor in the formation, implementation and monitoring of poverty reduction strategies... and the right to take part in the conduct of public affairs' (United Nations Commission for Human Rights, 2002: 2). Approaches that operate at the stronger end of the spectrum of participatory development emphasise poor people's 'leverage' and agency rather than 'voice' and consultation (Conway, et al., 2001: 36).

A Rights Based Approach to Development (RBAD) diverges from the idea of the Right to Development. It shifts priority back to the citizen-state relationship at the country level, and disentangles the policy focus from the wider question of equality between states and peoples at an international level, in relation to equal opportunity for trade, transfer of resources and investment. The practical political implications are not inconsequential. Unlike the 'Rights to Development' debate, articulations of rights-based approaches to development have largely prevaricated over questions about hegemonic states (Nyamu-Musembi and Cornwall, 2004: 5). The Rights to Development debate echoes some of the concerns of dependency theory and post-colonial inequalities (see Chapter 2), recognising the linkages between structural constraints in the south, and exogenous factors that have been an obstacle to development in poor countries. It is not surprising that development agencies have embraced RBAD enthusiastically, as it may provide an instrument to address some of their concerns associated with governance.

In reality the application of the Right to Development is more challenging than the Rights Based Approaches as it emphasises

> both sides of the equation – from claims for rights by citizens to the obligation and duties of the state to uphold those rights. The obligation/duty side of the coin is part of the reason that the right-to-development has not been promoted more widely and why commitment to rights by donor agencies has been only rhetorical in certain cases. (Pettit and Wheeler, 2005: 3)

What is more, RBAD do not present a framework for capturing the accountability, performance and obligations of International Finance Institutions, or Multinational Corporations, or the private sector in general. There is no clarity about what, if indeed any, human rights' obligations should be attached to corporate governance and the business conduct of countless multinational corporations and other business enterprises that operate in the south (Baxi, 2005: 15).

Critics suggest that the Right to Development is meaningless in the current global order and that international institutions 'mutate into working groups, commissions, and expert panels, each of which produce reports that are occasionally the subject of discussion in low level meetings' in the United Nations (Uvin, 2004: 43). In response, Uvin suggests that a Rights-Based Approach to Development would appear to be a better way to reduce poverty, even though it requires investment in a number of areas, not least to build the capacity of states to improve the rule of law, to empower local human rights through civil society organisations, and to carve out a clear purpose for international development agencies. Others have argued that despite concerns about how RBAD interfaces with RTD, RTD is making a 'comeback', invigorating the claim of countries in the south for a process of equitable development, including composite rights (Sengupta, 2005: 66). The right to development is indeed broader than the rights based approach to development, encompassing a critical examination of the overall development process, including planning, participation, allocation of resources and priorities within the context of international co-operation.

However, we should be cautious about suggesting that the two are separable, for in fact a human rights-based approach to development is an operational part of the right to development (Marks, 2005: 39). The Right to Development stipulates equality within and between nation states so that all states and their citizens can enjoy the benefits of trade and development. In theory, this all seems well and good. In reality, even though economic globalisation (see Chapter 4) has changed the nature of relations between the north and the south, and the world has become more interdependent since the Declaration on the Right to Development in 1986, the benefits of economic globalisation have not been distributed evenly. This is to a certain extent because the powerful states are in control of global institutions that direct the pace and nature of globalisation, leaving the poor countries with little voice in the decision-making process. It is no surprise that they consequently lose out (see Chapter 5). The United States plays a considerable role in this domination and its opposition to the Right to Development from its inception has been incredibly damaging (as discussed in Chapters 2 and 6). Effectively, the operation of the Right to Development term of office has been reduced to a report produced by independent experts and the task forces of various committees of the UN Human Rights Council. The Right to Development report of the High Commissioner for Human Rights is prepared annually for consideration by the UN Human Rights Council. This operates to the fairly restricted 'mandate' of evaluating progress on global development partnerships, as detailed in Goal 8 of the Millennium Development Goals (see table 3, UN Human Rights Council 2006).

Millennium development goals and human rights

The Millennium Declaration and its eight associated Millennium Development Goals (MDGs) were adopted by 191 UN member states in 2000. The objective of this 'New York Consensus' was to eliminate extreme poverty by 2015 by achieving the eight identified targets (See Table 3.1, Goal 1). The success criteria for goal one is measured on the World Bank 'one dollar a day' global poverty line which, as discussed earlier, has been subject to critical evaluation (see Pogge, 2004 for a comprehensive critique of Goal 1 of the MDGs). States that have made a commitment to the MDGs tend to be those that have ratified at least one of the human rights treaties and have an international legal obligation to put them into practice. The EU looks upon the international human rights framework as a prerequisite for achieving these goals. According to the rhetoric of the United Nations Commission for Human Rights (OHRC), the Millennium Declaration (2000) itself adopts a Rights-Based Approach to Development. Its guidelines for achieving the outcomes of the MDGs are based on human rights principles and standards. They promote freedom from hunger and from fear of violence, oppression or injustice; democratic and participatory governance based on the will of the people; equality of opportunity, in the sense that no individual or nation must be denied the opportunity to benefit from development; solidarity and co-operation between states; tolerance, that requires human beings to respect one another, for all their diversity of belief, culture and language; respect for nature, to ensure that resources are managed in a way that current and future generations can benefit; and shared responsibility for managing economic and social development globally and creating an environment of peace and security at the national and international level (UN 2000). The setting of global challenges facilitates managing the development process in a way that distributes the costs and burdens fairly in accordance with basic principles of equity and social justice. The UN is therefore required to play a central role to ensure the universal implementation of all these human rights' values for peace and security. Table 3.1 pulls together data from the OHRC and UN MDG to demonstrate the relationship between MDG and key human rights' indicators.

Table 3.1 Millennium development goals and human rights standards*

Millennium development goals	Indicators	Key human rights standards
Goal 1:	**Eradicate extreme poverty and hunger**	
Target 1: Reduce by half the proportion of people living on less than $1 a day.	Proportion of population living on < $1 per day;	Universal Declaration of Human Rights, article 25(1); ICESCR article 11
Target 2: Halve between 1990 and 2015 the proportion of people who suffer from hunger.	Poverty gap ratio; Share of poorest quintile in national consumption; Prevalence of underweight children (under-five years of age); Proportion of population below minimum level of dietary energy intake.	
Goal 2:	**Achieve universal primary education**	
Target 3: Ensure that, by 2015, children everywhere, boys and girls alike, will be able to complete a full course of primary schooling.	Net enrolment ratio in primary education; Proportion of pupils starting grade 1 who reach grade 6; Literacy rate of 15–24 year olds.	Universal Declaration of Human Rights article 25(1); ICESCR articles 13 and 14; CRC article 28(1)(a); CEDAW article 10; CERD article 5(e)(v)
Goal 3:	**Promote gender equality and empower women**	
Target 4: Eliminate gender disparity in primary and secondary education, preferably by 2005, and to all levels of education no later than 2015.	Ratio of girls to boys in primary, secondary and tertiary education; Ratio of literate females to males amongst 15–24 year olds; Share of women in waged employment in non-agricultural sectors; Proportion of seats held by women in national parliament.	Universal Declaration of Human Rights article 2; CEDAW; ICESCR article 3; CRC article 2

Continued

Table 3.1 Continued

Millennium development goals	Indicators	Key human rights standards
Goal 4:	**Reduce child mortality**	
Target 5: Reduce by two-thirds, between 1990 and 2015, the under-five mortality rate.	Under-five mortality rate; Infant mortality rate; Proportion of 1-year-old children immunized against measles.	Universal Declaration of Human Rights article 25; CRC articles 6, 24(2)(a); ICESCR article 12(2)(a)
Goal 5:	**Improve maternal health**	
Target 6: Reduce by three-quarters, between 1990 and 2015, the maternal mortality ratio	Maternal mortality ratio; Proportion of births attended by skilled health personnel.	Universal Declaration of Human Rights article 25; ICESCR article 12, CRC article 24; CEDAW article 12; CERD article 5(e) (iv)
Goal 6:	**Combat HIV/AIDS, malaria and other diseases**	
Target 7: By 2015 have halted and begun to reverse the spread of HIV/AIDS; Target 8: By 2015 have halted and begun to reverse the incidence of malaria and other major diseases.	HIV prevalence among 15–24 year old pregnant women; Contraceptive prevalence rate; Number of children orphaned by HIV/ AIDS; Prevalence of and death rates associated with malaria; Proportion of population in malaria risk areas using effective malaria prevention and treatment measures; Prevalence of and death rates associated with tuberculosis; Proportion of TB cases detected and cured.	Universal Declaration of Human Rights article 25(1); ICESCR articles 11(1) and 12; CEDAW article 14(2)(h); CRC article 24; CERD article 5(e)(iii)

Goal 7:

Target 9: Integrate the principles of sustainable development into country policies and programmes and reverse the loss of environmental resources.

Target 10: Halve, by 2015, the proportion of people without sustainable access to safe drinking water.

Target 11: Achieve significant improvement in lives of at least 100 million slum dwellers by 2020.

Goal 8:

Target 12: Develop further an open, rule-based, predictable, non-discriminatory trading and financial system. Includes a commitment to good governance, development and poverty reduction – both nationally and internationally. Some of the indicators listed below will be monitored separately for the Least Developed Countries (LDCs), Africa, landlocked countries and small island developing states.

Ensure environmental sustainability

Proportion of land area covered by forest; Land area protected to maintain biological diversity;

GDP per unit of energy use (as proxy for energy efficiency);

Carbon dioxide emissions (per capita);

Plus two figures of global atmospheric pollution: ozone depletion and the accumulation of global warming gases;

Proportion of population with sustainable access to an improved water source;

Proportion of people with access to improved sanitation;

Proportion of people with access to secure tenure

Develop a global partnership for development

Official Development Assistance

Net ODA as percentage of DAC donors' GNP (targets of 0.7% in total and 0.15% for LDCs);

Proportion of ODA to basic social services (basic education, primary health care, nutrition, safe water and sanitation);

Proportion of ODA that is untied;

Proportion of ODA for environment in small island developing states;

Universal Declaration of Human Rights article 25(1); ICESCR articles 11(1) and 12; CEDAW article 14(2)(h); CRC article 24; CERD article 5(e)(iii)

Charter articles 1(3), 55 and 56; Universal Declaration of Human Rights articles 22 and 28; ICESCR articles 2(1), 11(1), 15(4), 22 and 23; CRC articles 4, 24(4) and 28(3)

Continued

99

Table 3.1 Continued

Millennium development goals	Indicators	Key human rights standards
Target 13: Address the Special Needs of the Least Developed Countries. Includes: tariff and quota-free access for LDC exports; enhanced programme of debt relief for HIPC and cancellation of official bilateral debt; and more generous ODA for countries committed to poverty reduction.	Proportion of ODA for transport sector in landlocked countries.	
Target 14: Address the Special Needs of landlocked countries and small island developing states.	*Market Access* Proportion of exports (by value and excluding arms) admitted free of duties and quotas; Average tariffs and quotas on agricultural products, textiles and clothing; Domestic and export agricultural subsidies in OECD Countries;	
Target 15: Deal comprehensively with the debt problems of developing countries through national and international measures in order to make debt sustainable in the long term.	Proportion of ODA provided to help build trade capacity. *Debt Sustainability* Proportion of official bilateral HIPC debt cancelled; Debt service as a percentage of exports of goods and services;	
Target 16: In co-operation with developing countries, develop and implement strategies for decent and productive work for youth.	Proportion of ODA provided as debt relief; Number of countries reaching HIPC decision and completion points; Unemployment rate of 15–24 year olds;	
Target 17: In co-operation with pharmaceutical companies, provide access to affordable, essential drugs in developing countries.	Proportion of population with access to affordable essential drugs on a sustainable basis;	

Target 18: In co-operation with the private sector, make available the benefits of new technologies, especially information and communications.

Telephone lines per 1,000 people;
Personal computers per 1,000 people.

Notes:
*ICESCR (International Covenant on Economic, Social and Cultural Rights)
ICCPR (International Covenant on Civil and Political Rights)
CERD (International Convention on the Elimination of all Forms of Racial Discrimination)
CEDAW (International Convention on the Elimination of all Forms of Discrimination Against Women)
CRC (Convention on the Rights of the Child)

Sources: Office of United Nations High Commission for Human Rights, 2004 (http://www.ohchr.org/english/issues/millenium-development/ achievement.htm); and UN (2000) Millennium Development Goal (www.un.org/millennium/declation/areas552).

The human rights community has criticised the MDGs' reference to human rights as being patchy and imprecise. The full human rights framework is not reflected. Particular concerns have been raised that civil and political rights are referenced but not explicitly linked to any specific MDG (Alston, 2004). Despite this, it is hard to deny that the MDGs are geared towards achieving the universality of economic, social and cultural rights. They have also generated momentum for engagement in human rights debates. Some of the largest international civil society organisations such as Human Rights Watch and Amnesty International, which have traditionally pursued concern for political rights such as free speech, free election, and torture, have now taken on board the need to protect social, economic and cultural rights, such as concern for HIV/AIDS, health care issues, hunger, and the right to food and housing. Amnesty International's Annual Report 2004 concedes that 'despite the increasing discourse on the indivisibility of human rights, in reality economic, social and cultural rights are neglected, reducing human rights to a theoretical construct for the vast majority of the world's population'[8] (Amnesty International, 2004: 5). Several Civil society organisations have now started campaigning for MDGs to put pressure on states, International Financial Institutions and trans-national corporations to stand up to their responsibility to contribute to the achievement of the goals.

Some of the goals are unrealistic. Even Jeffery Sachs (2005), advisor to UN Secretary General Kofi Annan, admitted in Investing in Development that most of the goals are unreachable, in particular in Sub-Sahara Africa. This brings us back to the greatest of paradoxes and my most basic of questions – how can major improvements in human development indicators be achieved, such as universal primary education and lowering child mortality (Goal 2 and 4), when a state's ability to provide services such as education and health are eroded by a combination of privatisation and removal of state subsidies? How can the HIV/AIDS pandemic (Goal 4) be positively combated when pharmaceutical companies are permitted to charge high prices for essential drugs, which are not affordable for the poor? The MDGs promote both a state-focus and increasing privatisation policies that can make the state less capable of responding to the right claims that poor people are entitled to make.

The irony seems to be that this new far-reaching approach has its foundations in the development policy threads of the neo-liberalism of the Washington Consensus. The Millennium Declaration does not even try to build a bridge between the state and the private sector by making reference to the accountability of the private sector to meet human rights obligations. This is precisely why one should be cautious when interpreting some of the values attached to the MDGs, however novel they are.

A further source of apprehension is Goal 8. The first seven MDGs acknowledge that the states in the south should drive economic stability and fiscal discipline, while giving more opportunity for the private sector. Emphasis is on good governance in line with the values of social justice. The MDGs explicitly specify that achievement of the first seven goals depends on the poor countries themselves taking the main initiative. It is the primary responsibility of poor countries to build strong civil society relationships with good governance and accountable institutions. Secondly, to achieve these seven goals 'A global partnership for development' (Goal 8) is essential. Effectively this means that rich nations have an obligation to transfer resources to poor countries by way of fair trade regimes, debt relief, enhanced development assistance or aid, transfer of technology, foreign direct investment and other measures as specified in the MDGs targets. Goal 8 sets out the process for achieving the other seven goals, and the role of the poor nations, but it is conditional on the states of the rich countries adhering to their responsibility to be 'good'. In the words of Sachs: 'Poor countries have no guaranteed right to meet MDGs and to receive development assistance from the rich countries. They only have that right if they themselves carry through on their commitment to good governance' (2005: 269). Although the nature of the 'partnership' between the north and south has been somewhat shaky in the past, the hope is that a more robust partnership based on the 'mutuality of the obligations' can be established. The UN has put forward a development compact to ensure that countries are obliged to carry out these rights-based programmes and that they are matched by the international community's reciprocal obligations to co-operate and enable implementation of the MDGs. But the prospects for such reciprocal obligations being effective do not seem good, at least for the time being, and so long as structural constraints define the relationship between rich and poor countries. The UNDP (2003) annual report, 'A Compact among Nations to End Human Poverty', was dedicated to the Millennium Development Goals. The report, acknowledged that if the trade policy of rich countries remained highly discriminatory against poor countries' exports, achieving the MDGs remained remote:

It is hard to imagine the poorest countries achieving goals 1–7 without the policy change in rich countries to achieve goal 6. Poor countries cannot on their own tackle structural constraints that keep them in the poverty trap, including rich country tariffs and subsidies that restrict market access for exports; patents that restrict access to technology that can save lives; and unsustainable debt owed to rich county governments and multilateral institutions. (UNDP, 2003: 11)

The rich nations are only too aware that their obligation to support the social and economic rights of citizens of poor countries could cost more than US$50 billion a year if all goals were achieved by the target date of 2015. Reddy and Antoine (2006) estimate the cost to be much higher than this. The cost of only reducing income poverty (Goal 1) ranges from between US54 and US$62 billion. Other goals are likely to cost between US$35 and US$76 billion a year (UN 2002: 16). When the G8 countries met at the Gleneagles summit in 2005, they promised to raise this amount by increasing aid budgets to reach the UN target of giving 0.7 per cent of GDP in aid by 2015. Even though there has been some progress to fulfil this commitment, OECD report shows that the total aid figure still falls well short of this (OECD, 2007). Some countries that have increased aid have overshadowed the main objective of the Millennium Declaration by taking the opportunity to link aid to their own foreign policy agendas. The British Government's DFID has been reluctant to accept this, believing that aid should support pro-poor development objectives rather than address foreign policy or global security concerns. The empirical evidence, on the other hand, suggests that DFID 'has spent huge sums on consultancy firms to advise on privatisation in the south; firms whose own analytical frameworks reflect the privileges of investor interests. For example, the pro-privatisation Adam Smith Institute (international) received over £34 million from the UK aid budget in 1998–2005' (Pugh, 2005: 36).

The Millennium Challenge Account, launched by the United States in 2002, is fairly open in its objective to influence 'development' and further the US democratisation project. In March 2002 a UN conference on Financing for Development in Mexico was attended by 50 heads of state and others, including representatives from the private sector and civil society organisations. At the conference US President Bush announced a new initiative – a new Millennium Challenge Account (MCA) and a $5 billion annual increase in Overseas Development Assistance. This was to be devoted to projects in countries where conditions deemed essential for successful development existed – that is to say, where civil and political rights were upheld and where good governance and sound economic policies fostered enterprise. In 2004 Bush signed the law that established the Millennium Challenge Corporation. The reality is that most MCA funding has been directed towards 'pro-democratic programmes' for regime change in priority countries, indicating close links between the fund and Bush's 'Freedom Agenda'. The funding has been mainly used to neutralie states that do not follow conventional development policy, such as Venezuela whose President Chavez, went against the private sector and trans-national oil corporations by nationalising some of the country's oil refineries and distributing the benefits to the poor.[9]

The United States introduced parallel institutions to augment its ideology of building nations and regime change through a combination of 'soft power' and the aggressive interventionist approach witnessed in Iraq. The MCA was launched to assert US control and influence over 'development'. As an agency wholly controlled by the United States, it was a clearly contemptuous stab at multilateral institutions such as the UN. It was initially designed to overcome the limitations of structural adjustment lending on the part of multilateral institutions like the World Bank. However, in practice, the Millennium Challenge became a tool of the political gesturing of US foreign policy and the American democratisation programme. Thus the series of governance indicators specified for countries to qualify for the programme set a very clear context for where and how funds are spent. Initially, the United States proposed a fund of $5 billion, which in effect doubled US Overseas Development Assistance to poor countries, but this commitment was soon curtailed by US congress, which only funded $1.75 billion to poor countries in 2005 (Fukuyama, 2006: 147). By the beginning of Bush's second term, the administration had not disbursed a single loan, and was ready to pre-qualify only two countries – Honduras and Madagascar (both were not in need of such loans).

Pogge questions the moral value of wealthy countries and individuals and their growing reluctance to spend money on reducing world hunger, arguing that it reflects the increasingly popular idea that MDGs are best achieved through globalisation and free markets (2002). In other words, we have seen a discursive twist from 'human rights' to 'trade-related human rights'. Despite the Millennium Declaration, the dominant agenda continues to be trade-led economic growth, supported by conditional aid.

Conclusion

The main fall-out from the consensus forged in Washington has been a consistent pressure on nation states to reduce social protection measures to achieve economic growth through trade and privatisation, to the extent that the role of the state has changed to that of an unreceptive agent of justice and development. Neo-liberalism encourages the withdrawal of the state from the provision of many services essential for human rights, and its replacement by private sector and non-state actors. In this sense, the state's capacity to provide essential services to support the poor and most vulnerable is undermined by market forces.

Social justice theorists, in response to the resulting setbacks in social protection in human rights terms and in the increasing inequality and poverty, argue fervently for the need to ensure that development is about the importance of individual well-being and equality of opportunity. It is important to bear in mind that Sen and other egalitarian liberals are not opposed to the market but are critical of the fact that too much prominence on market forces is likely to produce a much divided society, making it harder to reduce poverty. Social justice theory attempts to bring together the market and the moral imperative for the elimination of conspicuous social inequality within societies; the most important feature of a human rights framework for development.

Incorporating rights into development provides an opportunity to challenge some of the basic neo-liberal assumptions about the nature of state-society relations. It also poses enormous challenges, in particular in the context of market-dominated development. There is a danger that the adoption of the language of rights as the ruling principles of the major international agencies, donors and powerful states, allows rights to be narrowed into a top-down agenda that is mainly geared towards market led development strategies that continue to undermine state obligations. We cannot be particularly reassured by current evidence that the reinvention of treaties and obligations, in the form of MDG 8, have failed to meet expectations; targets have quite simply not been met. Just how far the state and other agencies are able to fulfil their obligations in the context of economic globalisation is a question that I will explore further in the next Chapter.

4
Economic Globalisation and Global Social Justice

In the previous Chapter I explained how egalitarian liberals promote the idea of human rights for development, based on the principle of social justice, and how this challenges neo-liberal economists who prefer to talk of individual freedom, under the guarantors of minimal state activity and a free market. In response to the increasing interdependence of states in the course of economic globalisation, the concept and applicability of social justice is considered to extend far beyond the parameters of the nation state. This builds upon Rawls' idea that the principle of justice in a 'self-contained society' is limited to the basic structure of the nation state. However Pogge rejects an inside/outside distinction, in promoting a theory of cosmopolitan global justice that 'aspires to a single, universal criterion of justice which all persons and peoples can accept as the basis for moral judgments about the global order' (2002: 33). On this basis, cosmopolitan scholars keenly apply the notion of a 'difference principle' to the well-being of disadvantaged or poor people globally, based on equality of opportunity between people and not necessarily between nation states. What does this mean in terms of nation state responsibility and accountability? Cosmopolitans, like Griffin (2003), Beck (2006), Stiglitz (2006), and Pogge (2002) argue that the state system of the past 300 years is not designed to respond to the challenges of globalisation, which is one of the reasons why nation states are failing to protect the poor and the vulnerable. As a result we are wrapped up within an ineffective state system, when what we need is a twenty-first century, effective and democratic system of global governance (Kuper, 2005: 156).

In this Chapter, I argue that original assumptions about the right to development are tested by our increasing interdependence and interconnectedness through globalisation. The Chapter begins with an assessment of economic globalisation that has engendered new and contested questions about the relationship between human rights and development. It goes on to consider why there could be a need for new structures of accountability and democracy to avoid the current high risk of economic globalisation negatively impacting on the human rights agenda. If economic globalisation dis-empowers states so that they cannot control issues that impact on the provision of social protection, can they be accountable for addressing poverty and delivering human rights? Is there a need, as Held (2004, 2005) argues, for 'cosmopolitan democracy' which through 'cosmopolitan governance' operates to protect individual rights no matter where they live?

The making of globalisation

Globalisation is a web of complex processes that have had contradictory impacts on many countries. Most definitions of globalisation commonly refer to the closer integration of countries through communications, trade and migration generating the interconnectedness and interdependence of states and regions. In other words globalisation links distant localities in such a way that 'local happenings are shaped by events occurring many miles away and vice versa' (Giddens, 1990: 64). Intriguingly the concept of globalisation has only been widely used since the 1990s, appearing relatively recently in Anglo Saxon dictionaries. The social science citation index records no more than a few occurrences of the concept of 'globalisation' in the 1980s but shows its soaring popularity from 1992 onwards (Therborn, 2000: 149). It has certainly stimulated some critical questions in the social sciences in general, with development studies, in particular, calling for a paradigm shift in social analysis in order that the emerging form of globality can be explained and conceptualised in all its intricacy.

Although the discourse of globalisation and development, as we know it today, is as recent as the 1990s, the globalisation process originated during the early period of colonisation. There have been different historical forms of globalisation, and the current conjuncture is without doubt a new one. Robinson presents the idea that the contemporary form of globalisation is the outcome of the modernity achieved by three waves of globalisation – the first started with colonisation or the expansion of Europe into Asia and Africa. This was followed by the second wave in the guise of industrialisation and the expansion of technical change. The third wave, symbolised by the new global order under US hegemony, is the shift from increasing connectivity and dependency between states to the wider crosscutting global interdependence that we experience today (Robinson, 2004: 8–11). Globalisation has had significant transformational impact at both the global level as well as within nations. Not all outcomes are assumed to be positive, as I shall explore in this Chapter. Questions have been raised about the institutional capacity of all states to manage economic openness and participation in globalisation, and at the same time fulfil the role as protector of rights. A report from the Commission on Human Rights drew attention to tensions around roles and responsibilities arising from the increasing interdependence of states. The report acknowledged that: 'while globalisation, by its impact on, *inter alia*, the role of the state, may affect human rights, the promotion and protection of all human rights is first and foremost the responsibility of the state' (UN, 2000: 1).

Several political, social and economic changes since the 1980s have shaped the material basis of the current form of globalisation. These include: the end of the cold war, cheaper transport and communications networks; the growth of global trade and finance, the ascendancy of the world economy by Transnational Corporations (TNCs), the growth of civil society organisations and promotion of neo-liberal free market policies, and world-wide implementation of the 'Washington Consensus' as the mainstream framework for economic globalisation and poverty reduction. These reflect the increasingly active role and influence of global Institutions such as the World Trade Organisation (WTO), the International Monetary Fund (IMF), and the World Bank; the ostensible or self-styled centres of 'thinking for the world' that influence development policy making (Wade, 2004).

Economic globalisation and poverty reduction

Are current forms of economic globalisation supported by communication and technology advances driving 'closer economic integration of the countries of the world through the increased flow of goods and services, capital, and even labour' (Stiglitz 2006: 4)?. The basic premise of economic globalisation is the neo-liberal assumption that economic growth reduces poverty; provided countries participate in free trade and engage in the global economy. What has always remained uncertain is how direct the relationship between economic globalisation and poverty reduction is. Hyperglobalism and supporters of global economic convergence maintain that all countries would benefit from involvement in economic globalisation; for the reason that it has wider beneficial impacts, including the eventual narrowing of the gap between the rich and poor. Dollar and Kray (2002: 195) are convinced that 'the poor and the rich gain one-for-one from openness', supporting the argument that more globalisation not less will lift poorer countries from poverty (Bhawati, 2004). The selective and rather one-dimensional hypothesis that they uncompromisingly promote is that countries that integrate successfully into the global economy experience economic growth and, as a de facto benefit, achieve poverty reduction, and, therefore, economic globalisation can be the most powerful force for social good and protection of rights in the world today (Collier and Dollar, 2002; World Bank, 2002; Bhawati, 2004). The empirical evidence that is used to support this assumption is a rather narrow measurement of globalisation – the ratio of exports to imports over GDP.

The World Bank has ranked countries into three groups based on this measure: (1.) the more globalised (good) countries; (2.) the less globalised (bad) countries; and (3.)the non-globalised countries (World Bank, 2000; Wade, 2004). The first group is those that have experienced steady economic growth and are considered, as a result, to have witnessed a faster reduction of poverty than the other two groups. The more globalised countries – China, India, Argentina, Malaysia, Mexico, The Philippines, Thailand, Nepal, Côte d' Ivoire, Rwanda and Haiti – have all embarked on free trade in line with the idea of openness as a means of securing benefits for all. To what extent does this kind of success reflect human rights values and standards?

A globalised country and the right to development

The tendency to measure successful globalisation purely in terms of trade or the ratio of imports to exports over GDP and economic growth is indicative of the fact that little or no account is taken of indicators that assess a country's wider development – indicators on human development, rights, freedom, well-being and, most importantly, inequalities. If we take China as one of the most successful globalisers, as defined by economic indicators, we find a state that has been highly interventionist as an active agent of economic development but not as an agent of social justice and security for civil and political rights. A further paradox is that even though thriving globalisers such as China have followed a path of free trade they tend to remain highly protectionist and adopt a state-led development strategy (as discussed in Chapter 3). Stiglitz argues that China has been able to 'manage globalisation carefully' and well, not just because of openness or free trade but because it has been cautiously selective in respect of foreign investment criteria. The country was slow to open up its own markets to imports and it has engineered not to have short-term foreign investment for short-term returns (2006: 10).

Apprehension from the Western world to China's relationship with African states reflects another interesting angle to the Chinese globaliser model. China's ease with Africa's 'dictators' has led academics to argue that an alternative development strategy, the 'Beijing Consensus' is replacing the failed Washington Consensus. What we seem to be facing is a situation where 'developing countries around the world are looking to Asia, to the examples of success, to see what they can learn. It is not surprising that global support for the Washington Consensus has waned'. (Stiglitz, 2006: 44). On reflection, China in the past five years has triggered new trade deals worth more than $50 billion with African leaders indiscriminately. This includes widely condemned leaders, such as Mugabe in Zimbabwe who have abused the rights of their own citizens and Sudanese leaders whose atrocities in Darfur have resulted in the deaths of thousands of people and the displacement of millions. Despite evidence of violent acts, China has invested heavily in energy in Sudan purchasing nearly 70 per cent of Sudanese oil exports and, in actual fact, has blocked sanctions against Sudan in the UN Security Council. A recent report by Amnesty International points to China's massive arms export policy, estimated to be more than $1 billion a year, to countries such as Sudan, Nepal, Burma and South Africa.[1] China is the only major arms exporter that has not signed up to agreements that prevent the exports of arms to states that are known to be human rights abusers. The arms trade is one that is shrouded in secrecy; not only does Beijing not publish any information about arms transfers abroad, but it has not submitted any data to the UN Register on Conventional Arms in the last eight years (Amnesty International 2006: 1–3).

A further concern involves the way in which China has established special relations that guarantee loans to African leaders with no conditionality clauses. Reacting against this, the former World Bank President Paul Wolfowitz, unequivocally raised concern about the modus operandi of Chinese banks, arguing they ignored human rights and environmental standards when lending to African countries. There are also concerns that general aid and soft loans with no conditionality could lead to unsustainable debts, and ultimately undermine the World Bank's efforts to improve governance, transparency and accountability. Such a contradiction in terms on the part of the World Bank is discussed in Chapter 6. But suffice to say here that the conditionality that has been imposed by the World Bank does not exactly promote human rights standards – in effect the World Bank does not take into account the political dimensions of human rights in its lending decisions (see Chapter 5).

Does the Chinese case constitute an alternative model of development that could compete with the post-Washington Consensus? Western governments have endeavoured to prioritise individual civil and political rights, good governance and democracy. The Chinese model on the other hand clearly pursues development that shows little regard to individual civil and political rights but accords some priority to social and economic and cultural rights (see Chapters 1 and 2). This together with the growing influence of China has provoked unease among some of the northern powerful states. It is not surprising that Mugabe who has been one of the most enthusiastic to trade with China, has said that 'we have nothing to lose but our imperialist chain'. (Watts, J, *The Guardian*, Saturday 4 Nov 2006: 24–25).

Convergence: is it really that straightforward?

Whether the Chinese development model is going to be a real alternative to the current development paradigm for some countries remains to be seen, but it does seem to bring into disrepute the 'end of history thesis'. According to Francis Fukuyama, convergence in the pattern of economic reforms reflects convergence of politics and institutions and the triumph of liberalism on a global scale. In this sense it symbolises the 'end of history' and the end of the deep ideological cleavages that divided the world's societies, such as monarchy, fascism and communism, earlier this century. He argues that today virtually all countries have adopted, or are trying to adopt, liberal democratic political (economic) institutions and that 'a great number have simultaneously moved in the direction of market oriented economies and integration into the global capitalist division of labour' (1992: 1). Liberal democracy as a system of government is perceived to have defeated extreme rival ideologies by homogenising societies, regardless of their historical origins or cultural inheritance. Fukuyama argues that the 'end of history' is fundamentally an argument about modernisation. What is universal is not only the desire for liberal democracy but also the desire to live in a modern society, with its technology, high standards of living, access to health and education and access to the wider world. Economic growth and modernisation are perceived to drive demands for political participation by creating an educated middle class with property to protect (2006: 54–56).

The suggestion is that liberal democracy is one of the by-products of the modernisation process, and something that becomes a universal aspiration only in the course of historical time and not as a result of regime change by force, as recently pursued by US administrators (see Chapter 5 for a more detailed discussion). Even Fukuyama admits his theory may be questionable following 9/11 on two grounds, the first being his belief that capitalism can bring the whole of the world up to the current developed levels of rich countries, and the second that liberal democracy is spreading.

Fukuyama and supporters of the neo-liberal globalisation perspective have clearly assumed globalisation to be a 'benign force' for social transformation, creating, through the global market, free trade and capital mobility; a global civilisation in which there is less poverty, more wealth and widely diffused liberal democracy. What they fail to explain is the malignant side of globalisation that contributes to uneven development and increased poverty, inequality and environmental problems. Poverty has increased significantly over the past three decades. Around 40 per cent of the World's 6.5 billion people live in poverty, a sixth of those (877 million) live in extreme poverty. The worst failure is in Africa, where the percentage of the population living in extreme poverty has increased significantly. Given Africa's increasing population, the number of people living in extreme poverty has almost doubled from 164 million to 316 million since 1980 (UNDP, 2005). The conclusions are pretty stark. If we consider in more depth the idea that liberal democracies are an automatic by-product of economic globalisation, we surely have to question why there are only around 24 established liberal democracies in the world today out of 193 independent states. For many countries, the demands of the globalisation process have not gone hand in glove with increased democratisation and state capability to improve support and services for their own citizens. Rather they have worked to undermine state power and function, which is fairly crucial for the capacity of states to be a primary agent of justice and to rise to the increased challenge, from within the global arena, to states to deliver rights. The UN Commission for Human Right (2000: 9) concluded that:

> The opportunities provided by globalisation and integration into the world economy to developing countries have not, by and large, resulted in improved enjoyment of the right to development. That right implies a process of development, with a participatory, equitable and just process of economic growth with the progressive

realisation of all the recognized human rights.... The increasing globalisation of developing countries has not always resulted in increased economic growth and where it has, it has not been associated with increased equity and social justice and has not even always resulted in reduced poverty, the worst form of deprivation of human rights. Trade liberalisation, deregulation or globalisation, as such, are not ends in themselves, but are means to the end of rights-based development.

Chang and Grabel provide an interesting analysis of how neo-liberal globalisation has negatively impacted on both economic performance and living standards (2004: 25).

Uneven development and exclusion

When the benefits of globalisation are heralded, few take time to focus on the countries that are disadvantaged and in one way or another are excluded from participating in the global economy, including those marginalised for an assortment of historical reasons. In Sub-Saharan Africa, for example, increased poverty, inequality, social friction and human rights violations, reflect a pattern of uneven development that has made some areas of the world 'structurally irrelevant'. In the words of Wallerstein 'Within a capitalist world economy, all states cannot develop simultaneously by definition, since the system functions by virtue of having an unequal core and peripheral regions' (1984: 286). Globalisation has not only shaped inequality and tensions, it has actually harmed relations between states (Hirst and Thomson, 1996; Hoogvelt, 1997; Robinson, 2004; Wade, 2004).

The global picture of integration is complex and development has been extremely uneven. There is often an historical explanation for why the poorest countries and regions of the world have not benefited by economic globalisation. The discourse of development remains largely detached from its colonial past. Historical analyses of development remains linear, tracing either the evolution of development theories or the occurrence of key events and phases in development history. The omission of development's colonial roots has several implications for current understanding of development, as well as existing global relations and inequalities. Appreciation of the links between development and colonialism opens up possibilities for a better understanding of the current contexts of the south, as well as the complexities of its relations with the North (Khotari, 2005). Many are former colonies which were structurally exploited and which during years of colonialism were stripped of their resources by the rich nations.

Colonialism was not a historical accident. On the contrary, colonialism was a first step towards globalisation, bringing Third World nations into the global world only not in an open and fair way but through unequal relations that were determined by the need for raw materials and the strategic nature, for European countries, of some trade routes. In fact rivalries between nations intensified as countries competed over raw materials and the export of their commodities[2] (Bernstein, 2000: 242–245). Despite this heritage, proponents of economic globalisation like to suggest that colonisation was a 'benevolent force' – the good old 'invisible hand' that brought late 19th century technological progress to all corners of the world for the good of humanity. It may be convenient to leave the colossal felonies of colonisation in the past, but we cannot ignore the heritage of inequalities and human rights violations that colonisation generated in Africa and parts of Asia and Latin America. A leading article in *The Economist* summarises how little this heritage is acknowledged: 'Globalisation has already narrowed the overall gap between North and South. But some countries, notably in Africa and the Middle East, have *chosen* not to take part in that process, and misery there has increased' (emphasis is added; *The Economist*, 2002: 11). What choice Sub-Saharan Africans have, tied as they are to aid and conditional loans from donors and bound through these to pursue the World Bank and IMF's restrictive monetary and fiscal policies as part of adjustment. They are encouraged to promote exports to service national debts and to ease their balance of payments, but have been relatively unsuccessful as productivity is low and access to the global market is limited because of trade barriers to agricultural and other commodities. For many years, since independence from colonial powers, new nation states have been demanding equal rights on trade and fair trade (Rights to Development), but generous high subsidies in the United States and EU for local agricultural commodities have been an obstacle for southern goods. This has depressed the incomes of 75 per cent of the population in the south who do not get subsides and are dependent on agriculture for their livelihoods. Despite the fact that WTO trade agreements have outlawed subsidies for many commodities, subsidies for agriculture have remained high in the north. Furthermore liberalisation has failed to entice capital investment in Africa and in recent years, allowing foreign goods to continue to pour into African countries at a time when exports of oil and minerals have reached their height because of Chinese and Indian demand for their primary commodities.

Customary rights vs property rights

It is hardly surprising that the past three decades have been called the 'lost decades' for Africa. Life expectancy and access to health and education have little improved. Mortality rates from HIV/AIDS continue to increase (estimated to be 12 million) and there are approximately 25.8 million HIV positive people (Akukwe, 2006) across the continent. Millions of people are displaced as a result of devastating civil wars. So what choice do people from African countries have? Can economic globalisation work for them? What role has colonisation and subsequent post colonial development policy played?

Inequality over the course of history and linked to a variety of factors, such as social relations, underpins present levels of social, economic and cultural development. In the case of sub-Saharan Africa the early phases of globalisation, associated with colonisation set the historical context for inequality and human rights violations. The formation of export economies under colonialism required reorganisation of the economic activities of local people under the new ruling elites of the colonial state – white settlers and companies mainly from Europe. The mobilisation of labour broke down traditional social relations and impacted on the whole way of life, forcing the black population to move to communal or reserved areas while white people occupied the large areas with the most fertile lands. Tribal chiefs were given rights to land through lineage leadership and therefore were empowered to allocate land for homes, crop cultivation and grazing land in the communal areas. What was constructed in Africa was a rural, tribal identity as a means of political administrative control over customary rights.

Traditional authority and forms of social organisation or customary rights have tended to contradict modern forms of social organisation and neo liberal development ideas that promote individual property rights and which have been introduced in the wake of colonisation. This dualism is often judged as being a prime obstacle to development. In response land tenure reforms have been encouraged that substitute customary rights with individual private ownership through legal recognition. The basic assumption is that land tenure reform does not have to be based on the principle of redistribution, or reflect local definitions of customary communal land. What is uniformly promoted instead is market related individual title to land or private property rights, on the grounds that it has 'worked' in other parts of the world to reduce poverty. How capitalism can work for the poor is wrapped up in the need for formal property rights to be supported by legal institutions.

The right to property is the backbone of capitalist social relations. As discussed in Chapter 2, John Locke and Bentham and other Enlightenment writers associated political freedom with the individual ownership of property. In England, Oliver Cromwell was adamant that the 'voting rights were granted only to those who owned freehold land' (Ishay, 2004: 92). It took until the first amendment of the American Constitution before freedom was defined as giving the individual the right to life, liberty and property, and was therefore fully inclusive of all, for example women and the poor. The idea of property rights and individual ownership extended to other countries during the post colonial period since when it has been popularised by development agencies and other contemporary writers. The right to property rights and the supporting accessible legal system is one of the ten principles of the Washington Consensus (discussed in Chapter 3). Recent publications from the World Bank (2005a) accept that the historical inequitable distribution of land remains a pervasive source of poverty, and will continue to cause conflict if it is not addressed. The World Bank's solution for the agrarian question lies with market-led reform and effective community driven projects that involve the poor. This model is promoted as a more robust and efficient means of managing land distribution and ensuring beneficiaries secure land than resettlement by the state through a process of expropriation. Based on a *voluntary* 'willing buyer-willing seller' model, this replicates the idea of individual property rights as freedom and equity. Landowners are given incentives to sell to poor farmers, such as one-time payments at full market value rather than staggered compensation payments (Deininger, 1999: 663). However the World Bank acknowledges that the land issue is particularly complex in Africa because 90 per cent of land continue to be governed under customary tenure and therefore lies outside state registered property and by implication, the legal 'land market'. Only 10 per cent of people have formal title to freehold property that can be exchanged in the market. The current structure of land distribution based on customary rights produces in de Soto's words 'dead capital', because the feudal structure of communal areas (which permits a chief to move people off the land they farm) and consequential lack of secure tenure results in inefficiency and low productivity. Several farmers suffer the consequences of poor land management practices, such as land degradation induced by continual cultivation because of their insecurity.

De Soto provides a structural explanation of why capitalism, despite its success in the north, has failed to realise development in Africa, in some parts of Latin America and South Asia De Soto argues that the catalyst for inequality and poverty is nothing to do with the market economy but access to rights to land deeds, homes and other assets: 'What the poor lack is easy access to the property mechanism that could legally fix the economic potential of their assets so that they could be used to produce secure or guarantee greater value in the expanded market (de Soto 2001: 14). The poor have limited access to formal credit and opportunities to develop their income because they do not have land or assets to use as collateral to access inputs. To prove his hypothesis De Soto estimates that the total value of land and homes that are owned in Sub-Saharan Africa without deeds is approximately $1 trillion, more or less three times the total annual GDP and far greater than the aid received from rich nations (*The Economist*, 2006). He argues for a need to turn this 'dead capital' into 'live capital' which provides opportunities in the market for the poor to have access to credit and loans that would enable them to invest in land, seeds, machinery, home, business and in essence to increase their productivity.

Some civil society organisations counter argue that the principle of individualistic land title ownership cannot work in areas where land is collectively managed through kinship. It could exclude women and vulnerable groups from livelihood support and is underpinned by a fallacy that customary land tenure systems mean that land is not owned communally. Chimhowu and Woodhouse (2006) argue that the right to occupy land depends on being accepted as part of a community, under the jurisdiction of the village headman who allocates the community's estate. Thus individuals have rights of control which are as secure as ownership could be, through the mechanism that no one has the right to dispose or alienate the land individually, except after consultation with the lineage, family and the village headman. Even the village headman, after allocating land, cannot subsequently reverse this decision without consultation with members of the village. Such customary arrangements place land in the trust of village chiefs and headmen, and do not require legal frameworks, as traditional authority and responsibility is embedded within the moral obligations of a leader. Of course in many cases this power is abused through patronage and generates resistance to change that could undermine authority, as one head of village told me in Zimbabwe: Title deeds are good because it gives you a guarantee that the land belongs to you. If you have a plot of your own it means you have power. But as a chief I see the awarding of title deeds creates the problem of controlling the people. Even if a person does wrong you cannot control them because they have title to the land. A title deed will not make any difference in the up-keep of the land. But a person with title deeds can refuse you entrance to his property' (Interview by the author 2000, Zimbabwe).

Critiques argue that instead of promoting individual property rights, customary rights need to be reinforced because they provide a system of ownership that recognises tribal and village structures in relation to land rights. A good example is Communal Land Rights Bill in South Africa which allows individuals to use land and even own land within the prevailing tradition of customary rights. Empirical findings suggest that under this arrangement individuals invest in land improvements such as tree planting, water pump and irrigation or buildings and such investment is seen as a legitimate way to claim more secure rights to the land. Studies from Zimbabwe, Tanzania, Zamina, Malawi and South Africa conclude that there is a pervasive land market in communal areas which has enabled many individuals to purchase land. Such is the characteristic of what Chimhowu and Woodhouse (2006) describe as a 'Vernacular land market' which has become prevalent since the 1980s and liberalisation policy that encourages an export oriented economy. A strong market for agricultural commodities and growth of horticultural produce has been a key element of the recent development of land markets.

Land issues are extremely complex and require an understanding of how colonial history links to current attempts at development. The Western model of property rights may apply in one context and yet in other localities can be manipulated by the rich and elite and therefore deteriorate access to land and land rights for women, the poor and vulnerable groups. There can be no assumptions that, as de Soto suggested in 2001 when his book was published, poor people with titles to land are more likely to obtain a loan from a commercial bank. Even *The Economist* who paid tribute to de Soto's ideas has questioned his original assumptions to be unrealistic. According to a recent report by *The Economist*,

> Capitalism is the only system that can lift billions out of poverty. But no recipe can achieve this overnight. History suggests that as well as property rights and a decent legal system, it requires sound economic policies, an educated workforce and political arrangements capable of regulating conflicts and minimising the risk to investment. Then again, if development were easy, everyone would have already developed. (*The Economist*, 2006)

It also necessitates institutional reforms and enhancing state capacity to manage such a process. The issue of land reform emphasises for us that development after all is contextually determined, as different patterns of inequality from those of South Africa, Zimbabwe and Nigeria, to Brazil, Sudan and the Philippines demonstrate. This is something that the World Bank has never really conceived of. Many of its programmes and lending policies are universally packaged and ignore the particularity of a situation, its uniqueness and history (Wolford, 2005: 243). A more context-sensitive universalism would make a lot of social economic sense. Land inequality and reform should be taken seriously to address fundamental entitlements of all citizens to rights for land. The point I want to make is that a 'one size fit all' development policy and strategy has been very harmful for people in the south. It may be the case that land distribution is not necessary in some countries, but in others many farmers are desperate to own land to secure livelihood survival. In the poorest of countries the state has to drive physical distribution of land, as the poor are not able to compete with the rich and more powerful landowners to determine market prices.

There is plenty of empirical data that shows the complexity of conflict over land in different parts of the world. In Brazil there has been pressure for agrarian reform not only from the Landless Rural Workers Movement, but also by agrarian reform movements at the national level. The colonial legacy of the under-resourced rural landless in Brazil is now fully recognised and well documented (Bales, 2000),[3] as are grotesque inequalities that have persisted after colonialism, facilitated by the political structures left in place.[4] As growing unrest mounted in the 1960s, 'Liberation Theology' began to strengthen commitment amongst certain elements of the Catholic Church for social justice for the poor. Land concentration grew under the dictatorship's industrialised plan of agriculture, and land distribution persists today as being among the most unequal in the world. Almost half of all fertile land is owned by 1 per cent of the population. Furthermore, intensified mechanisation has also precipitated a massive exodus of unemployed workers from rural areas into the cities (Wolford, 2005: 243).

In Turkey, differentiation within the Kurdish south-east region is a source of both socio-economic and political conflict. The extreme unequal distribution of assets in the area represents the historical 'political settlement' that is the balance of power between groups affected by a given institution, in this case landlords known locally as Aga[5] (Morvaridi, 2004). The Aga, a legacy of the Ottoman Empire, represent families that over generations have inherited lands which were transferred to tribal leaders during the Ottoman Empire, to ensure their political support when the south-east was strategically important. These landlords perpetuate traditional kinship/tribal relations through patterns of common patrilineal descent and control through loyalty ties that impact on social and political relations and institutions, reinforcing the Aga strength at the expense of poorer families (Yalcin-Heckmann, 1991). In fact tribal ties are highly influential in all spheres of life from political behaviour to marriages and family structures. In this area there are a number of villages where only one or relatively few families (Aga) possess all cultivated land, with the land ownership of families extending beyond the boundaries of one village alone. Land tenure and property rights are problematic, particularly around proof of ownership. There are high levels of landlessness (approximately 35 per cent are landless) and continuing land disputes. Around 50 per cent of rural people in the area, mainly smallholders are unable to prove ownership, as they do not hold registration deeds. Although there was some pressure for land expropriation, and reform in the 1970s, since the 1980s liberalisation of market programmes and Structural Adjustment policies, rights to land and land reform in the area have not received support from the state.

The institutions of global governance have failed to respond to the problems associated with the inequalities that have persisted since colonisation which impinge on development. The current neo-liberal development programme has provided an inadequate understanding of local issues, customary rights and why it is important that they are appreciated in strategic approaches. In essence, neo-liberalism risks are seen as more detrimental than remedial. Demands that states restructure the economy in the direction of integration into the globalisation process, and measures such as conditional lending, export oriented expansion, secure property rights, privatisation, and reduction in state intervention, renew the global economy rather than the individual national economy and integration into the globalisation process.

Economic globalisation: withering away the state

In the Declaration of Human Rights 1948 and Rights to Development (1986) the state is regarded as the primary agent of justice. Social justice scholars, who promote a responsibility approach to human rights for global justice, have recently argued for the need to reconsider this role in the context of globalisation. There are several reasons why it is no longer considered to be workable. First some authors support the assumption that economic globalisation has effectively 'washed away' the primary role of the nation state (Beck, 2006: 61), changing both the form and political power of states (Held, 2004). The sovereignty and autonomy of territorial states in many countries and their ability to control or regulate their national economies have 'eroded' (Griffin, 2003), 'declined' (Hoogvelt, 1997; Robinson, 2004) and 'weakened' (Stiglitz, 2006). Secondly in the globalised world that we live in a multiplicity of agents, institutions and agencies seek to provide the administration necessary to protect and nurture human rights (Pogge, 2002; Griffin, 2003; Held, 2004; O'Neill 2005; Beck, 2006). The approach of these Cosmopolitan scholars who support the concept of global justice has, therefore, been to question the value of Article 3.1 that encapsulates a state-centric approach of the Declaration of Rights to Development (1986) that clearly positions the state as the primary agent of justice: 'States have the primary responsibility for the creation of national and international conditions favourable to the realization of the right to development' (Article 3: 1). In this conception development implies 'a comprehensive economic, social, cultural and political process, which aims at the constant improvement of the well being of the entire population and all individuals, on the basis of the fairer distribution of benefits resulting there from' so that 'all human rights and fundamental freedoms can be fully realised' (Article 1). Such a development process should be integral to national development policies that states have the duty to formulate (Article 2, paragraph 3) to ensure 'equality of opportunity for all in their access to basic resources, education, health services, food, housing, employment and the fair distribution of income' (Article 8). The objectives of development in policy terms are expressed in terms of the claims or entitlements of individuals as rights' holders, that is to say as the beneficiaries. It is equally clear that the state has responsibility for the promotion and implementation of rights to development and to protect them as duty bearer; this was reaffirmed in The Vienna Declaration (1993).

Griffin (2003) argues that within the current processes of globalisation and integration of the world economy, the sovereignty and autonomy of territorial states and their ability to control or regulate their national economy has gradually been eroded. In other words the right to development as configured is false 'methodological nationalism'. In the contemporary form of globalisation national problems can no longer be solved on a national basis, and the concept of state is as a result being hollowed out '... human rights are being turned against statism and are being "defended" by states against other states, and because highly mobile capital is forcing territorially fixated states to dis-empower and transform themselves' (Beck, 2006: 37).

Cosmopolitanism

In the context of the complex transformation that the world is experiencing through economic globalisation, the meaning of accountability and democracy at the national level is shifting. When the state is no longer empowered or effective at controlling the issues that impact on the provision of social protection, there is a risk that the poor and marginal might suffer. Acknowledging this risk, should the human rights and development discourse incorporate the cosmopolitan concept of global justice (Nussbaum, 1999; Pogge, 2002) and cosmopolitan democracy (Held, 2004)? This approach takes the individual as the unit of analysis and frames the individual's rights within 'a single human community'. The cosmopolitan theory is based on three key concepts – individuality, universality and generality. To see human beings as individuals means that family lines, tribes, ethnic, cultural, or religious communities, nations, or states have only indirect concern. This is reinforced by the concept of universality and the understanding that every living human being is equal and not part of some subset of society (e.g. men, aristocrats, whites, Muslims etc.). Lastly, the concept of generality suggests some kind of special status of global force which recognises that persons are ultimate units of concern for everyone and not only for those that they appear to fit with – other citizens, members of a religious group, socio-economic band etc. (Pogge, 2002: 169).

Global democracy frames the nation state as less important than the individual person who is considered to be the 'ultimate unit of moral concern'. Each person is regarded as equally worthy of respect regardless of geographical location or the community in which they were born or brought up (Held, 2004: 170). This reciprocal recognition allows individuals to form social relations based on equality of opportunity. If individuals have equality of status before the law and institutions that govern them, they may have to put up with loss, disadvantage and marginalisation. This is 'not because they are inferior to others but because they have no or less opportunity to participate in the process of development and institutions that shape their lives'[6] (Held, 2005: 192). This reflects a commitment to universal standards, human rights and democratic values which apply, in principle, to everyone. These principles can be universally shared to form the basis of the individual's interest in the determination of the institutions which govern their lives. These shared values are already enshrined in human rights law and other international rules and legal arrangements, including the Declaration of Human Rights 1948.

Cosmopolitans would have us believe, therefore, that individual rights can be protected no matter where people live through properly managed global governance. Ultimately geographical location and citizenship should make no intrinsic difference to the rights and obligations of individuals (Kuper, 2005: xii). We no longer live in a world of disconnected national or political communities, but one of 'overlapping communities of fate where the trajectories of countries are deeply enmeshed with each other, where the fate of nations is significantly entwined' (Held, 2005: 187). Globalisation has resulted in a multiplicity of actors and agents providing administration to protect rights and achieve development, some of which are transnational and have overlapping legal competencies. In this conception other agents are equally important, such as non-government organisations, and transnational actors, including global institutions, that could complement the state to achieve justice, the reduction of poverty and the delivery of rights.[7] Since many development issues such as global warming, poverty, migration, and disease are no longer national issues but cut across borders, such an approach could be seen to respond to a *cosmopolitan social standard* which reflects shared principles about the equal worth of all individuals irrespective of the geographical location in which they live. This restates the Kantian notion of 'cosmopolitan law' where individuals have equal rights, concern and opportunity as 'citizens of the earth' rather than citizens of a particular state in which they were born or brought up' (Held, 2005: 194). This universality of the individual is the first principle of the cosmopolitan position, with other associations by nationality or tribe, for example, considered to be important, but secondary. Anderson suggests we need to move away from a state-centric 'international law of a traditional kind, regulating relations between states', and towards 'a cosmopolitan law, establishing individuals as the subject of universally enforceable rights' (Anderson, 2005: 3). Within this context the right to development would be defined in terms of individual rights, rather than in relation to national or group rights. There would be no need for a dualism between poor and rich countries, Muslim/Christian, because 'all positions involving the negation of individual are transcended to the equality of the basic rights of all human beings' (Beck, 2006: 141). However, this does not necessarily mean the end of the state or national political strategies, but it would rely on the regulatory capacity of states increasingly being 'matched by the development of collaborative mechanisms of governance at supranational, regional and global level' (Held, 2004: 15).

Can global institutions solve development issues?

The thrust of the discussion on the cosmopolitan standards of governance is captured in the recently edited book by Bhargava (2006) 'Global Issues and Global Citizens', contributed to by 27 staff from the World Bank. Their main concern is that in the interconnected world in which we live many issues of development could be considered to be global concerns that cannot be handled by nation states alone because the risks of failure cross national boundaries. These include global poverty; climate change; fair trade; stability of the global financial system; conflicts, genocide, and failing states; migration; diseases without borders; access to education for all; debt sustainability and relief; biodiversity; and management of the world's resources (oceans, forests, water and energy). The general view is that global issues are expected to become even more acute due to population growth, expansion in the global economy, and growing imbalances in terms of the environment and social stresses (Bhargava, 2006). These need to be addressed by reducing the obstacles they present to movements of people, goods and capital, that necessitate proactive global institutions and co-operation of states. The concept of 'global governance' mechanisms to address these challenges, including international laws treaties and institutions, has become the unofficial ideology of mainstream development thinking. However, there is still the question of how global institutions such as the World Bank, the IMF, the WTO, influence international forums that promote cosmopolitan rights. What is the consequential impact on the delivery of the right to development, given that they have neither the power nor political will to respond to rights claims? Enhancing the influence of major global institutions is problematic. They are not open and transparent elected institutions and most decisions taken by them do not represent all perspectives, such as those of poor countries (see Chapter 6). It is partly because these global institutions are not accountable, that we face global injustices such as poverty, inequality and human rights abuses.

Cosmopolitan scholars remind us of the proliferation of international institutions that already exist to support global justice and rights, such as the International Criminal Court (ICC) where human rights abuses may be challenged; the Kyoto Protocol on climate change; conventions on arms control; and other forums through which global institutions yield influence. However, these global institutions lack the governmental powers and political will to respond to rights claims or to formally assign responsibilities for rights to the multiplicity of agents and institutions (see Chapter 5). Moreover, often the more powerful nations, such as the United States of America, rule out the legitimacy of these institutions (as we have discussed in the previous Chapter). If we take the ICC, for example, we find an innovative form of cosmopolitanism, which goes much beyond Kant's conception of 'cosmopolitan law' and represents the trend to do away with the principle of the absolute subjection of individuals to the state and develop the status of individuals under international law. The move to see individuals as the bearers of certain rights under international law cuts through the shield of state sovereignty. This may have been why the United States of America withdrew as a signatory to the ICC in 2002, exactly at the time that they were planning a pre-emptive attack on Iraq. The United States of America has vehemently opposed the recommendation of a UN report that the violators of human rights in Darfur, where more than one million people have been killed, two million internally displaced, and 200,000 have become refugees in neighbouring counties (UN, 2005: 65), be tried by the ICC, because according to Bush no one should be prosecuted in 'a foreign court ... where unaccountable judges (could) put our troops and officials at the unacceptable risk of politically motivated prosecutions' (*The Economist*, 2005). The United States instead has proposed different ways to deal with the situation that do not require the involvement of international courts, such as an ad-hoc tribunal based in Tanzania under the auspices of the African Union to try those responsible. And yet the ICC exists to undertake this role. Since the United States withdrew its signature from the ICC in May 2002 it has waged a relentless campaign against the court, threatening to cut US aid to countries which have ratified its statutes unless they sign bilateral agreements pledging not to hand over US suspects to the court, and threatening to withdraw its support from UN peacekeeping missions.

In the context of economic globalisation, we cannot simply assume that the existing pattern of global institutions will guarantee delivery of rights. The legal base of global institutions and their ability to enforce human rights law and treaties in their current forms have been overestimated by cosmopolitans. Although they suggest the need to deconstruct roles and responsibilities with the Human Rights Declaration (O'Neill, 2005), the fundamental issue is where ultimate responsibility for the delivery of rights rests. This currently lies with nation states and it is the interpretation of rights by nation states that affects how they are translated into national jurisdiction and policy paradigm. This continues to be the case, irrespective of how much international conventions, legal frameworks and global institutions posture about securing rights.

Post-globalisation: back to the state

Critiques of economic globalisation consider the current conjuncture to be one of rising protectionism and nationalism. According to Saul, we have reached 'the end of globalisation' (Saul, 2005), with the model of the 1970s and 1980s now faded away, and it is unexpectedly over (Rosenberg, 2005). 9/11 is seen as a catalyst for a reinvigoration of US nationalism, which has raised doubt about globalism that advocates the idea of integration of states and the disintegration of statism. Nevertheless the global economy continues to blossom but building on regionalism rather than globalism. US nationalism has become a primary force in undermining the old 'global project' by encouraging increasingly weaker states to seek protection under regionalist relationships with the major powers. Typical forums for this include South African Development Community (SADC), the Arab Cooperation Council, the EU and so forth which show that 'nation states and their own view of their national interest are still far more important than any international economic theory' (Saul, 2005: 35). In other words the state has not been displaced or lost its potential but it has reshaped and in some cases changed into a 'neo liberal state' (Robinson, 2004: 124).

We have to recognise that globalisation has certainly changed the form, character and economic direction of many states. The extent to which it has eroded the sovereignty of all territorial nation states, as Griffin and others maintain, is disputable. Across the world we find complex and diverse forms of state, verifying the enduring significance of the nation state. In fact after major political shifts such as decolonisation and the end of the cold war, and the disintegration of socialist states, the number of states has increased. With 33 new states becoming members since 1980, the United Nations has numerically grown by 20 per cent (UNDP, 2003).

However, on the global stage while some powerful states, such as the United States and the G8, are the more dominant actors, other states particularly in the south are weak or 'fragile states' and have less voice. A typical weak or fragile state tends to be powerful within its own sovereignty, but corruption and nepotism are often widespread. A weak state tends to have limited material resources, or limited infrastructure to exploit them, and its economy is often unhealthy or in debt. Of course, poverty among these states tends to be high. Such characteristics render these states weak at the global level and exclude them from the benefits of globalisation. In one way or another they face the problem of exclusion from the global market and the institutions of global governance are often biased towards the more powerful countries. Fragile states can be found across the world in Sub-Sahara Africa, parts of Latin America, and some regions of Asia. There are also ideologically oriented states that resist the current global order and seek an alternative form of state-society relationship. Basically for these states justice, rights and equality coexist with the idea of sovereignty, culture and spirituality. This is demonstrated in the internal relations between state and society, found in states such as Iran and Saudi Arabia. Other states, such as Venezuela, Ecuador, Peru, Bolivia, are looking for alternative pathways to development that contract the neo liberal economic agenda of the United States, the IMF and the World Bank. They pursue policies geared more towards social protection, and are sceptical about the benefits of free trade, but wish to pursue their interest in South-South regional co-operation. We also have states that are considered to be 'failed states', such as Somalia, Liberia and Iraq, etc. where institutions and internal order have crumbled.

Other forms of state failure include states that beleaguered by fragile institutions, poor governance and widespread corruption. These states are unable to protect their own citizens and often violate human rights. Others, referred to as *strong states*, accept some aspects of global norms, such as free trade, but reject others and pursue a state-led development strategy while still participating in globalisation. These include China and the developmental states of South East Asia.

The newly industrialised Asian states are characterised by a notion of the 'Developmental State', comprising powerful and competent bureau-crats and developmental elites with relative autonomy, a weak civil society and poor human rights record, but a strong commitment to economic growth and nationalism. National developmentalism and economic development are driven by the political structure of the state, shaped by factors such as nationalist ideology and a wish to 'catch up' with the West. This is added to by defensive and security military concepts that fuel regional competition and hostility (Leftwich, 2000). Although this model of the developmental state has largely been developed in the context of East Asian countries, Taylor (2005) argue that it can also apply to other states, despite variance with the Taiwanese or South Korean exempla. Others maintain that developmental states are the upshot of unique historical circumstances and that similarities are difficult to establish across national settings (Onis, 1991). Several states aspire to be developmental states; the real issues are differences in capacities and this depends highly on the ability of the state to recruit competent bureaucracies with the authority to direct and manage the broad shape of their economic and social development.

China and the developmental states of South East Asia in general have been able to sustain their autonomy, with minimal intervention from outsiders. None of these states have practiced the economic policies of the Washington Consensus, but they have achieved economic growth through state intervention behind protectionist barriers. In China, the government tends to control large portions of the country's industrial assets and shape development by investing heavily in infrastructure. India is not dissimilar and both countries have clearly seen modernisation from a national and not a global point of view, with emphasis on building the strength of the nation state. Weiss (1998) and Evans and Rauch (1999), in criticising those who believe the state has declined, argue that to achieve social and economic development a 'strong state', that can sustain its autonomy, irrespective of international pressures for external intervention in directing or influencing the way in which the economy should run, is essential. In fact successful development in these countries is often attributed to the significance of the 'embedded autonomy' of the state, which explains the ability of bureaucracies to manage sustainable growth. Using the Weberian model of bureaucracy, there appears to be a close correlation between an effective and capable bureaucracy and economic growth and this is evidenced by India and China. This leads me to consider that the success criteria of an effective developmental state are, firstly, the degree of independence it displays through competent decision-making without reliance on external sources or the conditionality of global institutions, and, secondly, its capacity to implement social and economic programmes and policy with confidence. Bureaucracies that achieve this are distinguished by decision-making procedures that are based on their own intuitive structures and are characterised by meritocratic recruitment that values long-term career rewards and leads to an effective form of organisation. Corruption and nepotism is less likely to be found in this type of bureaucracy.

Henderson et al. (2003) press forward with this hypothesis, albeit with a slightly different focus on poverty reduction strategies. In an analysis of data from 29 middle income countries they conclude that effective Weberian bureaucracies and public institutions have the ability to reduce poverty through their ability to achieve economic growth. Their research finds that investment in education, health and other social policies is likely to increase as a result of additional public finance generated by economic growth and this has an 'automatic' impact on the reduction of income poverty and capability deprivation. States with higher quality and more effective public bureaucracies achieve poverty reduction, therefore, on two fronts – through increased investment, and through the effectiveness of the services they provide. As people become more literate and morbidity is reduced, they are better placed to take advantage of income opportunities that present. Thus we find evidence of how addressing aspects of capability poverty indirectly reduces income poverty. Schemes that seek to alleviate poverty directly by providing poor people with such resources as food aid, subsidised loans, and training and technical advice, also help to raise their productivity. Schemes such as these are likely to be both better designed and implemented in states with Weberian circumstances, than in countries where public bureaucracies are not meritocratic and where corruption may be higher. Poverty Reduction Strategies assume that state agencies can play a major role in planning for poverty reduction. Their capacity and efficaciousness is therefore key.

State capacity is generally defined as a state's autonomous ability to formulate and implement development policies that achieve economic and social goals. This is not just about the ability of public institutions but it also requires a strong civil society that allows social critiques of established powers in relation to rights. The problem with Henderson et al.'s analysis of the model of the developmental state is that it seems to accept that where the state acts as an authoritarian manager of development policy and programmes, there can be an absence of civil and political rights, civil society institutions and non-state actors. As I have argued in previous Chapters, it is a state's capacity to be inclusive and to effect equal rights to development that is essential for social justice, not merely its capacity to stride towards economic growth. I would, therefore, question the extent to which economic growth, even when it has indirect or indirect impact on individual productivity, achieves development.

Conclusion

In this Chapter I have explained the cosmopolitan conception of global social justice that provides a helpful challenge to the uneven forces of economic globalisation that have intensified inequality and poverty. However the cosmopolitan approach not only misses the point that international treaties and laws are often flawed, but it also undermines the power and influence of the north and major actors in globalisation, such as transnational corporations and hegemonic states. This means that reforming global institutions alone will not be sufficient to achieve improved outcomes for the poorer nations. Cosmopolitans are sceptical about the operational value of rights to development at the national level, arguing that the best possibility we have of tackling global development issues will be a new form of global democracy, derived from universal human rights standards. So how would 'cosmopolitan democracy' and 'cosmopolitan governance' work? The next Chapter considers this question with regard to institutions of global governance and multinational corporations.

5
Global Governance and Rights to Development: Opportunity or Charade?

Introduction

The complex and asymmetric relationship between the nation state, 'capital' and global structures of governance makes the pursuance of rights to development easier said than done. As I have discussed in previous Chapters, the global capital market has shifted the locus of effective political power away from the nation state, while at the same time testing its regulative authority. This also impacts on the distribution of roles and responsibilities between state and non-state actors in a world that is politically and economically interconnected. Although the current global political and economic order continues to be based on local territorial sovereignty, its prospect is clearly shaped by global and intergovernmental networks. The network of organisations, which effectively governs the new 'global order', is captured by the umbrella term 'global governance' (Risse, 2005: 350). In this Chapter I will consider whether institutions of global governance can, as suggested by proponents of Cosmopolitanism, be reformed and restructured to deliver a mechanism for addressing inequality, poverty and environmental issues at all levels from the local to the global. In other words could institutions of global governance enhance state capacity to deliver rights? How expedient is it to engage a diversity of agents in development, thereby extending responsibility for delivering rights beyond the state? Could the concept of global justice be the key to the effective delivery of rights for the individual or community?

Previous Chapters have documented just a few of the many examples that exist of how economic globalisation has induced the withdrawal of the state from the imperative of social protection, substituting it with the private sector or the vagaries of the market. This Chapter questions more directly the accountability of institutions of global governance, the major intergovernmental organisations and the private sector or transnational corporations, in relation to rights delivery, given that their actions have extraterritorial effects. How does the activity and influence of these institutions fit with the notion of state obligation and responsibility? Is there a need to question who the agents of justice are, given the range of actors involved in development (O'Neill, 2005) and how global development issues might make an effective contribution to rights delivery?

Several studies suggest that it is no longer appropriate to attribute effective and legitimate power solely to states, because of the increasing trend to devolve responsibility to a variety of non-state actors (such as NGOs, and MNCs), in particular where states are weak, unjust or unwilling to act (Kuper, 2005). The relationship between national states and global institutions and rights is very complex. In calling for the deconstruction of the Declaration of Human Rights and The Right to Development, O'Neill advocates the idea of redistributing responsibilities and assigning justice and development obligations to non-state as well as state actors. Kuper argues that in the current global order states are failing their citizens, especially the poorest, because their systems are not designed for the pressures of economic globalisation. Essentially states struggle to manage the intensity and scope of cross border interactions and their impact. This leaves 'gaping holes, where governance should be' (Kuper, 2005: 224).

Less government, more governance

Before exposing the paradoxes of global governance institutions, it is important to demystify the core concepts. Hirst explains for us that 'Governance is often confused with government, presenting governance almost as if it were an autonomous administrative capacity, detached from politics and the structure and principle of the state' (Hirst, 2000: 24). The state comprises institutions that set the rules, make law, formulate development policy and provide security for people within a specific territory. The function of the state is executed by governing institutions – the police, army, civil service and other bureaucracies. Governments manage development by forming development policy and poverty reduction strategies in negotiation with the international development agencies such as the World Bank and the International Monetary Fund (IMF) (primarily for financial support). These institutions often describe governments in the south as powerful and forceful when it comes to managing development, although there are distinctions to be made between states 'not in their type of government, but in the degree to which the government really governs' (Hyden, Court and Means, 2003: 10). This is a pretty fundamental issue of course. States are often characterised as corrupt, unrepresentative, and unaccountable; violating individual civil and political rights. In fact widespread poverty and uneven economic growth are frequently attributed to irresponsible and corrupt elites who use and abuse their power.

In this context, there appears to be circumstances in which agencies other than the state could support the effective delivery and protection of individual or community rights. Such an approach to deliver rights focuses on less government and more governance or dispersed governance, based on multi level networks and partnerships. A multi-agency approach through which public bodies, and voluntary and public sector organisations assist communities, households, and individuals to manage and overcome risks and vulnerabilities is perhaps a necessary response to the far-reaching impact of globalisation. But only so long as the state continues to act as the primary agent of justice and development, if only in a regulatory capacity, could such an approach to protect individual rights be of any use. In Britain, for example, the network of public, private voluntary/charitable providers that is charged with meeting the basic needs of forced migrants provides a classic example of devolved governance or a dispersed state. Decentralisation has reduced the role of the state from that of a redistributor to that of a regulatory agent or a market manager. In this sense it is also a vehicle for promoting neo-liberal ideals, with individuals charged with increasingly taking responsibility for their own well-being as they become engaged with a host of agencies and institutions (Dwyer and Brown, 2005). Neo-liberals would suggest that we could do away with the idea of public good and community, replacing it with individual responsibility. Let's be clear – the involvement of a range of agencies in providing protection for the poor does not necessarily reflect greater commitment to their protection, but in most cases reflects attempts to contain the amount of welfare accessible to them, with the voluntary/informal sector essentially left to pick up the pieces.

In poor countries the problem of poverty is increasingly attributed to the problem of governance, or rather the lack of 'good governance', which is why the World Bank so keenly promotes the idea of achieving institutional reform, where needed, from within. 'Bad governance' is considered to be an obstacle to investment, innovation and a primary cause of delays to programme delivery, which in turn raise the overall cost of development. Corruption, bribery and the abuse of public office for private gain are characteristics associated with bad governance and incapable governments. According to the World Bank 'good governance' is an essential component for economic growth, as it sets the context for the way in which power is employed to manage the market and determines a nation's social and economic resources for growth and development (World Bank, 2001). This conception of governance clearly promotes the idea of the state, civil society, and the market as a triad. Using the vocabulary of 'donor agencies', development is the partnership between these institutions. Governance is determined as 'good', when it operates to make the market work well, or in other words when the state limits the scope of its action only to what is necessary to ensure that the market works and to provide appropriate low costs social units like education and health (Hirst, 2000). This suggests that good governance sets parameters on the power of the state, and in line with a liberalist strategy clearly marks a separation between a limited state, a largely self regulating civil society, and a market economy. The state becomes less of a service provider and develops a role as a commissioner and regulator of other non-state agents that are delegated to deliver social and economic rights.

Governance has been widely used in development literature to assess the accountability of governments. There are numerous definitions of governance, but here it is referred to as *a network of organisations consisting of government agencies, NGOs, private sector agencies and civil society organisations that share common social standards and values and which together rally around effective management of the market and development processes.* The retreat of the state and the reconfiguration of responsibilities to other agencies are increasingly immersed in discussions about global governance under the influences of international development and global financial institutions. The concept of governance at a global level is directly linked to the economic globalisation of the past 25 years and its undermining of state power and function.

Global governance

The concept of global governance is traditionally related to the political theory of international relations and in this sense it is not new. It has been co-opted into the discourse of development and not without contention. To start with let us consider a working definition for our clarification – *global governance is conceived as a network of transnational and intergovernmental organisations that have shared values and principles and follow a structured route of regulation and law. This network of organisations works on the belief system that poverty will be reduced through market-led development.* It is important that we make a distinction between global governance and government, which refers to rule and law on the basis of citizenship (defined through a constitution and relevant institutions). Despite the claim that we are all 'global citizens', a global constitution, through which membership or citizenship of a global civil society is established, does not exist. There is, therefore, no such thing as global government. Global governance however refers to collective action that may impact on individual states but is more likely to impact on groups of states or regions across the world. Global governance essentially operates through the activities of intergovernmental organisations such as the World Bank, IMF, the World Trade Organisation, Kyoto Protocol, various UN agencies and other agencies that represent civil society and have joined this complex in recent years. Their collective action to address the causes and consequences of adverse transnational or global problems, such as environmental destruction and poverty, reflects shared principles. The dynamic of global governance institutions lies in their ability to manage global issues that not only operate at a national level but also have wider trans-border implications. To provide a list of all such global issues would be exhaustive. It would, however, include trade, Intellectual Property Rights, corruption and money laundering, competition policy, international product standards, human rights (including crimes against humanity and torture), labour rights, refugees and humanitarian assistance, development and poverty reduction, Millennium Development Goals, environmental problems such as climate change and the depletion of the ozone layer, and so forth.

There seems to be inevitability that institutions of global governance have a role to play in determining our lives. According to the UN Commission on Global Governance, the current structure of global governance provides an institutional design for managing globalisation. The Commission defines global governance as 'the sum of many ways individuals and institutions, public and private, manage their common affairs. It is a continuing process through which conflicting or diverse interests may be accommodated and co-operative actions may be taken'[1] (Commission on Global Governance, 1995: 2). For Murphy, however, global governance has a clear ideological basis in the sense that it is 'a world-wide management strata for sharing neo-liberal ideology'. The delivery mechanism is the growing network of both public and private regimes that extend across the world's largest regions, some of which are relatively autonomous and powerful, and many of which carry out traditional service functions associated with public agencies, while at the same time working to establish new systems of international integration (2005: 139).

The contention of this Chapter is that the current institutions of global governance are not designed to manage development issues, as they have failed to ensure that the benefits of economic globalisation are symmetrically distributed. In a way 'Global governance has become the catch word for efforts at dealing with the political consequences of globalisation and subjecting them to political intervention' (Risse, 2005: 136). Whether we like it or not, protection is devolved to a variety of non-state actors, in particular where states are fragile or fail to deliver. Some schools of thought, such as the cosmopolitan managerialists, would have us believe that a reform of the institutions of global governance would lead to a realisation of the benefits of globalisation for the poor. If global governance were more transparent and inclusive would development strategies and policies that are more effective at poverty reduction be forthcoming? Could social and economic transformation be collectively managed through democratic global institutions that facilitate participation on the equal basis of all states? Beck suggests that such a form of 'institutionalised cosmopolitanism' would seek to structure and order the globalised world beyond the national and international (Beck, 2006).

There are some fairly simple presumptions in the Cosmopolitan position, not least that there can be consensus between states on complex issues and that this would take precedence over local or national policy drivers. The very global issue of refugee movement provides us with a good case study of the complex relationship between global and national institutions and rights. It demonstrates the difficulty that global institutions confront in terms of local implementation when accountability and responsibility remains with the nation state.

Institutions of global governance and refugees

International laws and treaties embrace protection for refugees with responsibility for delivery resting with signatory states. The principles that underpin the concept of protection for trans-border migrants are grounded in the UN Convention of 1951 and the 1967 Protocol Relating to the Status of Refugees, which set the protection of refugees within the framework of the Universal Declaration of Human Rights (1948). States who have ratified the Convention accept responsibility for protecting refugees' rights within their territory, not as a charitable gesture but under the obligation of international legal norms and in compliance with the Convention. In the context of the duality of the state versus the individual, a refugee is perceived to be an 'unprotected alien' that neither has the diplomatic protection accorded by states to nationals when abroad, nor the benefit of internal protection in their country of origin (Fortin, 2001). This lack of protection has driven the need to establish a substitute system of protection, based on the manner in which a refugee is defined.[2] Thus the concept of 'international protection' is used to denote protection that is directly accorded to individuals and groups by international agencies, based on international conventions and international laws. In a normative sense, the protection of refugees is set within a rights and morality framework. The United Nations Commission for Refugees (UNHCR) has responsibility for 'overseeing' the Convention's implementation, under an overall mandate to protect the rights of refugees, although compliance and enforcement with international human rights is problematic as there is no common legal system within which they are embedded (Brown, 1999). There are no enforcing institutions other than the UNHCR, which is in essence non-political and humanitarian, and can, at best, only apply diplomatic pressures to states that violate the UN Refugee Convention. In Asia and the Middle East some states have not signed up to UN refugee conventions, which effectively mean that they are not committed to asylum legislation or institutional arrangements for the protection of refugees that reflect universal human rights. Evidence shows that states which have signed the Convention often apply it loosely and rely on their own legal and cultural interpretations of rights, which increasingly reflect an agenda geared at ensuring national security and cultural identity (Dunne and Wheeler, 1999).

In practical terms, when 'protection' is translated into policy, it tends to be limited to legal and physical protection, rather than protection of social, economic, cultural and political rights. This is fundamentally determined by the fact that the plight of forced migrants is considered to only require temporary protection measures, with financial or other assistance provided as emergency relief only with 'a budget line on a par with an interstellar black hole'. Western European states have more capacity to deliver social protection for refugees than the majority of poor nations. In Europe it has been promoted through 'welfarism' and typical policy measures that protect forced migrants 'against the risks of inadequate incomes associated with employment, ill health and invalidity, parental responsibilities, old age ... and guaranteeing access to services that are essential for a life in dignity' (European Council on Refugees and Exiles, 2004). However, there have been moves to exclude forced migrants from access to the full range of welfare rights granted to citizens, reflecting the crisis of modern citizenship (Lister, 2004). Empirical evidence from western European countries suggests that the welfare rights of forced migrants have been systematically reduced to the extent that the whole idea of social protection and social rights is increasingly giving way to the idea of conditional entitlement (Dwyer and Brown, 2005). Stringent efforts to keep forced migrants out have been combined with attempts to reduce the welfare entitlements of those who enter to seek asylum. Such legislative changes have consolidated the link between immigration/residency status and welfare entitlement. In the United Kingdom the welfare rights of forced migrants have been systematically reduced by five pieces of legislation in the past 11 years. All people seeking asylum are now subject to a distinct system of welfare provision under the management of the National Asylum Support System (NASS) that is responsible for the co-ordination and funding of accommodation and financial support. Several asylum seekers are placed in detention centres or in social housing, without the right to work or to be productive. They find it difficult to integrate into the host society and are often the subject of racial tension. In an empirical study from Leeds, Dwyer (2005) provides evidence of destitution among asylum seekers and failed asylum seekers. Since 2002 asylum seekers have been disallowed the right to work and other privileges such as family reunion have been withdrawn. Asylum seekers, while waiting to hear the outcome of their application, live on basic-needs benefits even though some are skilled and could contribute economically to their host society.[3] Only those who have been granted refugee status have the same welfare rights as full citizens. Even those who have permission to work struggle to find employment that fits their skills and qualifications or because their own qualifications are not recognised as transferable and often 'doctors and professors end up as sandwich makers and security guards' (Hayter, 2004: 105). In fact UK anti-migration policies and justification for border control, to Hayter, reflect nothing but protection of nation state interest in a climate of racism, and to support the thesis that cites processes and practice that violate individual rights because they allow asylum seekers and their children to be labeled, for example, as 'voucher kids'. A truly open border migration policy would give people the opportunity for free mobility and secure this universal human right. The fear that numerous people from poor countries would come to the rich countries is, according to Hayter, over exploited as it would be very unlikely that several people would chose to migrate. However, this cosmopolitan notion of individual rights fails to consider the institutional problem of managing population flows in a global context, in today's world which is still nation-state centred.

While northern states have the capacity to offer social protection measures to deliver rights (even if they choose not to), the countries in the south tend to be less well placed. In these states refugees are forced to depend on what is offered through UN support or their own constrained resources and relatives and friends to manage poverty and risk. Poverty Reduction Programmes (PRSPs) aimed at achieving social protection for the vulnerable and the poor in over 70 poor countries have not addressed the problems faced by forced migrants (Marcus and Wilkinson, 2004). The main focus and priority of PRSPs is income poverty, while other deprivation concerns linked to forced migrants (gender inequality, rights, nutrition etc.) are ignored or treated as secondary (Conway et al., 2002: 26). In a similar vein, the Millennium Declaration makes only one reference in passing to refugees as vulnerable populations, requesting states to 'strengthen international co-operation, including burden-sharing in, and the coordination of, humanitarian assistance to countries hosting refugees, and to help all refugees and displaced persons to return voluntarily to their homes, in safety and dignity, and to be smoothly reintegrated into their societies' (UN, 2000: 5).

In the south most refugees and internally displaced people live in camps that were established for an initial period of five years, but which have remained open for more than two decades. In Africa alone, there are more than four million people living in perpetual poverty in one of the 170-plus camps that form the main structure of refugee assistance. In settings where facilities and basic necessities are minimal and where individuals have limited access to education, health, employment, and secure incomes, chronic poverty is widespread. Some refugees have lived for more than 15 years in camps where persistent shortages of food have resulted in acute malnutrition. As a result of recent budget cuts by UN institutions, bilateral donors, and NGOs, refugee food rations are often reduced and African refugees have been particularly affected with cuts of up to 25 per cent in some camps. According to UNHCR (2003a) there are rising rates of malnutrition in the refugee camps in Tanzania that house around 400,000 Burundian and Congolese refugees. In late 2004 the distribution of cereal and pulses was halved for refugees in Zambia and cuts have placed as many as 87,000 at risk of malnutrition. Lack of food is not simply a cause of transient poverty, but is a contributory factor to chronic poverty where subsequent generations are characterised by capability failure and deprivation. Even though many refugees have been living in camps for more than a decade they cannot come and go at will, nor do they have the right to work. Alongside malnutrition and poor living conditions, numerous human rights violations are believed to be committed within camps, including arbitrary detention and violent acts, such as rape and severe beatings. The oppression of women is particularly acute. Empirical findings show that camp inhabitants have to find their own strategies for survival and these include the collection of wild food, begging and vagary, prostitution, child placement, petty crimes, and so forth (Golooba-Mutebi, 2004).

The plight of Somali refugees in Kenya is indicative of the ineffectiveness of current policy frameworks to protect refugees. Kenya like many African[4] states has signed the UN Refugee Convention (1951), but there are no institutions or national legal procedures that apply to refugees and offer them legal protection or legal status within Kenyan territory. It is, therefore, impossible for refugees to seek asylum, and they are forced to live in designated camps, located in the remotest and poorest areas bordering a desert-savannah region that lacks vegetation and natural resources (Crisp, 1999). A number of people fled from their homes, land and villages during the civil war in Somalia in the early 1990s to take refuge in Kenya, and since then the UNHCR has provided food and shelter for up to 120,000 refugees in camps in Dadaab. Most refugees live in crowded, harsh conditions and, because they are confined to the camps, are mostly dependent on humanitarian aid. They live in makeshift shelters that provide little shade from the heat and poor protection against heavy rains. For example, on one rainy day over 600 shelters were destroyed and more than 300 refugees were left without shelters, exposed to scorpions and other insects. Although the World Food Programme and UNHCR recommend refugees receive 2100 kilocalories per day, this fluctuates and has been reduced at times of insufficient donor funding, such as in 2002 when normal daily food rations were reduced by approximately 25 per cent (Human Rights Watch, 2003). More than 8000 refugee children and hundreds of pregnant refugees suffer from malnutrition in the camps, according to a survey undertaken by the UN (UNHCR, 2003b). The problem of security and sexual violence in the camps is severe and the UNHCR has revealed that in one year alone women reported 70 incidents of rape in Dadaab (Montclos and Kagwanja, 2000: 204–208). More than 80 per cent of all rapes occurred when women were collecting firewood and building material outside the camps. Added to this is significant tension and violence between the locals and refugees, a number of whom have been killed. Several studies have documented evidence of the chronic poverty experienced by refugees and IDPs in camps in poor countries (Van Damme, 1995; Black, 1998; Bakewell, 2000; Arafat, 2003).

In response to concerns about the scale and costs of asylum in this era of economic globalisation and security issues post 9/11, support measures that offer temporary protection are being actively promoted in a political climate of 'containment' and increasingly restrictive protection.[5] The reconstruction of refugee protection policy in the north reflects concerns over the economic costs of asylum, state security and uncontrolled migration (UNHCR, 2006). In Castle's view it illustrates that forced migration is 'a pivotal aspect of global social relations, linked to an emerging new political economy in the context of US political and military domination, economic globalisation, North-South inequality and transnationalism' (1999: 23). As part of the so-called war against terrorism or 'political Islam', restrictive immigration policies have made it harder for individuals to seek asylum and indicate that states have largely regressed in their commitment towards protecting refugees and their rights.[6] Chimni (2000) attributes this to an ideology of humanitarianism that is peculiar to hegemonic northern states that use the vocabulary of human rights to legitimise concern with security issues.

Managing globalisation

As I discussed in previous Chapters a number of scholars have articulated the need for more transparent and accountable institutions of global governance that could operate on the basis of a cosmopolitan human rights standard. These have tended to focus on how the global economy could be directed, picking up on the fact that addressing the politicisation of global institutions is key to achieving more equitable globalisation. According to Griffin the problem that we have is not economic globalisation but the fact that we do not have global institutions to govern our global markets: '...the institutions that exist are unrepresentative, many people do not have a full voice in them, and they fail to conform to democratic ideals' (2003: 805). Moreover, these innumerable international and intergovernmental institutions lack the ability to manage global issues such as equal rights to trade because they do not have a clear shared vision, but rather compete to shape global public policy. The current pattern of global institutions is fragmented. The World Bank, IMF, WTO, the UN systems, and the G7 and G77 reflect different groupings of countries that also work alongside a number of national social initiatives (Held, 2004: 94). In reality, what exists is domination of the global institutions by the more powerful countries and this translates into restrictive and protectionist strategies, for example agricultural subsidies and protection measures in the United States of America and Europe. These effectively exclude the poorer nations from the benefits of free trade and economic globalisation. This is compounded by restrictions on the movement of low skilled labour and the creation of 'intellectual property rights' regimes that restrict the flow of knowledge, ideas and technology to the south. Preferential treatment protects the rich and powerful, by making it almost impossible for the poor and weak to participate in the global economy. The problem is not with trade liberalisation, but with the skewed distribution of the benefits of globalisation in favour of rich countries and discrimination against products such as foodstuffs, textile, clothing, footwear and leather products etc., from low income countries.

Griffin and Stiglitz both argue that greater globalisation, rather than less, will accomplish poverty reduction and increased incomes in poor countries. They suggest that if globalisation is managed properly then it does not have to be bad for the environment, contribute to inequality, or only advance corporate interests at the expense of the well-being of ordinary citizens. The successful development of much of East Asia and China is heralded as an example of the positive benefit of globalisation, regardless of position or location. Although Stiglitz does not use the term, he presents an economic cosmopolitan perspective, promoting 'at the international level the kinds of democratic global institutions that can deal effectively with the problems globalisation has created' (Stiglitz, 2006: 21). In effect, economic globalisation has outpaced political globalisation, generating a rather chaotic, uncoordinated system of global governance within which an array of institutions and agreements deal with a range of different problems, from global warming to international trade. Stiglitz acknowledges the weaknesses in current international institutions which suffer from democratic deficit. Lack of confidence in these institutions reflects that decisions made are too often not in the interests of those in the south. In a similar vein to Fukuyama, Stiglitz is confident that there is cohesion at one level, as states no longer have to worry about ideological clashes of the market with 'localised' political philosophies such as communism. Capitalism has a progressive role to play and can bring the whole of the world up to reasonable standards of living if economic globalisation is well managed. But what we need to understand is how responsible institutions of global governance can be established in order to raise living standards throughout the world: to give poor countries access to overseas markets so that they can sell their goods; to allow foreign investment to create new production at cheaper prices; and to open borders so people can travel abroad to be educated and work, and to send home earnings to help their families and fund new businesses (2006: 4).

What is clearly being suggested is that states and the institutions of global governance endeavour to fix the problems of capitalism by focusing on improving market operation. This requires a fundamental shift in the approach of the Washington Consensus, that relies upon market liberalisation, to one that views market operation in relation to other factors that shape poverty (see Chapter 3). To make globalisation work global institutions have to target foreign assistance and debt relief and tackle global poverty and protection of the global environment. Stiglitz argues that while the Millennium Development Goals are a response in the right direction, there is need for fairer trade regimes between countries if poverty reduction targets are to be achieved. A key motivation for his Post-Washington Consensus was to understand why some countries have failed to integrate into the globalisation process (in particular African countries), while others have been more successful (such as China and India). Stiglitz points to China as a successful country that has managed globalisation well (see Chapter 4). This suggests that although a welcome shift in thinking is coming out of Washington, economic patterns of managing globalisation continue to be policy focused. There is still insufficient engagement in how this can be at the cost of social, political and cultural rights. In the case of China, Stiglitz has been uncomfortably silent about distributional issues, inequality and human rights abuses and misses the point that managing globalisation entails a complicated set of processes operating in several arenas besides economics.

Redistribution and moral issues

Ethical cosmopolitism, on the other hand, raises wider moral questions about the unacceptable level of poverty and inequality to which globalisation contributes. It calls upon global institutions, the wealthier countries and the wealthy themselves to address the problems of injustice. In Frontier of Justice (2006a) Nussbaum extends her earlier work (see Chapter 2) to focus on the concept of global justice or justice across national boundaries, challenging the traditional social contract theory of Rawls.[7] She argues that justice is not particular to one nation but applies to all individuals universally. Using the language of human rights as the measure of the equal worth of all human beings, she considers how a theory of global justice might provide a mechanism for the protection of human dignity. As Gasper points out, however, 'an adequate theory of justice does not come simply out of bargaining rights. The language of human rights appropriately conveys an entitlement grounded in justice' (Gasper, 2006: 1233). Nussbaum develops her list of capabilities into principles for global justice, which are equally relevant to individuals everywhere. However, unlike other proponents of universalism she distinguishes her liberalism as a 'culture-sensitive form of universalism' (2006b: 1316). The idea that the richer nations have a moral obligation to assist the less advantaged, seems to cling fairly closely to the distributional ideal. Nussbaum and others, such as Singer, promote the notion that individuals in richer countries should contribute part of their income to poverty alleviation.[8] Although global institutions are defined as having a key role to play in supporting the achievement of global justice, the affluent are tasked to give at least 2 per cent of GDP to poorer people, which is above the current 0.7 per cent that has been internationally agreed by rich countries (2006b: 1327). From this point of view it is important that affluent national governments accept primary responsibility for the protection of the capabilities of their own citizens; they are also assumed to have responsibility to promote the capabilities of citizens from the poorer nations. It is in this context that Nussbaum argues that the unit of analysis should be an individual person not a state. She suggests that this would give individuals 'salience in a theory of justice... We cannot say, in a similar way, that the state is a necessary moral starting point' (Gasper, 2006: 236–237). States are not able to guarantee the security and protection of citizens through a social contract at the national level, requiring the state to provide goods and services to meet basic citizen rights, as specified in the capabilities list. Such social protection tends to be framed in relation to citizenship, although human rights are universal and apply to all, including non-citizens (refugees and migrants) minority or indigenous groups that may be denied full citizenship; and even women, who may have lesser rights in both statutory and customary law, for example in relation to land ownership or inheritance. Any approach that is limited to citizenship is considered to be inadequate to deliver protection for all unless the granting of citizenship is also 'human rights-based'.

For Pogge, the important question about the global justice thesis is not just its merits per se, but the fact that the poor tend to be largely viewed as recipients of charity, and not as individuals with equal rights and entitlements.

We should not think of our individual donation and of possible institutionalised poverty eradication initiatives... such as helping the poor, but as protecting them from the effect of global rules whose injustice benefits the rich countries. We should not only think about remedial measures, but also about how the injustices of the global order might be diminished through intuitional reforms that would end for such remedial measures. (2002: 23)

The idea that it is possible to remedy the suffering of the poor through transfers of resources, aid and money from the rich countries of the north to the south does not embrace the moral imperative of global redistribution of resources and wealth. Instruments of redistribution, such as the Global Resource Dividend (GRD), would allow individuals to engage in poverty alleviation, by using the tax system to divert a proportion of individuals' income in rich countries towards poverty reduction. In practice approximately $312 billion annually could be raised through this route to improve the standard of living of those who are living on less than $1 a day (Pogge, 2002: 197–199). Other proposals for obtaining funds for development purposes that are discussed in global justice literature include the insistence that governments fulfill the UN-recommended obligation to contribute 0.7 per cent of GNP as official development aid; taxes on environmentally undesirable activities (carbon use), or socially problematic activities (weapon trading); the Soros proposal to donate 'special drawing rights'; and the Currency Transfer Tax (Tobin Tax), or a more general tax on financial markets, in the style of a Value Added Tax on financial transactions. What Pogge has in mind when he claims that there is a 'feasible' alternative to the current global order is that redistributive measures of this sort could contribute to the eradication of at least absolute poverty. This requires, however, global institutions that could effectively redistribute these resources towards greatest need. Whether the current structure and operation of institutions of global governance are apposite to promote social justice will be discussed in the following sections.

What is the World Trade Organisation's contribution?

Theoretically, trade liberalisation and openness allows all countries to participate in the global market through a flow of goods, capital, and services. In practice this has worked for rich countries, and China and India to some extent, but not for those countries whose trade agreements depend on their primary exports. Rich countries tend to endorse high tariff levies on goods produced in poor countries so that when these goods reach the consumer they cost five times more than locally produced goods. At the same time as countries through conditionality are being forced to reduce or abandon subsidies on agriculture and other goods, their exports are discouraged. This makes one wonder exactly what institutions of global governance, such as theWTO with its responsibility to regulate trade and ensure that poorer countries are able to participate in the global economy, are actually doing.

In sum, the WTO treaties make no reference to human rights and rights to development. They, therefore, operate in a fairly narrow vacuum. Established in 1995, the objective of the WTO is to facilitate the rules of free trade, handling trade disputes between nations, and strengthening the capacity of states to participate in international trade negotiations. Based on the current state of play, I can only conclude that the WTO has failed the poor countries that it sets out to support. Poor countries have called for free trade in real terms but cannot compete with the world's two largest trading blocks, the United States and the EU, which do not implement the trade liberalisation they insist that other countries adopt. They continue to subsidise and protect sectors, such as agriculture and textiles, to avoid poor countries having comparative advantage. For example the United States pays more than $20,000 to each farmer per annum in the form of subsidies; EU farmers receive similar amounts. Cotton producers from West Africa have suffered most in recent years because of the fluctuating price of cotton in the global market as a result of the high subsidies the United States of America pays in protection to US farmers. The rich countries have flooded African markets with heavily subsidised and, therefore, artificially cheap food and products. African farmers and other producers find it even harder to compete and export, and struggle to operate efficiently. Ghana, for example, used to export rice, but now imports $100m of rice a year (*The Guardian*, 27 May 2002: 17). Why have institutions of global governance not been able to address what are imbalanced and unequal relations?

The poor countries raised their concerns and detailed the difficulties that they faced in implementing WTO agreements, in particular in the face of rich countries protectionists subsidies,[9] at the fourth WTO Ministerial Conference in Doha, Qatar, in November 2001. What came out of this was the Doha Development Agenda, through which the WTO promised to establish fairer trade regimes for all countries, and in particular to make sure that poor countries have access to rich nations' markets, in particular the agricultural and textile markets. The WTO promised that detailed concerns would be resolved at a future meeting, and through a better deal for the countries in the south. But so far this meeting has not taken place, and in September 2003 conflict between rich nations and the other countries led to the breakdown of the WTO Ministerial Conference in Cancun, which halted the progress of the Doha negotiations (Rittberger and Zangl, 2006: 153).

The other contentious issue that the WTO has failed to address is the impact of the Trade Related Aspects of Intellectual Property Rights (TRIPS) Agreement, which operates to give patent rights to genetic resources for agricultural products to companies from the north, and ignores the rights of poor farmers to their own resources, such as seeds. Rich and powerful transnational corporations have promoted the ownership of ideas or 'intellectual property rights', as it facilitates their monopoly over products. For poor countries this can inhibit both their own production of technology and the transfer of technology to the south, as it increases the costs of acquiring knowledge. If we take the example of multinational pharmaceutical companies, we find that their patent rights to drug production allows them a monopoly to price drugs in the global market at a price unaffordable for the majority of people in poor countries. The cost of antiretroviral drugs to treat an HIV-positive person, to prevent the development of Acquired Immune Deficiency Syndrome (AIDS), is around $360 per annum in Africa in 2006 prices (Akukwe, 2006). This equates to the income per capita per annum of the majority of people in Africa, 70 per cent of whom earn less that $1 a day; (using the World Bank criteria for our convenience). Most people simply cannot afford to purchase these drugs and die earlier than they might if they had lived in rich countries. The Doha Declaration of 2001 supported poor countries' need for cheaper drugs and to some extent has allowed them to buy cheap copies of desperately needed drugs produced in India and Thailand, where the manufacturing capacity exists. However the United States is trying to prevent these countries from making and selling cheaper generic versions of drugs, so as to preserve the monopolies of drug companies, even if this means breaking the Doha Declaration. When contested in court, producers from rich countries are unable to afford the same legal representation as the large multinational corporations, placing them at a distinct disadvantage when attempting to enforce their rights in a court of law. That said, Indian firms are now making most of the cheap drugs' cocktails that are being rolled out to people with HIV in Africa and according to Oxfam report these drugs are keeping more than a million people alive. The price of a basic three drug cocktail has come down from $1000 a year to the $360 it is today (Oxfam, 2006: 10). The problem with diseases such as AIDS, is that over time the virus becomes resistant to the basic drugs, generating a need for new ones which then have to go through the patenting process.

The WTO is more politically open than the IMF and the World Bank as it allows each member state to have an equal vote in the organisation. However, that does not mean to say that it has not 'institutionalised the current system of global economic equality' (Bello, 2002) by pursuing the Washington Consensus development agenda. None of the global institutions promote equality between nations on trade, or encourage foreign assistance and debt relief by reducing conditionality on loans and more aid for poorer countries. As Stiglitz rightly points out the poor countries have to spend whatever they earn from exports on paying back their debt service to Banks. Unless the debt burden is reduced, they will struggle to progress. The poor countries owe approximately $1.5 trillion to creditors including the World Bank and IMF. Despite the fact that there have been some gestures from the G8 to write off some of the debts of the 14 Sub-Saharan countries, poor countries continue to be the highest debtor to the World Bank (Stiglitz, 2006).

International financial institutions, governance and human rights

The International Financial Institutions (IMF and the World Bank) have advocated the first generation of human rights (civil and political rights) through the promotion of 'good governance'. But they have been less forthcoming about the need to consider the political dimensions of rights in terms of their interactions with the south. Hence, we have seen very little active support from within these institutions for rights to development. Kaufmann (2005) a leading economist at the World Bank provides empirical cross-country evidence that shows that social and economic rights (second generation rights) 'are (inter alia) found to be dependent on first generation of human rights' (2005: 381). Perhaps this helps to explain why the IMF and the World Bank believe that good governance – controlling corruption, establishing the rule of law, and transparent and accountable government – is the basis for improving civil and political rights. States are encouraged to focus on governance that promotes civil liberties that enhance aid effectiveness, even though the mandate of international finance institutions preclude explicit political conditionality, as specified in the World Bank Articles of Agreement, IV, Section 10: 'The Bank and its officers shall not influence the political affairs of any member, nor shall they be influenced in their decisions by the political character of the member or members concerned. Only economic considerations shall be relevant to their decisions'.

In other words the bank does not take into account the political dimensions of human rights in its lending decisions. Ann Krueger, the first deputy managing director of IMF, expresses this even more robustly:

> The function of the IMF is to make sure that macro economic and financial stability is managed appropriately. Therefore it should not deal in microeconomic issues; IMF should not (and does not) take a position on issues such as worker rights, core labour standards, and environmental policy, except in those rare instances where macroeconomic stability is threatened as, for example, when labour legislation has rendered the labour market so inflexible as to constitute a major barrier to economic growth. (Krueger, 2006: 61)

The IMF and the World Bank are at pains to point out that efficiency is impaired, not by politics, but when market forces conflict with social goals.

The International Financial Institutions (IFIs) have an ambiguous and often incongruous position on human rights. In a discussion of the reasons why they do not provide a framework through which rights could be articulated in their programmes, the former president of the World Bank pointed out that

> ...when I came to the Bank we were not allowed...to mention...the 'c' word. I was told within days of getting to the institution by the general council and in great secrecy, 'Don't mention the "c" word.' And, I said, 'What's the "c" word?' He said, 'Corruption...Well, maybe we need to mention the "r" word, which is "rights." And, maybe coming down the line we will talk much more about rights as we move forward...to some of our shareholders the very mention of the words human rights is inflammatory language. And, it's getting into areas of politics; and it's getting into areas that they're very concerned about. We decide to just go around it and we talk the language of economics and social development.' (Wolfensohn, 2005: 22)

Slow progress is being made. In the latest World Development Report (2006) the World Bank added the concept of equity to development. This draws on the work of Rawls and Sen who have developed, as I discussed earlier, theories of distributive justice based on individual freedom. Development is now defined as 'equality of opportunity' for individuals to pursue a life of their choosing, and suggests the intention of removing some of the structural constraints that make this impossible. The assumption that equity is good for growth accepts that inequalities in capabilities could be a source of poverty. The report acknowledges that past development policies have been less effective than anticipated and that poor people have remained poor because they have very little or no access to essential services, such as health centres, schools, and credit, that could enhance their capability. What is not surprising, however, is that the report concludes that equity must be relative to efficiency and the pursuit of overall well-being requires some balance between competing goals of equity and economic efficiency, as well as other individual freedoms and rights (World Bank, 2006). From this point of view equity does not raise the question of inequality in outcomes, such as income and assets. In a market economy inequality of this sort is considered to be inevitable. The World Bank asserts that assets and income distribution are obstacles to growth as they damage the efficiency that can be achieved by prudent expenditure and robust budgetary measures in selective areas such as education and health, It supports 'building up human capital and physical assets of poor people by judiciously using the redistributive power of government spending and, for example, market based and other forms' (World Bank, 2001: 56–57). The implication is that there is has to be a trade-off between human rights and development.

Even though the World Bank has recognised the importance of human rights in development practice, this is not backed up by its lending strategy. Privatisation and the rolling back of the state in the economy remain the focus of the Bank's development programme. As Wolfensohn said

> although the Bank is already engaged in human rights work, the sense of many on the Board of Directors is that the Bank's job is not to enforce rights; it's a neutral institution. This is consistent with the legal opinion done some years ago that indicated that the Bank is not an enforcement agency. Of course, the Bank does enforce prohibitions against slavery and abuse of children and many other things. But generally the best way for us to proceed has been in a sort of step-by-step way, doing it quietly, trying to assert the delivery of rights, but not necessarily couching it in the terms of human rights. (Wolfensohn, 2005: 3)

Paradoxical as it may be, the World Bank continues with the strategy of conditionality and in this sense mocks the whole notion of ownership and rights to development. Funding is only given to countries that have a good record of governance on the grounds that a poor development record is attributable to indigenous factors such as bad governance and corruption. What we are left with is a technocratic approach to governance that supports effective government intervention to reform institutions including legal reform and anti-corruption measures. Conditional lending is imposed on countries that do not go along with these measures. When Paul Wolfowitz, former US defense secretary, was appointed as the president of the World Bank in 2005 he outlined his vision of development, pointing out that the biggest obstacle to development was corruption. He withdrew loans from some of the poorest countries such as Kenya, India, Chad, Bangladesh, and The Congo because of corruption and poor governance. He promoted anti-corruption measures as the only way in which poverty could be fought to ensure 'that the bank's resources go to the poor and don't end up in the wrong pockets'. Clearly the president of the bank was pursuing the US agenda of democratisation, rather than representing the interests of the world's poor. Even the UK Department for International Development threatened to withdraw £50m from the World Bank out of concern that the poorest countries were suffering as a result of too much emphasis being placed on corruption, and the extent of conditionality attached to the bank's loan. The bank has been criticised for allowing the development of double standards, with countries that ally with the United States getting an easier time than those that take a more independent stand. The Bank's rather simplistic approach suggests it is not concerned about how aid reaches those who have the misfortune of living in the most corrupt countries, who are effectively punished twice, 'once for being poor and again for having corrupt government' (*The Guardian*, Monday 12 September, 2006).

Governance has a strong normative bias because it is 'a consensual process of accommodating parties whose aim is to reconcile conflict cooperatively' (Overbeek, 2005). There is an undeniable need for the IMF to become a democratic institution, which allows participation on an equal basis at the global level of all states, if social transformation is to be collectively managed. The normative dimension of governance gives hope that global governance has the potential to be reformist and counter hegemonic structures and processes, but this depends on support for a more equitable world. Simply reforming the accountability of global governance will be only one step towards justice. The relationship between the powerful rich nations and the south will not change unless there is a genuine commitment and political will for the goal of ending world poverty and equality.

Global governance and power relations

> No nation can make itself secure by seeking supremacy over all
> the others
>
> (Kofi Annan, 2006)

The golden thread that runs through this book is my concern at how hegemonic states use institutions of global governance to exercise control over the others. The global order has shifted into a new era of imperial power, in which the more powerful countries frame the agenda for development for those who are not represented on equal bases in the global institutions of governance. In the words of Cox 'Hegenomy frames thought and thereby circumscribes action' (1992: 179). The member states of the main multilateral development institutions are unequal. The more powerful nations dominate senior appointments at the World Bank and the IMF, reflecting that they pay the larger share of contributions from member states to the funding of these institutions. Countries like the United States, United Kingdom, France, Germany and Japan are represented on the Board of Executive directors, whereas the 19 other board members represent 178 countries.

To date nobody from the poorer countries of Africa or Asia has been the president of either institution, whatever their qualifications or background. The fundamental inequality of this governing structure is unlikely to change in the near future. Similarly asymmetries in the Security Council of the United Nations have been the subject of contest, with the most powerful nations dominating crucial decisions as permanent members of the Council. As Sen rightly points out – 'I do not believe the Bank and the IMF have really considered any major reform of governing arrangements, and given the fact that these are financial institutions, they probably will not.' (Sen, 2004: interview). Kofi Annan in his final farewell speech as Secretary-General of the UN, in a critique of Unilateralist of the United States pointed out that:

> It is only through multilateral institutions that states can hold each other to account. And that makes it very important to organize those institutions in a fair and democratic way, giving the poor and the weak some influence over the actions of the rich and the strong. That applies particularly to the international financial institutions, such as the World Bank and the International Monetary Fund. The south should have a stronger voice in these bodies, whose decisions can have almost a life-or-death impact on their fate. And it also

applies to the UN Security Council, whose membership still reflects the reality of 1945, not of today's world. (Annan, 2006)

Such an imbalance of power within the major global governance institutions persisted in the 2006 appointment of World Bank president Paul Wolfowitz, who as former US deputy defence secretary was directly involved in the pre-emptive attack on Iraq (which he considered a preventative measure against nuclear threat and global terror). Despite an international row over his appointment in such a major development institution, Paul Wolfowitz pursued a neo-conservative anti-corruption agenda that undermined social protection and rights issues. Whether the anti-corruption drive was an arbitrary process or tied to a development agenda is questionable, as it was applied with vigour in some countries but not others, such as Pakistan. Similarly conditionality is being used as a weapon to fulfil the corruption agenda and the British government has raised concerns about the merits of this approach.[10]

Benevolent hegemony – what about the UN?

For global governance to be effective this requires the commitment of all national states and parties on the grounds of equality. However, the current global order works well for powerful states, which can choose to ignore global institutions, while continuing to enjoy the benefits of economic globalisation. US unilitarism has clearly demonstrated its view that global institutions, in particular the UN, are too weak to achieve democratisation or civil and political rights, and indeed the US is critical of the role of the UN as arbitrator or enforcer of global justice (citing campaigns of contention such as the oil for food programme).[11] In fact when the UN fails to serve 'as an instrument of US unilateralism on issues of elite concerns, it is dismissed'[12] (Chomsky, 2003: 29). Although the United States remains in support of the collective action of some international institutions, such as NATO, the WTO, and the IMF, the distance between global institutions and the United States has widened since neo-conservatism became the dominant ideology of US foreign policy. The current US administration is clearly sceptical about the UN as an effective, legitimate seat of global governance. This has taken place against the backdrop of consolidation of the UN and the universalism of a rights regime based on the sovereignty of nation states through treaties and their gradual acceptance into national legislation (e.g. human rights laws). The modus operandi of previous nation building exercises mainly involved UN delivery of a peace keeping mission, whereas we have clearly seen a different strategy in Iraq where the UN has had no formal involvement.

The underlying premise of the US position is that other nations would support intervention to achieve *regime change* where necessary to preserve the *global order* and suppress perceived threats to global peace. In those states that violate human rights, regime change is promoted as a means to address poverty through the establishment of democracy. We have seen unilateralist 'benevolent hegemony' put into practice in the Middle East.[13] Reflecting as a reformed neo-con, Fukuyama points out that 'What goes on inside other countries has now become the business of the US' (2006: 114). There is, however, no agenda to address development problems, evidenced by the lack of concern from the United States on the problems of poverty in the countries of Africa and Latin America, which only become of interest when they are considered to be a security threat or appear on the 'freedom agenda'.[14] Laymen on the streets of the Middle East are justified in asking why the United States has not intervened in countries such as Sudan or Rwanda where millions have either died or been displaced as a result of civil war and state mismanagement of the economy. Indeed the invasion of Afghanistan was motivated as part of the 'geo-political management' of terrorism and political Islam associated with Al Quaida. Similarly, the invasion of Iraq was closely linked to the political priority to secure sufficient oil sources for the global capitalist economy and that of the United States in particular. These have all taken place, while countries like Saudi Arabia and other Gulf states that are known for domestic human rights abuses have gone unchallenged and while the profits of large oil companies like Shell and BP have soared. In this respect contradictory engagement with other states and geopolitical priorities, 'transcend the boundaries between national and international domains, but at the same time they revitalise the asymmetries of power between states' (Beck, 2006: 177). Thus, we see states maximising national interests through 'benevolent' international activity. In effect the United States stipulates rights but not responsibilities, imposing its view of the new global order on weaker and poorer nations in order to maintain its hegemony, with little reflection on cosmopolitan laws and rights.

Conclusion

In this Chapter I have argued that the concept of cosmopolitanism relies on a generic interpretation of global governance for the co-ordination of agencies that protect individual rights, and it is unclear about where responsibility actually lies. The current structure of global governance, as we have seen, has undoubted shortcomings and it is biased towards the powerful nations and their representatives. This is symptomatic of a global order in which the capacity of states to direct national economies has been restricted by supranational forces. We cannot ignore the part that Transnational Corporations play in ensuring that private, rather than national interests, dominate the global economy. Transnational corporations provide a key part of the network that transcends national and regional boundaries, while at the same time they achieve vertical integration into local economic systems (Sklair, 2002). Their activities also support the argument that it is no longer appropriate to attribute effective and legitimate power solely to states, as power really lies with a variety of local and international non-state institutions that include Transnational Corporations (TNCs) as well as major development agencies, and this is explored in the next Chapter.

6
Transnational Corporations and Corporate Social Responsibility: Does It Really Work?

Rights are a weapon of the weak against the strong.

(Vincent, 1986: 7)

As I discussed in the previous Chapter, the current structure of global governance is based on unequal relations that allow the transgressions of powerful states who are in control of these institutions to go unchallenged even when they harm the least advantaged and poorer nations. This is symptomatic of a global order in which the capacity of states to direct national economies has been restricted by supranational forces and 'the creation of a supranational economy, within which transactions are largely uncontrolled or even uncontrollable by states' (Hobsbawm, 1995: 272). The emergence of a range of transnational actors that work across national boundaries, supporting cross and trans-border flows of materials and non-material goods (people, information and communication, capital and labour) illustrates just how imperious the concept of 'transnational' is in the globalisation process. Operating within their own codes and regulations, transnational corporations tend to be somewhat independent of states and subject to little effective government intervention, such that their activity can undermine or conflict with that of nation states with little challenge. Transnational Corporations provide a key part of the network that transcends national and regional boundaries, while at the same time they achieve vertical integration into local economic systems (Sklair, 2002). A few indicators show the scale and size of Transnational Corporations' (TNC) capital accumulation at a global level: the revenue of the five largest corporations that are active in more than 50 countries accounts for more or less double the combined GDP of the 100 poorest countries together (Utting, 2000: 19). TNC activities also support the argument that it is no longer appropriate to attribute effective and legitimate power solely to states, as power really lies with a variety of local and global non-state institutions, including TNCs and major International Financial Institutions.

Just as the major institutions of global governance have avoided acknowledgement of their direct role in the rights agenda, even though they may quote the rhetoric, so have their private sector counterparts. This is why so many civil society organisations openly campaign in opposition to the practices that TNCs adopt. UN draft norms clearly place some responsibility on private sector organisations for securing the rights of individuals:

> Recognizing that even though States have the primary responsibility to promote, secure the fulfilment of, ensure respect of, and protect human rights, transnational corporations and other business enterprises, as organs of society, are also responsible for promoting and securing the human rights set forth in the Universal Declaration of Human Rights. (UN, 2003: 2)

To what extent have current institutions of global governance and their private sector counterparts acknowledged this responsibility?

This Chapter looks at the increasing pressure on TNCs to accept the notion of corporate social responsibility from local and global civil society organisations and analyses the potential for changing practice that could make a difference. Can responsibility for human rights regimes be transferred from governments and on to companies, and if so which legislative framework would apply? Could TNCs use their capabilities to complement the state in the construction of justice and delivery of rights? What responsibility would they have towards communities and would they be expected to engage in development and poverty reduction strategy?

Transnational corporations and corporate social responsibility

Increasing attention has been directed to the human rights records of non-state private actors such as TNCs. Failure to consider the role of TNCs, especially given the diminishing capacity of states to rectify the injustices brought about or sustained by the activities of business organisations, undermines attempts to accurately assess the global human rights regime and displays a very narrow understanding of the discourse (Campbell, 2006). The discourse around responsibilities and rights has tended to focus on individuals and nation states, even though more and more we find that transnational corporations are being endorsed with responsibilities, not only to their employees, but also to the people in whose communities they operate. The United Nations is considering making TNCs legally responsible and liable for human rights, including abuses by their suppliers and customers. Hypothetically this could shift some of the responsibility in international rights regimes away from governments and onto private companies. The draft UN Norms on the Responsibilities of Transnational Corporations and Other Business Enterprises with Regard to Human Rights (2003) proposes a shift in national and international law for human rights away from governments and onto companies which are liable to national legislation. Concerns have been raised that the norms would provide unions with ammunition for negotiating agreements, and the opportunity to exploit, and unfairly to 'name and shame', firms they want to attack. It has been suggested that obligations on multinationals could damage rather than help the poor countries (*The Guardian*, 18 March 2004).

In response to this agenda and increasing criticism of TNC activity, there has been a gesture on the side of some TNCs to integrate an ethical position into their business principles through the adoption of Corporate Social Responsibility (CSR) policies. What challenge does the concept of 'Corporate Social Responsibility' pose to policy and practice?

Transnational corporations are large private corporations that operate in several countries. They have the potential to be more powerful than a single state, as they are mostly independent of regulatory restrictions.[1] The parent companies of the majority of TNCs are in the north, to which profits are repatriated. Ninety per cent of global corporations have their parent companies in the United States of America, Europe or Japan. However, there has been a noticeable increase in the number and size of TNCs originating from the south, like India, Brazil, South Africa, Mexico and Malaysia (Sklair, 2001). These now represent 2 per cent of the total number of TNCs. TNCs are principal drivers of economic globalisation, but by and large they operate as a law unto themselves and are little regulated by national laws because they do not operate within the bounds of local sovereignty. It is also true that some states, desperate for capital investment and development opportunity, encourage multinational companies' operational activity by relaxing criteria they could impose such as environmental pollution controls, or allowing them to pay a low level of corporate taxation. Similarly some states choose to ignore working conditions of labourers, even though they have the obligation to protect citizens against large private corporations who violate human rights, such as in sweatshops, or when they employ child labour to work in inhumane conditions.

Private companies have been under pressure for some time from civil society organisations, the UN and regulatory bodies to operate within the realms of a global corporate responsibility that reflects the aims of sustainable development and human rights principles. This prescribes a clear mandate for TNCs not to support projects or investment that risk jeopardising those aims. In addition the interests of large corporations in terms of their operations are increasingly challenged in relation to specific areas, namely human rights, labour standards, corruption, local social relations and environmental impact. In a proactive sense, business activities should be geared towards working effectively with communities, for example, by providing infrastructural support for education systems and health centres, and making sure that the impact of their business activity is environmentally friendly. CSR provides the framework for private sector involvement and participation in rights and poverty reduction measures. In this sense it is a plank of the neo-liberal strategy to disperse state responsibility in line with declining social expenditure. By definition it would seem that the private sector is under a moral obligation to contribute towards the objectives of development in order to improve the well-being of local people, communities, individuals, the environment and wider society in a way that, according to the World Bank (2006), is good for business and development. Thus, according to the World Bank

> Corporate social responsibility is the commitment of businesses to behave ethically and to contribute to sustainable economic development by working with all relevant stakeholders (employees, their families, the local community and society at large) to improve their lives in ways that are good for business, the sustainable development agenda, and society at large. (Jorgensen, 2003: 10)

Sklair (2002) takes the rather sceptical position that in fact CSR does nothing more than provide a convenient tool for private companies anxious to protect their reputations. In reality the risk of loss of reputation is the prime motivation for private companies adopting CSR. Since the late 1990s TNCs have widely used voluntary codes of conduct that are directed at endorsing their operation in a socially responsible way, both in relation to the community and the environment, to demonstrate their commitment to global corporate citizenship. Several corporations have revised their business principles to focus on corporate governance, including relations with their employers, community development, and health and safety measures for consumers and citizens in countries where they operate to improve the quality of their lives. A major weakness in this approach is that codes are often voluntary, are not legally binding, and therefore they can be affected by day-to-day business pressures. Voluntary codes are promoted by institutions such as the World Bank and the EU, even though there is data from different corporations that suggest practices vary greatly and are generally ineffective.

The debate on CSR has tended to focus on the actions of individual corporations in terms of classifying them as 'good' or 'bad' and this has diverted attention away from more basic and fundamental questions of global governance and responsibility. Our concern should be with the democratic accountability of transnational corporations that tend to wield more economic, and as a consequence political, power than many states. According to Sklair (2001), the current global order sustains domination of the processes of globalisation by a transnational capitalist class who are mostly major investors in or owners of TNCs. His 'global system theory' is based on the concept of transnational practices that cross state borders but do not necessarily originate with state agencies or actors and in terms of scale are increasingly unsustainable in the ecological sense. A raft of statistics can be provided to demonstrate just how powerful the actions of TNCs are. For example, in terms of trade, the revenue of the 350 largest TNCs amounts to one-third of the industrialised world's GNP and outstrips the GNP of the entire countries in the south. The top five corporations have an annual revenue that is more than double the total GDP of the 100 poorest countries. TNCs control around 70 per cent of world trade and 90 per cent of all technology and product worldwide. Analysis of aggregate data estimates that TNCs are responsible for around 50 per cent of annual contributions to global warming and ozone depletion (UNCTC, 1992). Despite this alarming picture, the current system of economic globalisation is sustained by the ideology of consumerism that encourages people to purchase goods and services that TNCs produce for private profit. In terms of a global governance structure that addresses cosmopolitan human rights, TNC activity cannot be ignored. There are two essential problems associated with the practice of TNCs that have to be considered in the discourse of CSR for human rights. The first is their contribution to increasing poverty within and between communities and societies (the class polarisation crisis). The second is the unsustainability of the current system or, what could be known as, the ecological crisis.

TNC activity and the violation of human rights

Several human rights abuses and environmental disasters resulting from TNC activities have attracted grass roots civil rights and social justice protests. For example, the case of Shell in Nigeria and the death of the Nigerian environmental and human rights campaigner Ken Saro Wiwa in 1996 hit global headlines. There have been demonstrations against the dumping of the Brent Spar oil rig and oil spills, such as the Valdez; European TNC exportation of hazardous and toxic wastes to West Africa; and Japanese TNC exploitation of Malaysian rain forests. Some of the most significant protest campaigns have been against Shell's activities in the Niger Delta, resulting in death and injuries of many people, and the activities of Balfour Beatty in Southern Africa and in Ilisu in Turkey. These are examples of the 'big' stories that make the headlines. However, there is little documentation of TNC activity at the local level where the process of environmental decline can be directly or indirectly advanced by TNC actions. Continued abuses of this kind demonstrate that it is particularly difficult to regulate TNC activity within the context of local environments despite their global impact.

Countries from the south are striving to find their place within the global economy and do not want to discourage TNC investment that is perceived to play a vital role in assisting economic development. Furthermore, in terms of development, countries from the south tend to be uneasy about the international community's stress on concern for the environment. The UNCTAD (2002) Benchmark Corporate Environmental Survey found that the extent to which TNCs have incorporated environmental concerns into their management strategies and practices depends on the company in question and the locality in which they are operating. The environmental problems associated with TNC operations are in countries where there are few environmental regulations or little enforcement. TNC commitment to environmental concerns varies, but on the whole TNCs tend to make broad policy statements in relation to appropriate conduct, and then operate within the local legal environmental framework. Few companies actually operate strategies geared to address environmental challenges or the wider question of global sustainability unless there is a direct capital advantage to the company (Robbins, 1996). TNCs are unaccountable, undemocratic, powerful corporations that manipulate national and international trade negotiation to their advantage regardless of the fact that their decisions may evidently be the reason for untold hardship to people and environmental degradation, particularly in host countries.

Global and local processes are entwined and globalisation reinforces the need to understand local situations and to design local strategies for dealing with particular problems. However, trends in global interdependence, in which essential decisions affecting the livelihood of millions are taken by transnational firms only minimally accountable to any political constituency, give rise to several questions of social and environmental concern. How they are dealt with is likely to prove a key factor in the success or failure of the achievement of the right to development.

It is my view that the failure of TNCs to challenge poverty, human rights abuses, environmental problems, child labour, and global hunger, questions the moral legitimacy of capitalism.

Global compact: a regulation nightmare?

To encourage TNCs to support the protection of international human rights within their sphere of influence and to ensure that their operations are not complicit in human rights abuses, the idea of a Global Compact between the United Nations and the private sector has been promoted. This is symptomatic of a commitment to a concept of global governance that embraces collective actions and interactions between public and private actors to manage development problems. As a measure it aims to secure responsible corporate behaviour in support of development from a range of agencies and actors. In reality governance is likely to be more effective if there is a high degree of compliance with established standards, rules and norms than cosmopolitanism advocates. The Global Compact was launched in 1999 to encourage the corporate world to become directly involved in the implementation of the core values of universal human rights through their operations. In the words of Kofi Annan (2006), the UN Secretary-General, the compact is an attempt to find a way of entrenching the global market in a network of 'shared values'. The Compact contains 10 principles (listed in box 6.1 below) which originate from globally agreed standards that focus on human rights, labour standards, the environment and corruption, as demonstrated in the following documents: The Universal Declaration of Human Rights (1948), The International Labour Organisation's Declaration on Fundamental Principles and Rights at Work (1998), the Rio Declaration on Environment and Development (1992) and the United Nations Convention on Corruption (2005).

Because they are not enforceable the Global Compact and Corporate Social Responsibility Policies risk being nothing more than a PR exercise

---

Box 6.1   Core Values of the Global Compact

Human rights

1. Businesses should support and respect the protection of internationally proclaimed human rights;
2. Businesses should make sure that they are not complicit in human rights abuses.

Labour standard

3. Businesses should uphold the freedom of association and the effective recognition of the right to collective bargaining;
4. Businesses should eliminate all forms of forced and compulsory labour;
5. Businesses should abolish child labour;
6. Businesses should eliminate discrimination in respect of employment and occupation

Environment

7. Businesses should support a precautionary approach to environmental challenges
8. Businesses should undertake initiatives to promote greater environmental responsibility
9. Businesses should encourage the development and diffusion of environmentally-friendly technologies.

Anti-corruption

10. Businesses should work against all forms of corruption, including extortion and bribery.

Source: UN (2006) The Ten Principles of Global Compact. Available at www.unglobalcompact.org

---

to uphold the public image of private companies. Sometimes spurts of development activity by large companies are driven by nothing more than the desire to improve their public image (Christian Aid, 2004). The rhetoric can also mask corporate activity that makes things worse for communities they engage with as suppliers or consumers. Empirical evidence of various corporations supports the reputation-risk thesis. A study of pharmaceutical and tobacco companies shows that self-regulation and voluntary codes, that many TNCs have initiated since the 1990s, have failed to impact on their activities, even though they have incorporated the 10 principles and core values of human rights. The codes of marketing practise, for example, lack transparency and public accountability because consumers are not involved in monitoring and enforcement, and because the codes omit to address major areas of concern and lack timely and effective sanctions. The main problem is that voluntary codes are often aspirational and do not represent company commitment, to stakeholders to undertake necessary action. 'Voluntary' implies that companies cannot be held accountable under the law and there is concern that self-regulatory efforts have the effect of eroding societal commitment to universal rights and entitlement.

Shell in the Niger Delta

Shell was one of the first TNCs to adopt the Global Compact principles following altercations with environmental campaigners over the disposal of the Brent Spar oil platform and in response to human rights activists protesting about the company's operations in Nigeria, where the military government executed Ken Saro Wiwa, a leading opponent of Shell's operations in Ogoniland (see later). Following the Brent Spar fiasco, when the company had to abandon plans to dump the platform in the Atlantic, Shell executives acknowledged they had been too introverted and too concerned with government relations, rather than those with the wider public. Subsequently Shell disseminated its corporate responsibility agenda in respect of sustainable development principles and made a further commitment to support fundamental human rights. Shell unremittingly promotes the idea that the company is dedicated to its core values of honesty, integrity and respect for people. The Chairman of Shell went further than ever before in acknowledging the environmental dangers of burning oil and gas and the likelihood of climatic change necessitating 'prudent precautionary action' (*The Guardian*, 18 March 1997). In 2005 Shell revised its business principles to reflect 'growing concern about security' following the attacks of 9/11, placing even more emphasis on community involvement, diversity and inclusiveness. Without doubt Shell 'talks the talk', but actions are what we need to consider.

The Nigerian National Petroleum Corporation (NNPC) has developed a series of joint ventures with private companies such as Shell, ExxonMobil, Chevron, Elf, Agip Texaco, and others. Since the 1960s the Niger Delta Region has been a land of opportunity for large TNCs with the infrastructure to invest in the oil and gas industry. Crude oil is primarily concentrated in the Delta region of the country, accounting for 75 per cent of oil production and over 50 per cent of government gross revenue.[2] However, the UN Human Development Report (2006a) reveals particularly high rates of poverty in the Niger Delta region with lower GNP per capita per annum than the national average at only $280, and high mortality rates and lower life expectancy than other regions of Nigeria. The report also shows a disproportionately high level of fatality rates related to water-borne diseases, malnutrition and poor sanitation, and limited social infrastructure with only a few schools and poor services.[3]

Ample documentation demonstrates that the Shell Petroleum Development Company, which has been involved in the exploration, exploitation and production of oil for more than 30 years in the Niger Delta, has disregarded the needs of local people and the environment throughout this period (Fryan, Beck and Mellahi, 2000). The impact of TNC investment on the livelihoods of the local population of around 20 million people has been limited. Many in the region rely on subsistence farming and fishing and live in isolated communities, only accessible by boat. These communities have not experienced any visible benefits from the proceeds of the oil industry. In fact the exploration of oil has resulted in conflicts among different ethnic groups over compensation for loss of land and territories. For example, in the Warri area of the Niger Delta there are three ethnic groups the Itsekiri, The Urhabs, the Ijaw. Conflict between these groups intensified after the discovery of oil in the area, as they all claimed ownership of the oil wells in order to benefit from compensation from the oil companies. These conflicts have been compounded by competition for quality farm land in an area where land has become increasingly degraded as a result of oil exploration. This has resulted in considerable violence. As the Niger Delta Human Development Report confirms:

> The Niger Delta is a region suffering from administrative neglect, crumbling social infrastructure and services, high unemployment, social deprivation, abject poverty, filth and squalor, and endemic conflict...for most people of the delta, progress and hope, much less prosperity, remain out of reach...if unaddressed, these do not bode well for the future of Nigeria or an oil hungry world.[4] (UNDP, 2006a: 6)

Local people have demanded development within an inclusive and participatory framework that views people not simply as the beneficiaries of development, but its rightful and legitimate claimants. Thus they challenge state and private companies, particularly Shell, to operate within an institutional framework that creates inclusive opportunities that empower all people, including the poor, women and the marginalised, to shape and mediate their entitlements and social, economic, cultural and political rights. However this demand has never been met and there have been a number of demonstrations against the state and against Shell's activities, which at times have been violent and have included the kidnapping of personnel from the oil company.[5] The protestors assert that they have not been provided with the jobs and development projects, such as water systems, health services, schools and roads, that they were promised. The key contentious issues that form the focus of local and transnational campaign networks against Shell, and the state, fit broadly into two groups – first there is the negative environmental impact of investment projects, in particular oil spills, and, secondly, the impact of Shell's operation on the rights of local people (Okonta, Douglas and Monbiot, 2003).

It is estimated that a total of 6817 oil spills occurred between 1976 and 2001. Negative long-term environmental impact on the livelihoods of local communities includes the degradation of forests and depletion of aquatic fauna and depletion of mangrove swamps and groundwater resources. Oil companies have constructed pipes and canals that have caused saltwater to flow into freshwater zones, resulting in significant environmental pollution. Although projects likely to have environmental impact are subject to Environmental Impact Assessment (EIA), laws requiring this assessment for *large* projects did not come into effect until the early 1990s, by which time it was too late for the Niger Delta, which had already suffered much damage at the hands of oil companies. Even if EIA had been undertaken it is unlikely that the social, political or human rights impact would have been identified as assessment of these is generally undermined within the EIA evaluation framework. Decision-makers in general show little enthusiasm for incorporating mechanisms for social-political and human rights issues into the terms of reference of environmental assessment procedures, which tend to dictate, and to some extent constrain, what information should be gathered and what should be prioritised and which privilege certain information or knowledge over others.

This brings me to the second, and perhaps most fundamental, issue which is the impact of TNC operations on human rights in Nigeria. The oil companies operating in Nigeria tend only to communicate with the elites of communities, such as local Chiefs, in relation to compensation, and contract and job opportunities. This contributes to the alienation of local people who perceive local leaders appropriate compensation for themselves and their extended family (Idemudia, 2005). In the case of Nigeria, since the late 1990s there has been an increase in violations of civil and political rights such as arbitrary detention, suppression of freedom of expression, and extra-judicial execution to suppress local protest against oil companies. In 2005 the Nigerian Security forces killed one person and injured more than 30 in order to stop a demonstration by Ijaw youths. Soldiers even used the facilities of Chevron (a helicopter and boats) to facilitate their attack on local people who were protesting for their rights. The company tried to distance itself from the army, claiming it had no choice but to allow the security forces access to its equipment. Local people feel that Nigerian society is violated by the lifestyle of oil workers, who are blamed for the increasing incidence of prostitution and its attendant diseases such as HIV and AIDS and the influx of young girls into the sex industry looking to make their livelihoods from 'petro-money' (Okonta, Douglas,and Monbiot, 2003).

This case provides a good example of complicity (the second principle of the UN Global Compact see box 6.1 above), where the company itself does not commit a primary abuse, but benefits from an abuse or human rights violation committed by someone else, and remains silent. In the current legal framework, it would be highly unlikely that companies would be legally liable for complicity. Although several cases and reports of complicity can be cited, few end up in court, and even fewer are successful[6] (Khan, 2005). More than 100 transnational companies operate in countries that have a bad record of human rights abuse – such as torture, extra judicial killings, hostage taking, denial of the freedom of expression, arbitrary arrests and detention, denial of women's rights, denial of freedom of association, forced child labour and forced labour displacement. The issue of corporate complicity is as much a moral question as a legal one, although this is an emerging area of law. TNCs tend to sidestep responsibility for the social and economic impact of their actions where possible, reflecting their position that the state is the agent responsible for social protection.

O'Neil argues that where there is political instability and the state itself uses violence against its citizens, TNCs are well-placed to develop a range of capabilities to contribute to greater justice and to take some responsibility for maintaining and sustaining cosmopolitan standards (2000, 236–238). There is undoubtedly an argument that corporate power could be used to support and strengthen states that are reasonably just but do not have the required infrastructure or administration to be effective in delivering rights. However, as the Nigerian case study demonstrates TNCs can just as easily accept the status quo, and collude with local elites and patterns of injustice. They can, in fact, use their powers to perpetuate or even make worse situations of injustice where states are weak, as in the case of the Niger Delta. In this sense, the simple distinction between primary and secondary agents of social justice blurs.

TNCs cannot fulfill the responsibility of the state, which has, therefore, to remain the primary agent of justice, but their activities do translate into a measurable impact on the rights agenda and, therefore, need to be effectively regulated within a legislative framework. Non-governmental organisations such as Amnesty International, Christian Aid, and Human Rights Watch, have been campaigning and advocating for effective regulation of TNCs. But a word of caution, too many regulations might impede investment in countries and in particular in poorer countries. NGOs have called for clear international standards to ensure that TNCs are part of the solution to today's problems and that they do not, knowingly or unknowingly, exacerbate them. Some corporations have engaged in development projects, as in the example in Box 6.2 about technology transfer, but if they really want to make a difference projects have to be relevant. In a country like South Africa where poverty is high and poor families cannot send their children to school, preventing child hunger is more important than providing computers.

Box 6.2 The way to 'do development': Technology and Poverty Alleviation in Africa

Some TNCs are actively considering how their products could contribute to poverty alleviation in poor countries. This question is currently being explored in South Africa where software giants Hewlett-Packard (in partnership with the South African government), chipmaker Intel Corp, and Microsoft are setting up 'digital villages' comprising IT labs and PC refurbishing centres in an effort to connect many thousands of people in the rural areas and townships to the internet.

The initiative also links local libraries, community centres, clinics and schools to the Web and facilitates access to micro-lenders. The intended benefits are many: the new technology will help trigger growth, create jobs, provide access to information, knowledge and educational services, and more generally, stimulate exposure to fresh ideas. It is hoped that the project activities are sufficiently grounded in business principles so that, rather than continuing to be dependent on grants, the i-Communities will eventually become self-funding, with the running of the centres being transferred to local entrepreneurs. The project directors are confident that the project can easily be replicated elsewhere on the continent.[7]

The project has nevertheless attracted criticism for being unrealistic, ill-timed and overambitious. How, can the I-Community visionaries attempt to address the so-called 'digital divide' when the country has not yet crossed the literacy divide? The project is being touted under the banner of 'poverty alleviation' yet many intended beneficiaries living below the poverty line will simply not be able to use the services provided. 'The poor' are certainly not a homogenous group. There are 'degrees' of poverty, both within South Africa and in other African countries. I-Community projects targeting the illiterate poor are taking on an impossible task unless the education and basic skills training required to use the technology are also provided. As literacy rates stand at the moment, few in Africa will be able to take advantage of such opportunities, making their creation a costly and inefficient exercise that is unlikely to be sustainable in the long term. Only private companies, elites and rich people can benefit from these schemes.

The IT initiative will no doubt empower a small number of individuals, but it certainly does not constitute the best strategy for overcoming the most pressing difficulties currently faced by impoverished Africans. Information access of this kind is the exclusive preserve of the literate. I-Community enthusiasts need to ensure that their poverty-alleviation activities do not end up underlining the inequalities they are meant to address.

Source: based on Harrison R (2005), 'Can Technology Ease Africa's woes?'. Available at http://today.reuters.com/news/newsArticle.aspx?type=technologyNews&storyID=2 005-11-16T012245Z_01_MCC604869_RTRUKOC_0_US-AFRICA.xml&archived=False Reuters, as viewed on 15 November 2005

Civil society organisations, and the transnational dimension of protest

Over the past three decades an increasing number and diversity of transnational organisations, including local and international NGOs, have framed protests over the case of the Niger Delta within a rights context. Transnational networks and group such as Human Rights Watch, Oxfam, Amnesty International have joined local NGOs, in actively protesting against lack of development at a local level and environmental pollution while large corporations such as Shell have profited from the oil industry in the region.[8] Amnesty International reflected the voice of local people in its 2005 report:

It is like paradise and hell. They have everything. We have nothing. They throw our petitions in the dustbin...If we protest, they send soldiers. They sign agreements with us and then ignore us. We have graduates going hungry, without jobs. And they bring people from Lagos to work here. – Eghare W.O. Ojhogar, Chief of the Ugborodo community, one of whose members died during a protest at Chevron Nigeria's Escravos oil terminal where demonstrators were assaulted and injured by the security forces on 4 February 2005. (Amnesty International 2005: 1)

Transnational networks that have a human rights basis typify much of the growing opposition to inequality between the north and the south, representing new sources of agency in the form of activists. Actions range form gatherings at G8 summit locations to protest in front of the world's media to more localised protests over communities afflicted by specific projects and environmental degradation. The common theme of protest is opposition to inequality and poverty, and civil, social and economic and cultural rights abuses and environmental issues. Protests focus on corporate globalisation, global capitalism and the neo-liberal order, in other words the principle targets are multilateral organisations (The International Monetary Fund (IMF) and The World Bank), Transnational Corporations (e.g. Shell and Balfour Beatty), the G8 and strong states that drive mega-development projects such as hydroelectric dams in an effort to raise GNP in order to 'catch up' with Western countries and to strengthen their position on the global stage. The protest movement is typically a weapon of the weak and marginal who are excluded from mainstream civil society and the global economy, but who seek to challenge, change or influence public policies and international protection regimes supported by the existing social and political structures.

Civil society organisations form a continuum from NGOs, at the most organised end of the scale, to groups of individuals involved in political actions at the other. My focus here is human rights and development oriented civil society groupings, which tend to take the form of NGOs. Accepting that civil society provides a model of social organisation, current theory leads us to categorise NGOs as they reflect the two common 'genealogies' of civil society within the development discourse – the first being co-opted by the system and the second operating in opposition to it (Howell and Pearce, 2001). The mainstream neo-liberal perspective sees civil society as an intermediate sphere of agency between the market and the state and one that should be strengthened as part of 'new development paradigm shifts'. These call for not only the regulation of the market economy, but also partnership based on the transformation of institutions, and participation that involves and supports groups in civil society. Within this perspective we find some development NGOs that are strategically co-opted by governments and institutions such as the World Bank to deliver their agenda. For example the World Bank and IMF provides funding to development NGOs that are in partnerships with governments and the private sector under schemes such as 'Grant competition for NGOs' or 'Competing for Just Cause'. These are targeted at projects that address various development needs from poverty reduction strategy, HIV/AIDS, women resource centres, biodiversity and environmental projects, micro credit, health, education etc.

Other NGOs have been quite independent from the state and these are the institutions that have been most involved in promoting rights-based approaches to development. In contrast, within the political economy approach, civil society exists in this context as a force in the Gramscian sense, (*albeit* not in class sense), or one that operates to 'counterbalance' the power of the states, private corporations, and neo liberal economic globalisation. In the words of Cox, 'Civil society is now understood to refer to the realm of autonomous group action distinct from both corporate power and the state' (Cox with Schechter, 2002: 102), and the varied ways in which the collective will of people 'independently of (and often in opposition to) established power, both economic and political'. Those who see an emancipatory or counter-hegemony role for civil society have appropriated the concept. Some would like to feel that civil society is a set of diverse non-governmental agents strong enough to counterbalance the powerful state, and prevent it from dominating society while undertaking its role as the keeper of the peace and arbiter between major interests (Gellner, 1994: 5).

Sen considers the transactional protests of NGOs to be the 'active agitation' route to expressing rights and the advancement of human rights and social justice. NGOs such as Human Rights Watch and Amnesty International, OXFAM, Médicins Sans Frontièrs, the Red Cross, Save the Children, Christian Aid and Action Aid, play an effective role in the struggle for rights issues through discussion and support, on the one hand, and publicising and criticising violations of human rights, on the other. Christian Aid consider that development projects should engage in a right – based approach rather than a charitable approach. The objective is to empower 'people to claim their fundamental and universal right rather than focusing purely on service provision, promoting self respect and dignity amongst vulnerable groups and advocating for increased government responsibility' (Christian Aid, 2005: 2). Campaigning on issues relating to child labour, street children, gender inequality, agricultural labour, orphans and advocating for changes to national legislation that enhance social, economic and political development.

Raising awareness is important: 'The rights invoked in this "agitation route" may or may not have any legal status in the country in question, but advocacy and support are not necessarily rendered useless by the absence of legal backing' (Sen, 2004: 329–330). Where Sen however sees these as the actions of only pressure groups, others see them as 'movements' or rather a new form of 'social movements'. A social movement is a 'collective identity', which relies on its social solidarity to challenge the state and authorities and to achieve socio-economic and political change through a sustained defiance of power structures (Cox, 2002).

A shift in the actions of both new and established sources of agency within domestic civil society whose ambitions lie not in replacing the current political status but in achieving greater recognition of local culture or 'identity politics' are considered to be 'new' social movements (Calhoun, 1993).

New social movements

Environmentalists, ecologists, feminists, human rights activists, churches, indigenous people's movements, pro-democracy campaigners, peace groups, socialists, small farmers etc. that tend to focus on achieving greater autonomy from the state through modifications in everyday policies and practice, have been defined as 'new social movements' (Calhoun, 1993; Escobar, 1995: 217). For post-developmental writers, it is resistance to mainstream development discourses and projects as 'conventional Western modes of knowing' that unites new social movements (Escobar, 1995: 217). The increasing influence of post-development ideas and post-modernity that calls for an end to development, is a critique of policy prescriptions that flowed from the theoretical presuppositions of modernisation and neo-liberalism theory (the Washington Consensus (WC), Post Washington Consensus (PWC) and Structural Adjustment Policies) which failed to bring about meaningful development. Instead they have come to represent the very 'crisis of development' (Cowen and Shenton, 1996; Escobar, 1995; Rahnama, 1997; Sachs, 1999). Post-developmental ideas focus on the failure of development (modernisation and economic growth) to improve, or manage the chaos and the pandemonium induced by modernity or capitalism, suggesting that rather than improving poor people's lots, economic expansion and growth has come up against its biophysical limits. In the words of Sachs:

> The idea of development stands today like a ruin in the intellectual landscape, its shadows obscuring our vision. It is high time we tackled the archaeology of this towering conceit; that we uncover its foundations to see it for what it is: the outdated monument to an immodest era. (1999: 3)

The arguments of new environmental and feminist social movements that act to defend their 'place' are, according to Escobar, centred on rights – rights to their identity (hence, the right to be different), rights to their territory (as the space for exercising identity), to a measure of local autonomy, and rights to their own 'vision of development and the promotion of democratic, egalitarian and participatory styles of politics' (Escobar, 1995: 219). In fact the emergence of new social movements testifies to the exclusionary nature of development and a fundamental lack of confidence in existing political institutions to protect the displacement of spaces that reflect the identity of local people. The rise of 'identity politics' based on local culture has shifted the focus of domestic social movements away from the struggle for political control of the state and towards demands for social change across a range of contentious issues. In sum, post development authors argue that the discourse of the south has to include explanations for cultural diversity and local interests, and therefore has the potential to provide an alternative to the conventional development discourse. McMichael explains how an 'alternative modernity' will sooner or later come from local people who are best placed to reconstruct and redefine different concepts of modernity from their own deeply rooted traditions. Indisputably people, communities and countries have to determine the substantive content of rights appropriate to their unique circumstances. Locals have to define their own way of life and their own rights 'in agriculture, labour, fishing, food and land policies which are ecologically, socially, economically and culturally appropriate' (McMichael, 2007: 5).

A tension exists however in the anti-developmental conception of new social movements in that there is in fact 'heterogeneity in the form and character' of many of these movements. Peiterse argues for example that social movements are not in fact anti-developmental, but promote access to development within an inclusive and participatory framework (2001: 109), that views local people not simply as the beneficiaries of development, but its rightful and legitimate claimants. Often the concerns of local social movements are articulated through transnational protest networks that hold up not for local solutions to poverty, but the need for fair and equal global free trade mindful that obstacles to free trade are 'opposition to the development of the south' (Desai and Potter, 2001; Ashman, 2004). Different protests are in fact fairly heterogeneous in their anti-globalisation stand, in that they oppose neo-liberal economic globalisation, not globalisation as such.

Economic globalisation certainly challenges the assumption that civil society is confined merely to the national setting in relation to development, by extending the spatial scale of the relationship between political struggle and contentious development. In a grass-roots or bottom-up sense, civil society is the realm in which those who are disadvantaged by the economic globalisation mount their protest and seek alternatives.

Sklair suggests that transnational social movements and advocacy groups involved in the struggle for the globalisation of human rights could drive 'from below' a new form of globalisation or transnationalism that is not dominated by capital, but based on a just global order. The crisis of capitalism is embodied in the values that these movements share – community, gender relations, ethnicity, religion, poverty, inequality, class polarisation and environmental issues, most of which are either ignored or seriously neglected by a capitalist globalisation which directly undermines human rights (Sklair, 2002: 306–319). States, development agencies and TNCs are continually being challenged to operate within a global institutional environment that creates inclusive opportunities that empower all disaffected people, including the poor and the marginalised, to shape and mediate their entitlements and social, economic, cultural and political rights. But to what extent do the new opportunities for collective transnational action constitute an international or 'global civil society' (Colas, 2002) and one that has the potential to erode state sovereignty and to reduce state power? To what extent do transnational networks empower people to effect change through collective action, especially in settings where states are strong and overpowering, or where the state is fragile, weak and rogue? Can transnational networks be conceptualised as 'transnational social movements'?

Increasingly we find that local issues are raised at the global level, and local people voice their concerns in global terms, demonstrating new alliances and new configurations of power. Both the actions of states and the interests of large corporations are increasingly subject to challenges from new alliances or transnational networks, operating outside the boundaries of the nation state. Although contentious development issues are localised, transnational networks articulate linkages between local impacts and wider global concerns in respect of a range of issues – ecology, human rights, feminism, the rights of ethnic and indigenous people and so forth. So what potential is there for transnational networks to influence the actions and policies of nation states and transnational corporations? Can they continue to prevaricate over the adoption of policies that promote social, community and human rights, in the light of the activities of transnational actors?

The political, legal and institutional changes, on which the resolution of most contentious development issues relies, have long been the focus of politically formed challenges from local civil society. However, social protests and 'contentious politics' no longer operate in isolation in national or local spatial dimensions, but, in the words of Tarrow (1994), are transnational, facilitated through an array of new technologies and telecommunications (fax, internet and so forth). Exemplars are well documented of how the interactions of international activists and their networks, that work across state borders, bring a distinct 'global' dimension to social protest in a range of countries. Members of transnational networks develop similarities and shared identities, as they operate with a common theme against the provision of global neo-liberalism and with focused targeted actions in opposition to TNCs and global institutions from the World Bank to the IMF, the World Trade Organisation (WTO) to the G8. Although they may have little else in common than their opposition to one or more of the global institutions, activists are developing a counter-structure of contention (Tarrow, 1994: 32–33).

In considering whether transnational networks comprising different actors are social movements, we should revisit the distinction between orthodox social movements as an organised collective force that struggles for socio-economic and political change through a sustained defiance of power structures and 'new' social movements that have local culture or 'identity politics' as their focus (Calhoun, 1993). Orthodox social movements are, by definition, transformative in their objective (Cox, 2002). Working class labour movements, that had a common framework and operated on the basis of collective action, are a good example of social movements. Tarrow (1994), in a global context, cites the Islamic Fundamentalist Movement as an example of a transnational social movement, based on his distinction between domestic social movements that actively embark on contentious political confrontations with elites at national state level and transnational social movements, that involve interacting 'with opponents – national or non-national – by connected networks of challenges organized across national boundaries' (Tarrow, 1994: 184). Given this definition, transnational networks that campaign against specific projects or issues are not orthodox social movements. Even though they may be effective in advocating alternatives and drawing attention to the need for changes in the social and political behaviour of global institutions of governance (The World Bank, IMF, WTO), states and TNCs, they are not driven by the objective of transforming a common political opposition.

At the local level, transnational campaign networks appear to have been most effective in drawing attention to contentious development – social and political issues arising from or concatenated with neo liberal development policy and projects. Transnational networks exist in essence as a communicative, information-sharing structure enabling political exchange between NGOs, individuals as well as governmental institutions by effectively linking locales and coordinating strategies for action. These conditions of interaction tend to make it difficult for the various movements that comprise a transnational network to be engaged with each other to the same degree of social solidarity as that which hallmarks 'new' domestic social movements. For Keck and Sikkink transnational networks operate as 'advocacy networks', representing a common discourse on particular contentious issues and 'include those relevant actors working internationally on issues, who are bound together by shared values, a common discourse, and dense exchanges of information and services' (1998: 2). What transnational networks achieve is 'a new form of political space beyond the state' (Robinson, 2002: 206) that transcends state boundaries and defies the traditional notion that development actors are bounded by local or national scales and within which they unite citizens across the world in networks that challenge global issues – environment, human rights, women's and indigenous rights.

Conclusion

Private companies are under pressure from civil society, NGOs and regulatory policy to operate within the realms of a global corporate responsibility that reflects the aims of global compact and human rights principles. This prescribes a clear mandate not to support projects that risk jeopardising those aims. Campaigns driven by environmental activists, NGOs and the media to disrupt large development projects argue that it is neither ethical nor socially responsible for states and companies to ignore social and environmental problems. This challenges the interests of large corporations in terms of their operations and in relation to specific areas, namely corruption, local social relations and environmental impacts. In reality 'corporate social responsibility' does nothing more than provide a convenient tool for private companies anxious to protect their 'reputations' when they are threatened by pressure and criticism both from civil society and transnational movements, in particular when their actions are not subject to a code of regulations.

The fact that some TNCs make efforts to change their culture and practice by, for instance, integrating the Global Compact into business principles is itself a step forward. However, there is still some way to go before we can confidently identify the contribution of companies to rights to development and poverty reduction. How a range of agencies with different capabilities can deliver cosmopolitan standards and values, while sound economic practice and the legitimate corporate interests are secured, is a complex that still eludes us. Baxi argues that the emergence of a market-friendly (or specifically trade-related) human rights paradigm, instigated by transnational agencies and encapsulated in current compacts and norms, is precisely constructed to protect the interests of global capital. According to Baxi:

> The paradigm of the Universal Declaration of Human Rights is being steadily, but surely, *supplanted* by that of trade-related, market-friendly human rights. This new paradigm seeks to reverse the notion that universal human rights are designed for the attainment of dignity and the well-being of human beings and for enhancing the security and well being of socially, economically and civilisation of vulnerable peoples and communities. (2002: 131)

7
Global Social Justice and Development

My aim in writing this book has been to show that the idea of social justice could be articulated in development theory and practice but political forces, in particular hegemonic states, and current institutions of global governance divest it of supporting relevance. I did not set out to provide a theory of social justice for development – that is too ambitious a task for my humble background, but I do believe that social justice provides the potential for a fresh theoretical approach to overcome the ongoing 'impasse' in development theory and practice, and challenge the hegemonic discourse. Social Justice for development is a critical ideal, one that incites change in our institutions and practices for greater equality, and increasing the voice of the powerless with the objective of reducing inequality. I have also argued that even though institutions of global governance exist, their structure does not render power equally across nation states and engenders as a result winners and losers. Disproportionate power within these institutions is vested in a few individual nation states, namely the hegemonic or powerful states that comprise the G8, and very little effective power is shared with other states, even though they constitute the majority. The result is that the goals of these institutions are defined by the privileged few and reflect very specific interests and agenda – Structural Adjustment Programmes, 'good' governance etc., all of which tend to reinforce the privileges of some states over others and to accord them an undeserved driving lead within the global order in development strategy and policy. If the poorer, weaker states do not have a voice in determining how development can be achieved, how can they be expected to deliver the Millennium Development Goals?

Reducing poverty is contingent upon reducing inequality between the rich nation states and the poor ones. A necessary condition for the realisation of development and the rights of individuals has to be the right of a nation state to develop. Few would question that the idea of the development of all countries is sound, although exactly what this means is fairly contentious. As this book evidences, it is increasingly apparent that while the south may demand some form of equality or social justice, a whole host of political forces undermine it becoming reality. One should also not dismiss the exponents of cosmopolitanism who argue that in the context of the complex transformation that the world is experiencing through economic globalisation, the meaning of accountability and democracy at the national level is itself altering and this has an impact on the securing of human rights. The processes of economic globalisation – rapidly growing flows of trade, cheaper communication technology, movement of capital and labour – increasingly impacts on state capacity in terms of both power and function. Concerns around national and global security since 9/11 add a further dimension to the capability of states to secure social justice, having effectively reconstructed the notion of protection for the poor and marginal as a temporary and containing measure. These forces have reduced the effectiveness of national development policy, compelling it to be considered within a wider global arena.

While there are international laws and pressures for social justice and global obligations to protect human rights wrapped up in UN declarations, the basic framework for the protection and enforcement of rights is still the nation state. The state remains therefore an important agent of social justice. Rights declarations continue to be articulated through the state and national legal systems, and therefore irrespective of which agencies deliver front-line services or development policies, it is the local political context that influences the delivery of rights. A crucial element in delivering rights is the political will to enforce them and the only real power base for this exists at a national level for international pressures and declarations do not sit within a jurisdiction framework, but are articulated through the state and national legal systems. In reality many nation states in the south are either undemocratic (choosing not to promote rights and social justice), or lack capacity to act as a vehicle for social justice because they are short of the necessary human, material and organisational resources to secure or improve justice within their boundaries. Those that fail to deliver social justice also tend to lack the capabilities needed for the coordination and enforcement of action and obligations by other agents and agencies and therefore are not able to be either enforcers or enablers. Global institutions have promoted a development agenda that focuses capacity building on democracy and good governance, to maximise states' efficacy within the global market in line with neo-liberal principles, but this has not necessarily worked when it has been linked to economic or political conditionality or forced by way of armed invasion. That does not mean to say that liberal democratic government is not preferable to non-democratic government. It will always be so, but we have to question what form of democracy is being promoted, given that accountable and democratic institutions that ensure involvement and participation of individuals and groups in decision-making only have meaning when governments are in control of the essential policies that impact on the well-being of their citizens. Without political freedom, a key plank of democracy, it would not be possible for states to fulfill the basic needs of their citizens. And yet the current form of economic globalisation is undermining the operation of liberal democratic governments.

Cosmopolitans conclude that if the state is no longer empowered or effective at controlling all of the issues that impact on the provision of social justice because of the global context, then there is a need to establish 'cosmopolitan democracy' and 'cosmopolitan governance' that operates to protect individual rights no matter where people live or their personal circumstances. This means the law to protect individual rights being linked in some way to global institutions that reflect a global commitment to a development or poverty reduction agenda. The cosmopolitan perspective indicates a relentless optimism that globalisation could work provided global governance institutions are reformed. But they underestimate the extent to which the hegemonic states influence the direction of economic globalisation through these institutions. Global institutions are essentially undemocratic and unrepresentative and this distorts their propensity to be efficacious. Campaigns and demonstrations in Seattle and Prague have recently drawn the world's attention to the undemocratic structure of the World Bank, The International Monetary Fund (IMF) and World Trade Organisation (WTO). Cosmopolitanism acknowledges that rich nations have a role to play in poverty reduction, but it trivialises prevailing asymmetric power relations and the hegemonic role of powerful states within institutions of governance. Reliance on some form of moral obligation and aid on the part of richer nations, global institutions and individuals to achieve poverty reduction and the inequality that it represents, has proved to be very limited. This is partly due to lack of political commitment from the wealthier nations to increase financial assistance (and not following through on a pledge to dedicate up to 0.7 per cent of their GDP to poorer nations) and partly because of the reluctance of hegemonic states to depoliticise the direction of journey of economic globalisation. It is now well documented that the MDGs will not be achieved by 2015. More importantly a just and equitable social contract can only be effective if it involves parties of equal power and resources. In the case of the current global order, as Nussbaum (2006a) points out, it is clear that there cannot be co-operation entrenched in 'mutual advantage' or a social contact between nation states on the grounds of equality, because there has always been a component of domination particularly of the rich nation states over the poor nation states.

Essentially the existing structure of global governance is impotent as it allows the transgressions of powerful states to go unchallenged even when they harm the least advantaged and poorer nations. The current idea of consensus blurs the fact that the development agenda is dominated by the more powerful states. Drawing on the imperatives of the moral economy, we need the principles of global social justice to shift the paradigm from the Washington/Post-Washington consensus to one that truly reflects global consensus. As a starting point for how 'people' can lead global governance there is a need to apply the core criteria of social justice to global institutions. The list of necessary changes that this would trigger is long, and here I present an eclectic selection of ideas.

- A reconfiguration of the composition of UN Security Council would be needed to ensure an equal voice for all member states: the principle of 'one country, one vote, one value' has not worked within the United Nations because not all nation states carry equal weight and powerful states tend to dominate the development agenda through the idea of consensus. The idea that some countries have limited capabilities, and therefore require some form of intervention, is undoubtedly associated with inequality of participation in the global economy and inequality of voice, which in one way or another lead us back to the shaping of the development agenda by the more powerful national states.
- There would also be need to structure an appropriate forum for the engagement of non–state actors, such as civil society organisations, NGOs, indigenous, local actors or non-experts who could also expand, through their action and local knowledge, development perspectives in the decision-making of the global institutions alongside nation states. The fullest extension of rights would set up ways in which local people select those who affect, govern and control our lives within these institutions.

- Issues of gender equality also need to be at the front of any debate as in the current structure very few women are in senior positions or influence decision-making.
- There is scope for human rights regimes to be strengthened through the rule of law as well as the moral economy at an international level.
- Fundamentally the decentralisation of decisions from Washington to other locations would make a real statement about the global community's commitment to social justice for development – why couldn't the headquarters of the World Bank be relocated from Washington to Africa or the IMF be based in Latin America or the WTO in Asia?
- More importantly Transitional Corporations must be made accountable for their activities and, through measures such as integrating the Global Compact into business principles and strengthening corporate social responsibility, encouraged to contribute towards poverty reduction and development. It is no longer appropriate to attribute effective and legitimate power solely to states, as some power clearly lies with a variety of local and global non–state institutions. The idea of devolving and redistributing responsibility to a variety of non–state actors and assigning justice and development obligations to non-state as well as state actors has to be explored further, but always within the context that the state at the end of the day is the primary agent of justice and development.
- The drive for global institutions to become more accountable, transparent and representative could only be effective if it is underpinned by an ideological commitment to global social justice based on redistribution. Suggestions about how global redistribution could be achieved include a foreign aid tax, such as the Global Resource Dividend or the Currency Transfer Tax or Tobin Tax. This is in itself a fairly narrow approach, and one that risks pampering to the conscience of wealthier nations, rather than achieving real step improvement in the current state of affairs. It is essential that affluent national governments assume some responsibility for promoting the capabilities of states and citizens from the poorer nations.
- The most important channel of global redistribution is trade, but in many ways the current trade regime has been the catalyst for inequality between nation states, with the dominant national states disadvantaging many states from access to the market through their use of protectionist measures and subsidies. All encompassing inclusive trade could benefit the poorer nation states, but this means rich

nations removing trade barriers and encouraging investment in the south. The distributional impact of such measures would be reflected in GDP.

- Finally nation states have to be accountable. Corruption, bad governance and human rights violations are not a construction of the hegemonic states and global institutions, although they may be used to legitimise control or intervention. Many nations states are responsible for travesties against their citizens.

Changes such as those outlined here that would redistribute power and income within the global order have been raised in national and international forums and by oppositional social forces or in the words of Robert Cox through the agency of social movements as a potential source of counter hegemony 'against core country dominance aiming toward the autonomous development of countries in the south' (1986: 237). Social justice, with its focus on rights that are equal and inalienable and apply to all human beings, provides a framework for 'emancipatory politics', reducing inequality and hierarchical notions of power within global governance. The crux of the development debate may no longer be the merits of competing models of economic and social transformation, but that does not mean to say that liberal capitalism has to provide the context of development and that we have reached 'the end of history'. Civil society has found ways of coping with the neo-liberal market economy and its injustices and in time it is likely, through the social struggle for rights and social justice, to find alternatives too. Our challenge is to support this by ensuring that development theory remains a critical enquiry into the dynamics of the global order to identify imperatives that would achieve a dignified and decent life for all people.

Notes

1 Introduction: Social Justice and Development

1. The positivist approach in its crudest form has dominated social science in general and development studies in particular. Positivists stress that the aim of research is to expand 'verifiable' knowledge, that is knowledge that enables a social scientist to explain, predict and understand empirical reality. Crucial to this approach is that the observer does not present or include his or her values or opinions as part of the interpretation of findings. This is considered to be the only form of knowledge that could be used to improve the human condition for a better life and to achieve development.
2. Before decolonisation in 1945 these ideas on development crystallized in the discourses and practices of new states in the south, under the influence of northern states and the newly established multilateral development institutions, the United Nations, the World Bank and IMF etc. which wanted to operationalise the agenda of development in poor countries through aid funding from ex-colonial powers. The architects of post-war aid and development were the World Bank or the International Bank for Reconstruction and Development and IMF, established in 1944 at Bretton Woods. The World Bank commenced with the reconstruction of Europe and then moved on to the south providing conditional lending to fund projects for economic development. Though promoting 'a world free of poverty', the World Bank and IMF have not made a commitment to the Right to Development on the grounds that as apolitical organisations they cannot intervene in politics. The slogan and claim that poverty could be abolished is the 'single most important pretention' of the mainstream development paradigm (Sachs, 1999: 254).
3. For a more detailed discussion see Todaro and Smith, 2006; Sen, 1999. For a more critical reflection see Leys, 1996; Peiterse, 2001; and Kothari & Minogue 2002.
4. Rostow's modernisation is anchored in the teleological conception of history that all societies evolve through more or less the same structural processes of social change that the Western countries went through, evolving from traditional to modern, industrial or high mass consumption societies. This formed the basis of modernisation theory and much development policy in the Third World.
5. Merquior distinguishes six types of liberalism: Classical Liberalism, Conservative Liberalism, New Liberalism, Neo-liberalism, Sociological Liberalism and the Neo-contractarians. They all share four fundamental points: the (negative) freedom of not being subject to arbitrary interferences; the (positive) freedom of participation in pubic affairs; the (interior) freedom of consciousness and beliefs; the (personal) freedom of self-development for each individual. Gellner and Cansino, (1996) point out that these four will always pertain to historical canons of liberal thought.

6. Recent attempts to promote fair trade are a politicised attempt to establish some kind of moral economic framework based on a fair exchange of commodities and to enable small producers to compete in the global market. Their impact, paradoxically, is to endorse neo-liberal policy and labour production in the south as part of an unequal system of economic exchange between the north and the south. Fair trade movements can only ever have limited impact for so long as they do not focus on the historical and structural inequalities in the global economic order.

7. The introduction of anti-terrorist laws, and the abandonment of the Geneva Conventions in Guatanamo Bay are regarded as a setback to human rights in the United States.

8. More or less in line with the Kantian conception of perfect duties, which correspond with the basic rights to freedom; the necessary condition for the exercise of all other rights. That is why so much of Kant's ethics focuses on what we might call negative duties, prohibitions against certain actions. These are generally correlated with perfect duties. Kant is concerned with describing those moral warrants that are consistent with and promote universal principles of freedom as they relate to rational beings.

2　The Right to Development

1. Although this has been the subject of debate among variants of the Marxist positions.

2. Cohen uses a good example of a social movement of his period to support his view that natural rights do exist. I have reconstructed this here to better relate to the current historical context. Suppose the government through legal means and/or constitutional law stopped people marching through Edinburgh as part of the Make Poverty History forum on the grounds of national security and concerns that the marchers might endanger peace in the region. Legally banning the marchers, including anti capitalist protestors, would mean that they would lose a platform to protest against the G8 leaders' agenda. They could express their protests at such action by suggesting that the government had removed their rights to express and reflect their anger on issues relating to the war in Iraq, global warming and poverty, which the G8 leaders had ignored for many years. In this hypothetical case people have no legal rights but they have, in the words of Cohen and Nozick, natural rights or moral rights. In fact the 'language of natural right (or moral) is the language of justice, and whoever takes justice seriously must accept that there are natural rights' (Cohen, 1995: 12). So what Cohen in fact points out is not that the notion of natural right or equality results in constitutional laws that protect the rights of the powerful or those who own the means of production, but that morally the ownership of private property is unjust.

3. The United Nations institutions that have been established to protect and endorse human rights are first the bodies launched under the UN Charter; such as the Human Rights Council which includes the Commission on Human Rights, and the international human rights treaties for which seven bodies have been established monitor the implementation of the core international human rights treaties.

4. The UN's 'Guiding Principles on Internal Displacement' defines IDPs as: 'Internally Displaced Persons are persons or groups of persons who have been forced or obliged to flee or to leave their homes or places of habitual residence, in particular as a result of or in order to avoid the effects of armed conflict, situations of generalised violence, violations of human rights or natural or human-made disasters, and who have not crossed an internationally recognised State border'. (Guiding Principle on Internal Displacement, 1998)

5. For more details of variants of the Dependency School see Frank 1971 and Wallenstein World System 1979, and Cardoso, 'dependent development' 1972. The rigor of Dependency theory was in cohesion and ability to give a causal explanation to the Satellite/Metropolitant, or centre (core)/ periphery relations. Frank identified the mechanism of capital accumulation in the centre with the reproduction of economic underdevelopment in the periphery; primarily caused by the extraction of surplus from the periphery through a kind of exploitation and oppression of weaker nations. In fact, this began in the sixteenth century, when capital penetrated third world countries and destroyed the traditional production relationship, creating instead a dependent economy in which cheap raw materials were sent to rich countries in return for expensive commodities and goods. The centre was equated with power and capacity to dominate. The periphery, on the other hand, was identified with subordination and marginality. Development in the metropolitan centre in this paradigm was associated with the reproduction of underdevelopment in the periphery as a result of the transference of resources on an unequal basis or unequal exchange.

6. For critiques of the Dependency school see Colin Leys (1996).

7. Since the 1950s United Nations declarations have been converted into treaty and international law. Almost all states ratified the Universal Declaration of Human Rights 1948 and The Convention on the Rights of the Child (CRC). 150 states have also ratified the International Covenant on Economic, Social and Cultural Rights 1966, (ICESCR) and the International Covenant on Civil and Political Rights 1966, (ICCPR). Most countries have signed the following conventions and declarations endorsed by the UN which augment the human rights agenda: Convention on the Status of Refugees (1951); Convention on the Political Rights of Women (1953); Declaration on the Granting of Independence to Colonial Countries and Peoples (1960), The International Convention on the Elimination of all Forms of Racial Discrimination (1965); The Universal Declaration on Eradication of Hunger and Malnutrition (1974); Convention on the Elimination of Discrimination Against Women (1979); African Charter on Human and People's Rights (1981); The Convention Against Torture and Other Cruel Inhuman or Degrading Treatment or Punishment (1984); 1986 Declaration on the Right to Development; The Convention of the Rights of the Child (1989); The Declaration on the Elimination of all Forms of Intolerance Based on Religion or Belief (1981); The Declaration on the Rights of People Belonging to National and Ethnic Minority (1992); The Declaration on the Elimination of Violence Against Women (1993); Arab Charter of Human Rights 1994 (revised in 2004); Treaty setting up the International Criminal Court (1998); The United Nations Convention on Corruption (2005).

8. Even though the Islamic declaration of human rights incorporates Sharia Law and upholds divine revelation that presents the equality of humanity before God, it remains fairly consistent with the UN Human Rights Declaration. In many respects the wording is similar to that of UN documents.

9. Nelson Mandela provides us with a nice example of how rights and social justice can be learned through customary practice, in his case through 'the wise men who retained the knowledge of tribal history and custom in their heads and whose opinion carried great weight'. He describes how tribal meetings represented democracy in its purest form with all tribal members allowed to attend and speak, with decisions taken jointly:

> There may have been hierarchy of importance among the speakers, but every one was heard ... People spoke without interruption and the meeting lasted for many hours. The foundation of self government was that all men were free to voice their opinions and were equal in their value as citizens ... Women I am afraid were deemed second citizens ... 'These institutions, and customary laws provide transparency, however their hierarchical relations should not be romanticised. The crucial point for us to take note of here is that what we recognise today as universal rights can have different cultural and historical origins.

10. In the fifty-sixth General Assembly (2001) the Islamic state of Iran called for a dialogue among civilisations as 'a critique of the prevailing human rights discourse'. A current accepted wisdom in the Islamic world, in particular after 9/11 and the invasion of Iraq, is that the West has been constantly attacking Islamic countries and misrepresenting their culture by equating Islamic fundamentalism with terrorism. There are those who believe that Islam can provide an alternative framework favouring the incorporation of rights of civilisation into the discourse of the protective framework of international law.

11. In February 2007 China's National People's congress passed a law on private property rights. However this does not give full property rights to individuals to own land, that is to say, the farmers do not have ownership rights to the land they farm nor are they able to sell their land. What this law will facilitate is protection for the farmers against land grabbers who illegally force them off their land, so it can be used for development, without offers of compensation. The problem relating to individual and collective rights remain unresolved.

12. This was in response to the United States' objection to the possibility of building up of nuclear weapons in Iran. The Iranian government in response argued vociferously that 'Iran has inalienable rights to nuclear energy for development' and the Prime Minister of the Islamic Republic of Iran told the UN Conference that 'hegemonic powers have misrepresented Iran's technological endeavours in the nuclear field as pursuit of nuclear weapons ... This is nothing but a propaganda ploy.' Declaring that Iran, in accordance with its religious principles, would never develop nuclear weapons, he said that his country was 'prepared to engage in serious partnership with private and public sectors of other countries in the implementation of an uranium enrichment program in Iran.' At the same time, he stressed that Iran, 'in its pursuit of peaceful nuclear technology, considers it within its legitimate rights to receive objective guarantees for uranium enrichment in the nuclear fuel cycle.' Mahmoud Ahmadinejad Speech in the sixtieth session of the United Nations General Assembly, 21 September 2005.

3 Neoliberalism and Social Justice

1. During this period 1945–1980 '... the goal of development was growth; the agent of development was the state and the means of development was national economic planning in the context of macroeconomic policy instruments ...' (Leys, 1996: 7).
2. The shift in policy paradigm was the culmination of a number of factors including the shock of the late 1970s recession, debt burden, the past policy failure of state-led development, the slow pace of economic growth, the ideological crisis of the left, the collapse of central planning, and the socialist model of development.
3. Williamson (1990) coined the term Washington Consensus and even went as far as to say that there was 'universal convergence' that with good institutions these policies would lead to economic growth and development.
4. For the World Bank, conditionality meant that governments would be 'focusing on critical issues, such as long-run structural and institutional policy programs, and giving greater emphasis to outcomes and to government accountability for and commitment to those policies'.
5. The Human Development Index of the United Nations uses capabilities but it has its value, in its particular context. Sen points out that Nussbaum use of capabilities list make contribution for the evaluation of gender equality and on human rights.
6. Sen himself was the main contributor and writer of the UNDP (2000) Human Development Report entitled 'Human Rights and Human Development'.
7. See 'The Human Rights Based Approach to Development Cooperation: Towards a Common Understanding Among the UN Agencies', in *Report of the Second Interagency Workshop on Implementing a Human Rights-based Approach in the Context of UN Reform*, (Stamford, USA, 5–7 May, 2003), available at http://www.humanrights.se/svenska/Common%20Understanding%20FN%20 2003.pdf
8. The Secretary General's message, 'Why human rights matter', in Amnesty International, *Annual Report 2004*, at http://web.amnesty.org/report2004/ message-eng
9. Among the grants channeled to Venezuela to support opposition to the present government are: $47,459 for a 'democratic leadership campaign'; $37,614 for citizen meetings to discuss a 'shared vision' for society; and of $56,124 to analyse Venezuela's new constitution. The Office of Transition Initiatives, which also works in such 'priority countries' as Iraq, Afghanistan, Bolivia and Haiti, has overseen more than $26m in grants to groups in Venezuela since 2002.

4 Economic Globalisation and Global Social Justice

1. Other contracts in Africa include iron ore with The Gabon ($3 billion); a contract with China's Simopec oil giant to sell crude oil in Angola; investment in the state run oil company Songangol in Congo; in Nigeria an investment in oil and gas to supply China's crude oil; in South Africa a number of business

contracts; hydro-electronic dams in Mozambique worth $2.6 billion; and a new contact to build dams in Ghana. (Meldrum and Watts, *The Guardian*, Thursday 15 June 2006; Rory Carroll, *The Guardian*, Tuesday 28 March 2006).

2. The concept of colonisation denotes the idea of the permanent settlement of a new territory by a group of people who have moved there from their original home and the political control or rule of the people of a given territory by a foreign state. This can include permanent settlement but does not have to.

3. In 1888, Brazil was the last country of the Americas where legal slavery was abolished. Up to the point of abolition, ten times as many slaves had been shipped to Brazil from Africa as were transported to North America, although, due to the extraordinarily high rates of mortality on Brazilian slave plantations, the number of slaves at abolition was only half that of those in North America (Bales, 2000: 124).

4. Most presidents for example, between 1898 and 1930, originated from coffee and dairy dynasties, being commonly referred to therefore as *'café com leite'* (coffee with milk) (Wolford, 2005: 411).

5. The Aga, a legacy of the Ottoman Empire, represent families that over generations inherited lands transferred to tribal leaders to ensure their political support during the Ottoman Empire, when the southeast was strategically important.

6. It is their 'imperial agency' that become the 'focus of concern' (Held, 2005: 192).

7. On the fiftieth anniversary of the United Nations Human Rights Declaration a proposal was put forward for discussion to the UN General Assembly which emphasised universal responsibilities and accountability, and which complemented the 1948 Universal Declaration of Human Responsibilities. But this proposal does not *clearly* specify or provide a guide on the duties and responsibilities of different actors towards extreme poverty within and between nations and the 'under-fulfillment of human rights today'. For critique of this see Pogge (2005).

5   Global Governance and Rights to Development: Opportunity or Charade?

1. Governance in the White Paper on EU refers to five principles and is defined as 'the rules, processes and behaviour that affect the way in which powers are exercised at European level, particularly as regards openness, participation, accountability, effectiveness and coherence.

2. A refugee is defined as person in fear of being persecuted for reasons of race, religion, nationality, membership of a particular social group, or political opinion, who is outside his/her country of nationality and has sufficient evidence of prosecution in their own country to justify seeking protection across an international border (UN Convention, 1951). IDPs are forced to move within the confines of national boundaries, for a range of reasons including conflict or as a result of development interventions, such as large dam projects. There are commonalities between the two (refugees and IDPs) that are not necessarily reflected in the policy domain.

3. Asylum is 'protection granted by a state on its territory against the exercise of jurisdiction by the state of origin, based on the principle of non – refoulement and characterised by the enjoyment of internationally recognised refugee rights, and generally accorded without limit of time' (UNHCR, 2003b: 2).

4. 30 per cent of the world's refugees and 50 per cent of internally displaced people are in Sub-Saharan Africa, mainly resulting from civil wars.
5. Increasingly restrictive refugee policies in Europe and North America include 'encampment' under in-country protection programmes; restrictions on access to key services and resources, such as work; and tighter visa and permit restrictions. In some cases, a new paradigm has emerged, aimed at preventing refugee flows before international borders are crossed through polices such as 'safe country', 'transit processing centres'; 'safety zones'; 'open relief centres'; and 'safe heaven zones'. Britain's proposed 'Regional Protection Programme' provides an example.
6. The shift in the refugee discourse from 'burden sharing' to that based on a 'threat to the security of states' has had the desired effect of reducing the number of refugees travelling to Europe and other Northern countries. Recent statistics indicate that since 9/11 asylum applications have dropped by 40 per cent. The number of refugees globally has declined from 18 million in 1992 to 9.2 million in 2003 (UNHCR, 2006).
7. She also applies justice for disabilities and justice for animals.
8. However Nussbaum argues that 15 per cent of GDP is rather generous and it is difficult to convince people in affluent countries to commit themselves to that proportion of income.
9. Other issues the agenda added to negotiations were on agriculture and non-agricultural tariffs, trade and environment, anti-dumping and subsidies, investment, competition policy, trade facilitation, and intellectual property.
10. The tension over the conditionality and corruption reached its height when the British Minister for the Department for International Development threatened to withhold $50 million of UK funding from the World Bank.
11. In the 1990s, following the Gulf War, a Security Council resolution imposed sections on Iraq. The UN oil for food programme, in fact, was initiated to offset the effect of the sanction on the poor, and for humanitarian reasons. When started in 1995 this programme allowed Iraq to sell oil in the global market in exchange for food and medicine. However, the US government, which funds 22 per cent of the UN budget, criticised UN officials, together with the Iraqi government, as being corrupt because some oil profits were pocketed by people administering the programme.
12. The US has vetoed many resolutions on the Security Council on a wide range of issues, in particular in recent years.
13. The justification for a pre-emptive military invasion in Iraq, that led to the overthrow of the Saddam regime, was the association of his dictatorship with human rights abuses of Kurds and Shiites and the perceived threat against Western nations.
14. Since 2002, covert and overt operations of the US administration, through Transition Initiatives, have invested in 'pro-democracy programmes' in priority countries such as Iraq, Afghanistan, Bolivia, Haiti, Venezuela, and Cuba. 'The goal of the programme is to strengthen democracy; a goal consistent with President Bush's 'Freedom Agenda'. There is clear evidence that the US administration has abandoned Clinton's 'soft power' approach and adopted one of forced military power.

6   Transnational Corporations and Corporate Social Responsibility: Does It Really Work?

1. TNCs are involved in the most profitable industrial and service sectors, such as the production of electronic equipment, automobiles, pharmaceuticals, chemicals, petroleum, tourism, telecommunication, transport, banking and finance, and information technology. TNC activity in such areas as vehicle and oil production, and electricity generation accounts for 50 per cent of carbon dioxide emissions, 10–20 per cent of methane emissions, 60–70 per cent of CFC emissions, and 50 per cent of gas emissions such as nitrogen oxides and tropospheric ozone (UNCTC, 1992).

2. Nigeria has the seventh largest oil and gas reserve and is the sixth largest exporter of crude oil. Nigeria permits one of the largest global corporations, Shell, to invest and produce oil, yet with income per capita per annum of just $300 Nigeria is among the *top* 20 poorest countries in the world, and approximately 65 per cent of the population lives on less than $1 a day. This is a clear indication of the level of absolute poverty (GDP per capita, in terms of purchasing power parity (PPP) is US$ 896). The oil sector only employs 5 per cent of the population but accounts for over 90 per cent of Nigerian foreign exchange.

3. The report came up with a seven-point agenda to address the issues and challenges in the region, namely: promoting peace as the foundation for development; making local governance effective and responsive to the needs of the people; improving and diversifying the economy; promoting social inclusion and improved access to social services; promoting environmental sustainability to preserve the means of sustainable livelihoods; taking an integrated approach to HIV and AIDS; and building sustainable partnerships for the advancement of human development between state and local governments, Niger Delta Development Commission (NDDC), oil companies, communities, non-governmental organisations and civil society organisations.

4. The Shell Petroleum Development Company and Nigeria Limited funded this report in partnership with UNDP.

5. Since the 1960s the Niger Delta Region has been the land of opportunity for large TNC's, including ExxonMobil, Total Nigeria, Chevron, Elf, Agip Texaco, PAN Ocean and Statoil, to invest in the oil and gas industries. Nigeria Liquefied Natural Gas (NLNG) also plays a major role in the region. The Nigerian National Petroleum Corporation (NNPC), over the years, has developed a series of joint venture activities with the oil majors. Some of the indigenous oil firms that operate in the region include Dubri Oil, Consolidated Oil, and the AMNI International Petroleum Company.

6. In the US there are currently no more than about twenty cases under the Alien Tort Claims Act, which allows foreigners to sue entities, including companies, for injury.

7. The number of multinational corporations is growing in countries with the highest inequality and poverty, for example Tata in India, and Cemex in Mexico, China, and South Africa. In South Africa the Anglo-American Corporation and De Beers are among the top mining companies in the world. SAB Miller has become a global brewing giant, Sappi is known world wide for its paper production, and MTN has become a household name in many African countries. Dimension Data (Didata), which provides computer services,

operates in over 30 countries. Sasal, an energy and chemical company, operates in over 20 countries across the globe. (*The Guardian* July 15 December 2006: 67–68). They all focus on particular markets, mainly in Sub-Saharan Africa, Russia and Eastern Europe.

8. There is also an armed social movement that believes in an independent state, struggle against environmental pollution, fair distribution of local natural resources and jobs for local people etc. The Movement for the Emancipation of the Niger Delta has been involved in a number of acts of sabotage on Shell and government oil installations.

References

Abouharb, R. M. and Cingranelli, D. (2006), *Human Rights and Structural Adjustment* (Cambridge: Cambridge University Press).

Afshari, R. (2001), *Human Rights in Iran: The Abuse of Cultural Relativism* (Pennsylvania: Studies in Human Rights).

Ahmadinejad, M. (2005), Speech in the 60th session of the United Nations General Assembly, 21 September.

Akukwe, C. (2006), *Don't Let Them Die: HIV/AIDS, TB, Malaria and the Healthcare Crisis in Africa* (London: Adonis & Abbey Publishers Ltd).

Albright, M. (1998), Speech on Human Rights, Atlanta, Georgia, 3 December. Available at www.usconsulate.org.hk/uscn/state/1998/1203.htm.

Alston, P. (2004), *A Human Rights Perspective on the Millennium Development Goals*. Paper prepared as a contribution to the work of the Millennium Project Task Force on Poverty and Economic Development, by the Special Adviser to the United Nations High Commissioner for Human Rights (Millennium Development Goals).

Alston, P. (2006), *Non-State Actors and Human Rights* (Oxford: Oxford University Press).

Amin, S. (1985), *Delinking* (New York: Monthly Review Press).

Amnesty International (2004), Secretary General's message, *Why human rights matter'* in Amnesty International's Annual Report. Available at http://web. amnesty.org/report2004/message-eng

Amnesty International (2005), China Annual Report. Available at http://web. amnesty.org/report2004/chn-summary-eng

Amnesty International (2006), *People's Republic of China: Sustaining Conflict and Human Rights Abuse, the Flow of Arms Accelerates*, Annual Report June. Available at http://web.amnesty.org/library/Index/ENGASA170302006

Anan, K. (2006), Farewell Address: Truman Presidential Museum and Library 11 December, Missouri. Available at http://www.trumanlibrary.org/annan.htm.

Anderson, P. (2005), Arms and Rights: Rawls, Habermas and Bobbio in an Age of War, *New Left Review*, 31, 5–40.

Arafat, J. (2003), Camps and Freedoms: Long – term Refugee Situations in Africa, *Forced Migrants Review*, 16, 4–8.

Ashman, S. (2004), Resistance to Neoliberal Globalisation: A Case of Militant Particularism?, *Political Studies Association*, 24, 2, 143–153.

Asian Source (2004), Interview with Sen, December. Available at http://www. asiasource.org/news/special_reports/sen.cfm.

Bakewell, O. (2000), Repatriation and Self-settled Refugees in Zambia: Bringing Solutions to the Wrong Problems, *Journal of Refugee Studies*, 13, 4, 356–373.

Bales, K. (2000), *Disposable People: New Slavery in the Global Economy* (London: University of California Press).

Barry, B. (2005), *Why Social Justice Matters* (Cambridge: Polity Press).

Baxi, U. (2002), *The Future of Human Rights* (Delhi: Oxford University Press).

Baxi, U. (2005), Market Fundamentalisms: Business Ethics at the Altar of Human Rights, *Human Rights Law Review*, 5, 1, 1–26.

Bayat, A. (2007), *Making Islam Democratic: Social Movements and the Post – Islamist Turn* (Stanford: Stanford Univesity Press).

Beck, U. (2006), *Cosmopolitan Vision* (Cambridge: Polity Press).

Bello, W. (2002), *De-globalisation Ideas for a New World Economy* (London: Zed Press).

Bentham, J. (2000), *Anarchical Fallacies: An Examination of Declaration of the Rights to Man and the Citizen Decreed by the Constituent Assembly in France*, in Bentham, J.; Harrison, R. (ed.), Selected Writings on Utilitarianism, (Herefordshire: Wordsworth).

Bernstein, H. (2000), *Colonialism, Capitalism, Development*, in Allen, T. and Thomas, A. (eds), Poverty and Development into the 21st Century (Oxford: Oxford University in association with Open University) 241–270.

Bernstein, H. (2006), *Development Studies and the Marxist*, in Kothari, U. (ed.), A Radical History of Development Studies (London: Zend Press).

Bhargava, K. V. (ed.), (2006), *Global Issues for Global Citizens: An Introduction to Key Development Challenges* (Washington: The World Bank).

Bhawati, J. (2004), *In Defence of Globalisation* (Oxford: Oxford University Press).

Birdsall, N. (2005), *The World is Not Flat: Inequality and Injustice in Our Global Economy.* (Helsinki, Finland: WIDER Annual Lecture). Available at http://www.wider.unu.edu/publications/annual-lectures/annual-lecture-2005.pdf.

Black, R. (1998), Putting Refugees in Camps, *Forced Migration Review*, 2, August 1–7.

Booth, D. (1985), Marxism and Development Sociology: Interpreting the Impasse, *World Development*, 13, 7, 761–781.

Booth, K. (1999), *Three Tyrannies* in Dunne, T. and Wheeler, J. N. (eds), Human Rights in Global Politics (Cambridge: Cambridge University Press).

Brown, C. (1999), *Universal Human Rights: A Critique*, in Dunne, T. and Wheeler, J. N. (eds), Human Rights in Global Politics (Cambridge: Cambridge University Press).

Bush, G. (2002), Remark by President George Bush at the International Conference on Financing for Development, Monterrey, Mexico, 22 March.

Bush, R. (2004), Poverty and Neo Liberal Bias in the Middle East and North Africa, *Development and Change*, 34, 4, 673–741.

Calhoun, C. (1993), New Social Movements of the Early Nineteenth Century, *Social Science History*, 17, 3, 385–428.

Cammack, P. (2004), What the World Bank Means by Poverty Reduction, and Why it Matters, *New Political Economy*, 9, 189–211.

Campbell, T. (2006), *Rights: A Critical Introduction* (London: Routledge).

Cardoso, H. F. (1972), Dependency and Development in Latin America, *New Left review*, 7, 483–495.

Castles, S. (1999), Towards a Sociology of Forced Migration Social Transformation, *Sociology*, 37, 1, 13–34.

Chambers, R. (1998), Poverty and Livelihoods: Whose Reality Counts? *Economic and Political Weekly*, November special issue.

Chambers, R. (2005), *Ideas for Development* (London: Earthscan).

Chang, H. J. (2002), *Kicking Away the Ladder: Development Strategy in Historical Perspective* (London: Anthem Press).

Chang, H. J. and Grabel, I. (2004), *Reclaiming Development: An Alternative Economic Policy Manual* (London: Zed Press).

Chimhowu, A. and Woodhouse, P. (2006), Customary v Property rights: Dynamic and Trajectories of Vernacular Land Markets in Sub-Saharan Africa, *Journal of Agrarian Change*, 6, 3, 346–371.

Chimni, S. B. (2000), Globalisation, Humanitarianism and the Erosion of Refugee Protection, *Oxford Refugee Studies Centre*, Working Paper 3, 1–23.

Chomsky, N. (2003), *Hegemony or Survival: America's Quest for Global Domination* (London: Penguin Books).

Christian Aid (2004), *Behind the Mask. The Real Face of Corporate Social Responsibility*. Available at http://www.christian-aid.org.uk/indepth/0401csr/csr_behindthemask.pdf

Christian Aid (2005), *Central Asia*, Regional Policy & Strategy Paper, *London Christian Aid*.

Cohen, A. G. (1994), Amartya Sen's Unequal World, *New Left Review*, 117–129.

Cohen, A. G. (1995), *Self-Ownership, Freedom, and Equality* (Cambridge: Cambridge University Press).

Colas, A. (2002), *International Civil Society* (Oxford: Polity).

Collier, P. and Dollar, D. (2002), *Globalisation, Growth and Poverty: Building an Inclusive World Economy* (Oxford: Oxford University Press).

Commission on Global Governance (1995), *Our Global Neighbourhood* (Oxford: Oxford University Press).

Conway, T. et al. (2001), *To Claim Our Rights: Livelihood Security, Human Rights and Sustainable Development* (London: Overseas Development Institute).

Conway, T., de Haan A., and Norton A. (2002), Nets, Ropes, Ladders and Trampolines: The Place of Social Protection Within Current Debates on Poverty Reduction, *Development Policy Review*, 20, 5, 533–540.

Cornwall, A. and Nyamu-Musembi, C. (2005), *Why Rights, Why Now? Reflections on the Rise of Rights in International Discourse*, in Pettit, J. and Wheeler, J. (eds), Developing Rights? *IDS Bulletin*, 36, 1.

Cowen, P. M. and Shenton, W. R. (1996), *Doctrines of Development* (London: Routledge) 4–5.

Cox, R. (1992), *Towards a Post – Hegemonic Conceptualisation of World Order: Reflection on the Relevance of Ibn Khaldun*, in Rosenau, N. J. and Czempiel, E. T. (eds), Governance Without Government: Order and Change in World Politics (Cambridge: Cambridge University Press).

Cox, W. R. (1986), *Social Forces, States and World Orders: Beyond International Relations Theory*, in Keohane, O. R. (ed.), Neo-realism and its Crisis (New York: Columbia University Press).

Cox, W. R. with Schechter, G. (2002), *The Political Economy of a Plural World: Critical Reflection on Power, Morals and Civilisation* (London: Routledge).

Crisp, J. (1999), *A State of Insecurity: The political Economy of Violence in Refugee – Populated Areas of Kenya*, New Issues in Refugee Research No.16 (Geneva: Evaluation and Policy Analysis Unit UNHCR).

Dan Zupan, LTC (2004), On the Obligation to Conduct World Police Work. Available at http://www.usafa.af.mil/jscope/JSCOPE02/Zupan02.html

Deininger, K. (1999), Making Negotiated Land Reform Work: Initial Experience from Columbia, Brazil and South Africa, *World Development*, 27, 4, 651–672.

Deng, M. F. and Cohen, R. (1998), *Masses in Flights: The Global Crisis of Internal Displacement* (Brookings: Brookings Institution Press).

Desai, V. and Potter, R. (ed. 2001), *The Companion to Development Studies* (London: Arnold).

De Soto , H. (2001), *The Myth of Capital: Why Capitalism Triumphs in the West and Fails Everywhere Else* (New York: Basic Book).

Dinc, C. (2005), Debating Islamism, Modernity and the West in Turkey, Unpublished PhD Thesis, University of Bradford.

Dollar, D. and Kray, A. (2002), Growth is Good for the Poor, *Journal of Economic Growth*, 7, 3, 195–225.

Donnelly, J. (2003), *Universal Human Rights in Theory and Practice,* (2nd edn) (London: Cornell University Press).

Dunne, T. and Wheeler, N. (1999), *Human Rights in Global Politics* (Cambridge: Cambridge University Press).

Dwyer, P. (2005), *Governance, Forced Migration and Welfare*, ESRC.

Dwyer, P. and Brown, D. (2005), Meeting Basic Needs? Forced Migrants and Welfare, *Social Policy and Society*, 4, 4, 369–380.

Ebadi, S. (2003), Interview with Nobel Laureate Shiriin Ebadi, UN Office for Coordination of Humanitarian Affairs. Available at http://www.payvand. com/news/03/oct/1133.html.

Elson, D. (2002), *Gender Justice, Human Rights and Neo-liberal Economic Policies* in Molyneux M. and Razavi, S. (eds), Gender Justice, Development and Rights (Oxford: Oxford University Press).

Escobar, R. (1995), *Encountering Development: The Making and Unmaking of the Third World* (Princeton: Princeton University Press).

European Council on Refugees and Exiles (2004), *Broken Promises – Forgotten Principles: An Evaluation of the Development of EU Minimum Standards for Refugee Protection* (Brussels: EU).

Evans, P. and Rauch, J. (1999), Bureaucracy and Growth: A Cross-National Analysis of the Effects of Weberian State Structures on Economic Growth, *American Sociological Review*, 64, 4, 748–765.

Falk, R. (2001), *Human Rights Horizons: The Pursuit of Justice in a Globalising World* (London: Routledge).

Fine, B. (2002), *Social Capital Verses Social Theory: Political Economy and Social Sciences at the Turn of the Millennium* (London: Routledge).

Fortin, A. (2001), 'The Meaning of "Protection" in the Refugee Definition', *International Journal of Refugee Law*, 12, 4, 548–576.

Foucault, M. (1976), *The History of Sexuality* (London: Penguin Books).

Frank, A. G. (1971), *Capitalism and Underdevelopment in Latin America* (London: Penguin).

Frank, G. (1967), *Capitalism and Underdevelopment in Latin America* (New York: Monthly Review Press).

Friedman, M. (1962), *Capitalism and Freedom* (Chicago: Chicago University Press).

Fryan, J. G., Beck, P. M. and Mellahi, K. (2000), Maintaining Corporate Domination After Decolonisation: The First Move Advantage of Shell–BP in Nigeria, *Review of African Political Economy*, 27, 85, 407–425.

Fukuyama, F. (1992), *The End of History and the Last Man* (New York: The Free Press).

Fukuyama, F. (2006), *After the Neo Cons* (London: Profile Books).

Gasper, D. (2006), Cosmopolitan Presumptions? On Martha Nussbaum and Her Commentators, *Development and Change*, 37, 6, 1227–1246.

Gaventa, J. (2002), Making Rights Real: Exploring Citizenship, Participation and Accountability, *IDS Bulletin*, 33, 2, April, 1–12.

Gellner, E. (1994), *Conditions of Liberty: Civil Society and its Rivals* (London: Penguin).

Gellner, E. and Cansino, C. (1996), *Liberalism in Modern Timse: Essays in Honour of Merquire* (London: Central European University Press).

Geras, N. (1991), *Justice* in Bottomore, T. et al. (eds), A Dictionary of Marxist Thought (Oxford: Blackwell) (2nd edn) 276–277.

Giddens, A. (1990), *The Consequences of Modernity* (Cambridge: Polity Press).

Giddens, A. (1998), *The Third Way: The Renewal of Social Democracy* (London: The Polity Press).

Giovanni, A. C., Jolly, R., and Stewart, F. (1987), *Adjustment with a Human Face: Protecting the Vulnerable and Promoting Growth, Vol 1* (Oxford: Clarendon Press).

Golooba-Mutebi, F. (2004), Refugees Livelihoods, Confronting Uncertainty and Responding to Adversity: Mozambique Refugee in Limpopo Province South Africa, *New Issues in Refugee Research*, Working Paper 15, UNHRC, 1–129.

Greige, G. Hulme, D. and Turner, D. (2007), *Challenging Global Inequality: Development Theory and Practice in the 21st Century* (London: Palgrave Machmillan).

Green, M. and Hulme, D. (2005), From Correlated and Characteristics to Causes: Thinking About Poverty from Chronic Poverty Perspective, *World Development*, 33, 6, 867–879.

Griffin, K. (2003), Economic Globalisation and Institutions of Global Governance, *Development and Change*, 34, 4, 789–807.

Gro Harlem Brundtland (1987), World Commission on Environment and Development, *Our Common Future* (Oxford: Oxford University Press).

Halliday, F. (1995), *Human Rights and the Islamic Middle East: Universalism and Relativism* in Halliday, F.(ed.), Islam and the Myth of Confrontation (London: Tauris).

Hanak, I. (2000), Working Her Way out of Poverty: Micro-Credit Programms Undelivered Promises in Poverty Alleviation, *Journal fur Entwicklungspolitik*, 16, 3, 303–423.

Hann, C. and Dunn, E. (eds), (1996), *Civil Society: Challenging Western Models* (London: Routledge).

Harrison, R. (2005), 'Can Technology Ease Africa's Woes?', Available at http://today.reuters.com/news/newsArticle.aspx?type=technologyNews&storyID=2005-11-16T012245Z_01_MCC604869_RTRUKOC_0_US-AFRICA.xml&archived=False Reuters, as viewed on November 15 2005.

Haugaard, M. (2002), *Power: A Reader* (Manchester: Manchester University Press).

Hayek, F. A. (1944), *The Road to Serfdom*, (2nd edn) (London: Routledge and Kegan Paul).

Hayek, F. A. (1976), *The Mirage of Social Justice*, Vol. II of Law, Legislation and Liberty (London: Routledge and Kegan Paul).

Hayter, T (2004), *Open Borders: The Case Against Immigration Controls* (London: Pluto Press).

Held, D. (2004), *Global Governance: The Social Democratic Alternative to the Washington Consensus* (Cambridge: Polity Press).

Held, D. (2005), *Globalisation, Corporate Practice, and Cosmopolitan Social Standards*, in Kuper, A. (ed.), Global Responsibilities: Who must deliver on Human Rights? (London: Routledge).

Henderson, J., Hulme, D., Jalilian, H. and Phillips, R. (2003), Bureaucratic Effects: 'Weberian' State Structures and Poverty Reduction. Working Paper 31, Manchester: IDPM/Chronic Poverty Research Centre (CPRC), 1–29.

Hickey, S. and Bracking, S. (2005), Exploring the Politics of Chronic Poverty: From Representation to a Politics of Justice? *World Development*, 33, 6, 851–865.

Hirst, P. (2000), *Democracy and Governance*, in Pierre, J. (ed.), Debating Governance: Authority, Steering and Democracy (Oxford: University Press).

Hirst, P. and Thompson, G. (1996), *Globalisation in Question* (Cambridge: Polity Press).

Hobsbawm, E. (1995), The Future of the State, *Development and Change*, 27, 267–278.

Hoogvelt, A. N. (1997), *Globalisation and the Postcolonial World: The New Political Economy of Development* (Basingstoke: Macmillan).

Howell, J. and Pearce, J. (2001), *Civil Society and Development: A Critical Exploration* (Boulder, Colo: Lynne Rienner).

Hulme, D. and Shephered, A. (2003), Conceptualising Chronic Poverty, *World Development*, 31, 3, 403–423.

Huntington, S. (1996), *The Clash of Civilisation and the Remaking of World Order* (New York: Simon & Schuster).

Hyden, G., Court, J. and Means, K. (2003), *Governance and Government in 16 developing countries*, World Governance Survey Discussion Paper (London: ODI). 1–28.

Idemudia, U. (2005), Corporate Community Relations in Nigeria's Oil Industry: Challenges and Imperatives, *Corporate Social Responsibility and Environmental Management*, 12, 1–13.

Ishay, M. (2004), *The History of Human Rights: From Ancient Times to the Globalisation Era* (Berkley: University of California).

Jorgensen, H. B. et al. (2003), *Strengthening Implementation of Corporate Social Responsibility* (Washington: The World Bank).

Kabeer, N. (2002), *Resources, Agency, Achievement*, In Razavi, S. (ed.), Gendered Poverty and Wellbeing (Oxford: Blackwell Publishing).

Kamrava, M. (2001), The Civil Society Discourse in Iran, *British Journal of Middle Eastern Studies*, 28, 2, 165–185.

Kaufmann, D. (2005), *Human Rights and Governance: The Empirical Challenge* in Alston, P. and Robinson, M. (eds), Human Rights and Development: Towards Mutual Reinforcement (Oxford: Oxford University Press).

Keck, M. and Sikkink, K. (1998), *Activists Beyond Borders: Advocacy Networks in International Politics* (Ithaca, NY: Cornel University Press).

Keddie, R. N. (1969), *The Roots of the Ulama's Power in Modern Iran*, in Keddie, R. N. (ed.), Scholars, Saints and Sufis: Muslim Religious Institutions Since 1500 (Berkley: University of California).

Khan, I. (2005), *Responsibility and Complicity and the Moral Expectation of Society* in The 2005 Business and Human Right Report: Exploring Responsibility and Complicity (London: Business and Human Rights Seminar Ltd).

Khotari, U. (2005), *From Colonialism to Development Studies: A Post Colonial Critique of the History of Development Studies*, in Khotari, U. (ed.), A Radical History of Development Studies: Individual Institutions and Ideologies (London: Zed Press).

Kothari, U. and Minogue, M. (2002), *Development Theory and Practice: A Critical Perspective* (London: Palgrave).

Krueger, O. A. (2006), Response to Allan Meltzer, *The Review of International Organisations*, 1, 1, 60–64.

Kuper, A. (2005), *Global Responsibilities: Who Must Deliver on Human Rights?* (New York: Routledge).

Laderchi, S. R, Saith, R. and Steward, F. (2003), Does it Matter that we do not Agree on the Definition of Poverty? A Comparative of Four Approaches, *Oxford Development Studies*, 31, 3, 243–274.

Lal, D. (1983), *The Poverty of 'Development Economics* (London: Institute of Economic Affairs).

Leftwich, A. (2000), *States of Development: On the Primacy of Politics in Development* (Oxford: Polity Press).

Leys, C. (1996), *The Rise and Fall of Development Theory* (Oxford: James Curry).

Lister, R. (2004), Poverty (Cambridge: Polity Press).

Little, D. (1982), *Economic Development: Theory, Policies and International Relations* (New York: Basic Books).

Littman, D. G. (1999), Islamism Grows Stronger at the United Nations, *Middle East Quarterly*, September, 59–64.

Locke, J. (1952), *The Second Treatise of Government* (Indianapolis: The Bobbs-Merrill Company Inc.).

Lopes, C. (1999), Are Structural Adjustment Programmes an Adequate Response to Globalisation, *International Social Science Journal*, 51, 162–512.

Lukes, S. (1985), *Marxism and Morality* (Oxford: Oxford University Press).

Magoke-Mhoja, M. (2005), *Impact of Customary Inheritance on the Status of Widows and Daughters in Tanzania: Challenge to Human Rights Activists*, in Bond, J. (eds), Voices of African Women: Women's Rights in Ghana, Uganda, and Tanzania (Durham, North Carolina: Carolina Academic Press).

Marcus, R. and Wilkinson, J. (2004), 'Whose Poverty Matters? Vulnerability, Social Protection and PRSPs', *Childhood Poverty Research and Policy Centre*, Save the Children Fund.

Marks, S. (2003), Obstacle to the Right to Development, Mimeo, 1–35.

Marks, S. (2004), The Human Right to Development: Between Rhetoric and Reality, Harvard *Human Rights Journal*, 17.

Marx, K. (1976), Capital, Vols.1 and 3 (New York: International Publisher).

Marx, K. (1979), *Early Writings* (London: Penguin books).

Marx, K. (2000), *On the Jewish Question*, in Mclellan, D. (ed.), Karl Mark: Selected Writings (Oxford: Oxford University Press).

Marx, K. and Engels, F. (1963), *Manifesto of the Communist Party* (Moscow: Progress Publisher).

Maxwell, S. (2005), *The Washington Consensus is Dead! Long Live the Meta Narrative!* (London: ODI), Working Paper 243.

Mbeki, T. (2003), The Icy Ideological Grip, *Progressive Politics*, 2, 2, 1–15.

McMichael, P. (2000), *Development and Social Change, A Global Perspective*, (2nd edn), (Thousand Oaks, California: Pine Forge Press).

McMichael, P. (forthcoming), Reframing Development: Global Peasant Movements and the New Agrarian Question, *Canadian Journal of Development Studies*.

Milanovic, B. (2005), *World Apart: Global and International Inequality 1950–2000* (Princeton: Princeton University Press).

Miller, D. (1999), *The Principles of Social Justice* (London: Harvard University Press).

Miller, D. (2005), *What is Social Justice*, in Pearce, M. and Paxman, W. (eds), Social Justice: Building a Fairer Britain (London: Politico).

Molyneux, M. and Razavi, S. (2002) (eds), *Gender Justice, Development and Rights*, (Oxford: Oxford University Press).

Montclos, M. A. P. D. and Kagwanja, P. (2000), Refugee Camps on Crisis? The socio-economic dynamics of the Dodaab and Kakuma Camps, Northern Kenya, *Journal of Refugee Studies*, 13, 2, 203–222.

Morvaridi, B. (2004), Resettlement, Rights to Development, and the Illisu Dam, Turkey, *Development And Change*, 35, 4, 719–741.

Morvaridi, B. (2005), *Contentious Development Issues, Displacement and Transnational Network* in Harrison, G. (ed.), Global Encounters: International Political Economy, Development and Globalisation (London: Palgrave).

Murphy, C. N. (2005), *Global Institutions, Marginalization, and Development* (London: Routledge).

Narayan, D. et al. (1999), *Voices of the Poor: Can Anyone Hear Us? Voices from 47 Countries* (Washington: World Bank).

North, C. D. (1990), *Institutional Change and Economic Performance* (Cambridge: Cambridge University Press).

Nussbaum, M. (1999), *Sex and Social Justice* (New York: Oxford University Press).

Nussbaum, M. (2002), *Women and Human Development: The Capabilities Approach* (Cambridge: Cambridge University Press).

Nussbaum, M. (2006a), *Frontiers of Justice: Disability, Nationality, Species Membership* (Cambridge, MA: Harvard University Press).

Nussbaum, M. (2006b), Reply: In Defense of Global Political Liberalism, *Development and Change* 37, 6, 1227–1246.

Nyamu-Musembi and Cornwall (2004), Putting the 'Rights-Based Approach to Development' into Perspective, *Third World Quarterly*, 25, 8, 1415–1437.

OECD (2001), *Economic Survey: Turkey* (Paris: OECD).

OECD (2007), More Effort Needed to Reach Foreign Aid Targets, Development Co-operation Report 2006, *OECD Journal on Development* (Paris: OECD).

Okonta, I., Douglas, O. and Monbiot, G. (2003), *Where Vultures Feast: Shell, Human Rights and Oil* (London: Verso Books).

Onis, Z. (1991), The Logic of the Developmental State, *Comparative Politics*, 24, 1, 109–126.

O'Neill, O. (2000), *Bounds of Justice* (Cambridge : Cambridge University Press).

O'Neill, O. (2005), *Agents of Justice*, in Kuper, A. (ed.), Global Responsibilities: Who Must Deliver on Human Rights? (New York: Routledge).

Overbeek, Henk. (2005), *Class, Hegemony and Global Governance: A Historical Materialist Perspective*, in M. Hoffmann and A. Ba (eds), Contending Perspectives on Global Governance: Coherence, Contestation, and World Order (London: Routledge), 39–56.

Oxfam (2006), *Patents Versus Patients: Five Years After the Doha Declaration*, Oxfam Briefing paper, 1–38.

Peiterse J. N. (2001), *Development Theory: Deconstruction/Reconstruction* (London: Sage).

Perry, E.G. et al. (2006), *Poverty Reduction and Economic Growth: Virtuous and Vicious Circles* (Washington: The World Bank).

Pettit, J. and Wheeler, J. (2005), (eds), Developing Rights? *IDS Bulletin* Vol. 36, No 1.

People's Republic of China to the United Nations (1995), *White Paper – The Progress of Human Rights in China, Information Office of the State Council of the People's Republic of China,* Beijing, 1–23 December.

Pogge, T. (2002), *World Poverty and Human Rights* (Cambridge: Polity Press).

Pogge, T. (2004), The First Millennium Development Goal: A Cause for Celebration, *Journal of Human Development,* 5, 2, 377–397.

Pogge, T. (2005), *Human Rights and Human Responsibilities,* in Kuper, A. (ed.), Global Responsibilities: Who must deliver on Human Rights? (London: Routledge).

Prendergast, R. (2005), The Concept of Freedom and its Relation to Economic Development – A Critical Appreciation of the Work of Amartya Sen *Cambridge Journal of Economics,* 29, 6, 1145–1170.

Pugh, M. (2005), The Political Economy of Peacekeeping: A Critical Theory Perspective, *International Journal of Peace Studies,* 10, 2, 23–42.

Rahnema, R. and Bawtree, V. (1997), *The Post – Development Reader* (London: Zed Press).

Ramadan, T. (2004), *Western Muslin and the Future of Islam* (New York: Oxford University Press).

Rawls, J. (1993), *Political Liberalism* (New York: Colombia University Press).

Redclift, M. (1987), *Sustainable Development: Exploring the Contradictions* (London: Routledge).

Reddy, S. and Pogge, T. (2002), How not to Count the Poor. Unpublished Manuscript (Colombia University).

Reddy, G. S. and Antoine, H. (2006), Achieving the Millennium Development Goals: What's Wrong with Existing Analytical Models? Economic and Social Affairs DESA Working Paper No. 30, 1–35.

Risse, M. (2005), How Does the Global Order Harm the Poor? *Philosophy & Public Affairs.* 33, 4, 349–379.

Rittberger, V. and Zangl, B. (2006), *International Organisation: Polity, Politics and Policies* (London: Palgrave).

Robbins, P. (1996), TNCs and Global Environmental Change: A Review of the UN Benchmark Corporate Environmental Survey, Global Environmental Change, 6, 235–244.

Robert, N. G. and Kay, C. (ed.), (1999), *Latin America Transformed, Globalisation and Modernity* (London: Arnold).

Robinson, W. (2002), Remapping Development in light of Globalisation: from a Territorial to a Social Cartography, *Third World Quarterly,* 23, 6, 1047–1071.

Robinson, W. (2004), *A Theory of Global Capitalism* (Baltimore: John Hopkins University Press).

Robinson, M., Weir, S., Brand, D. and Lindahl, L. (2007), *A Human Rights Approach to Social Justice* (London: Unlocked Democracy).

Rosenberg, J. (2005), Globalisation Theory: A Post Mortem, *International Politics,* 42, 2, 2–74.

Rousseau, J. (1973), *The Social Contract and Discourses* translated and introduced by G. D. H. Cole (London: Dent and Sons).

Rowntree, B. S. (1941), *Poverty and Progress: A second Social Survey of York* (London: Longman).

Russell, B. (1979), *A History of Western Philosophy* (London: Unwin Paperbacks).

Sachs, J. (2005), *The End of Poverty: How We Can Make It Happen in Our Life Time?* (London: Penguin Books).

Sachs, W. (1999), *Planet Dialectics: Exploration in Environment and Development* (London: Zed Press).

Said, E. (2003), *Orientalism* (London: Penguin).

Satterthwaite, D. (2003), The Millennium Development Goals and Urban Poverty Reduction: Great Expectations and Nonsense Statistics, *Environment and Urbanization*, 15, 2–187.

Saul, J. R. (2005), *The Collapse of Globalism* (London: Atlantic Books).

Sayer, A. (1998), *Moral Economy and Political Economy*, Lancaster University, May, Mimeo 1–39.

Sayers, A. (2004), *Moral Economy, Department of Sciology at University of Lancaster*, available http://www.comp.lancs.ac.uk/fass/sociology/papers/sayer-moraleconomy

Schuurman, F. J. (ed.), (1993), *Beyond the Impasse: New Direction in Development Theory* (London: Zed Press).

Sen, A. (1981), *Poverty and Famines: An Essay on Entitlement and Deprivation* (Oxford: Clarendon).

Sen, A. (1992), *Inequality Re-examined* (Oxford: Oxford University Press).

Sen, A. (1999), *Development as Freedom* (Oxford: Oxford University Press).

Sen, A. (2004), Elements of a Theory of Human Rights, *Philosophy and Public Affairs*, 32, 4, 315–347.

Sengupta, A. (2002), On the Theory and Practice of the Rights to Development, *Human Rights Quarterly*, 24, 839–889.

Sengupta, A., Negi, A., Basu, M. (eds), (2005), *Reflections on the Right to Development* (New Delhi: Sage Publications).

Sklair, L. (2001), *Transnational Capitalist Class* (Oxford: Blackwell).

Sklair, L. (2002), *Globalisation: Capitalism and its Alternatives*, (3rd edn), (Oxford: Blackwell).

Slaughter, A. M. (2004), *A New World Order* (Princeton and Oxford: Princeton University Press).

Soysal, N. Y. (1994), *Limits of Citizenship: Migrants and Post National Membership in Europe* (Chicago: University of Chicago Press).

Stammers, N. (1993), Human Rights and Power, *Political Studies*, 41, 1, 70–82.

Stiglitz, J. (2002), *Globalization and its Discontents* (London: Allen Lane).

Stiglitz, J. (2006), *Making Globalisation Work* (London: Penguin Books).

Tarrow, S. (1994), *Power in Movement; Social Movements and Contentious Politics* (Cambridge: Cambridge University).

The Economist (2002), Sustaining the Poor's Development, Leaders, 31 August, 11.

The Economist (2005), 21 May, 32.

The Economist (2006), The Leaders: Of Property and Poverty; Development, 26 August.

Taylor, I. (2005), *Botswana's Development State and the Politics of Legitimacy*, in Harrison, G. (eds), Global Encounters: International Political Economy, Development and Globalisation (London: Palgrave).

Therborn, G. (2000), Introduction: From the Universal to the Global, *International Sociology*, 15, 2, 149–150.

Thomas, A. (2000), Development as Practice in a Liberal Capitalist World, *Journal of International Development*, 12, 6, 773–787.

Thompson, E. P. (1968), *The Making of the English Working Class* (London: Penguin Books).

Thompson, E. P. (1978), *The Poverty of Theory* (London: Merlin).

Todaro, M. P. and Smith, S.C. (2006), *Economic Development* (Harlow: Addison Wesley).

Toner, A. (2007), Structure, Agency and the Popular Development Paradigm: An Ethnography of Development and Change in Uchira, Tanzania, PhD Thesis, University of Bradford.

Toye, J. (1987), *Dilemmas of Development* (New York: Blackwell).

Truman, H. (1950), *Inaugural Address, in a Decade of American Foreign Policy* (Washington: US Government Printing Office).

Tully, J. (1995), *Strange Multiplicity: Constitutionalism in an Age of Diversity* (Cambridge: Cambridge University Press).

Uvin, P. (2004), *Human Rights and Development* (London: Bloomfield Press).

United Nations Commission for Human Rights (2000), *Globalization and its impact on the full enjoyment of all human rights*, Commission on Human Rights resolution 1999/59 A/55/342. 31 August.

United Nations Commission for Human Rights (2002), *Draft Guidelines: A Human Rights Approach to Poverty Reduction Strategies* (Geneva: OHCR). Available at www.unhchr.ch/development/povertyfinal.html.

United Nations Commission on Human Rights (2004), *The Right to Development Report*. (United Nations Economic and Social Council: Geneva).

UNCTAD (2002), *World Investment Report 2002: Transnational Corporation and Export Competitiveness* (Geneva: UNCTAD).

United Nations Centre on Transnational Corporation (UNCTC) (1992), Climate Change and Transnational Corporations: Analysis and Trends (Geneva: UNCTC).

United Nations (2000), *Millennium Declaration*, General Assembly Resolution 55/2. Available at www.un.org/millennium/declation/areas552.

United Nations (2002), *Fifth Report of the Independent Expert on the Right to Development*, submitted in accordance with Commission Resolution 2002/69, U.N. document E/CN.4/2002/WG.18/6.

United Nations (2003), *Draft Norms on the Responsibilities of Transnational Corporations and Other Business Enterprises with Regard to Human Rights*, E/CN.4/Sub.2/2003/12.

United Nations (2004), *Human Rights and Poverty Reduction: A Conceptual Framework*, (New York: United Nations).

United Nations (2005), Report of the International Commission on Darfur to the United Nations Secretary General, Geneva. Available at http://www.un.org/news/dh/sudan/com_inq_darfur.pdf

United Nations (2006), *Humanitarian Situation in Zimbabwe*, No.8, June.

United Nations Development Programme (2000), *Human Rights and Human Development* (New York: UNDP).

United Nations Development Programme (2003), *Human Development Report 2003: Millennium Development Goals: A Compact Among Nations to End Human Poverty* (New York: Oxford University Press).

United Nations Development Programme (2005), *Human Development Report* (New York: UNDP).

United Nations Development Programme (2006a), *Beyond Scarcity: Power, Poverty and the Global Water Crisis* (New York: UNDP).

United Nations Development Programme (2006b), *Niger Delta Human Development Report* (New York: UNDP).

United Nations Economic and Social Council (2005), *Report of the United Nations High Commissioner for Human Rights on the Responsibilities of Transnational Corporations and Related Business Enterprises with Regard to Human Rights,* 15 February. E/CN.4/2005/91.

United Nations Economic and Social Council (2006), Situation of Detainees at Guantanamo Bay, Commission on Human Rights, E/CN.4/2006/120.

UNHCR (2003a), Africa's Refugee Need Urgent Food Aid, Available at http://www.unhcr.org/cgi-bin/texis/vtx/home/opendoc.htm?tbl=NEWS&id=3e4d2 3cc4&page=news

UNHCR (2003b), *The State of the World's Refugees: In Search of Solutions* (Oxford: Oxford University Press).

United Nations Human Rights Council (2006), *The Right To Development. Report of the High Commissioner for Human Rights,* E/CN.4/2006/26, para 77.

United Nations Universal Declaration of Human Rights, (1948), Adopted by General Assembly Resolution 217 A (III), 10 December 1948. Also available from the Office of the High Commission on Human Rights, and at www.unhchr.ch/udhr/lang.eng.htm.

Utting, P. (2000), Business Responsibility for Sustainable Development, UNRISD, Occasional Paper, No.2.

Van Damme, W. (1995), Do Refugees Belong in Camps? Experiences from Goma and Guinea, *The Lancet,* 346, 360–362.

Vidal, J. (2005), Flagship Water Privatisation Fields in Tanzania, *The Guardian,* 25 May.

Vincent, R. J. (1986), *Human Rights and International Relations* (Cambridge: Cambridge University Press) 7.

Wade, R. (2002), US Hegemony and the World Bank: The Fight over People and Ideas. *Review of International Political Economy* 9, 2, 215–243.

Wade, R. (2004), Is Globalisation Reducing Poverty and Inequality? *World Development,* 32, 4, 467–589.

Wallerstien, I. (1976), *The Modern World – System,* Vol.1: *Capitalist Agriculture and the Origin of the European World-Economy in the Sixteenth Century* (London: Academic Press).

Wallerstein, I. (1984), *The Politics of the World Economy: The States, The Movements and the Civilisations* (Cambridge: Cambridge University Press).

Watts, J. (2006), China a New Power Block? *The Guardian,* 4 November, 24– 25.

Watts, M. (1995), A New Deal in Emotions: Theory and Practice and the Crisis of Development, in Crush, J. (ed.), *Power of Development,* pp. 44–62 (London: Routledge).

Weiss, L. (1998), *The Myth of the Powerless State* (Cornell: Cornell University Press).

Williamson, J. (1990), *What Washington Means by Policy Reform,* in Williamson, J. (ed.), Latin American Adjustment: How much Has Happened? (Washington DC: Institute for International Economics).

Wolfensohn, J. D. (2005), *Some Reflections on Human Rights and Development* in Alston, P. and Robinson, M. Human Rights and Development: Towards Mutual Reinforcement (Oxford: Oxford University Press).

Wolford, W. (2005), Agrarian Moral Economies and Neoliberalism in Brazil: Competing Worldviews and the State in the Struggle for Land. *Environment and Planning.* 37, 2, 241–261.

World Bank (2001), *World Development Report 2000/2001: Attacking Poverty* (Washington DC: World Bank).

World Bank (2002), *Globalisation, Growth, and Poverty: Building an Inclusive World Economy* (Oxford: Oxford University Press).

World Bank, (2005a), Consensus, Confusion and Controversy: Selected Land Reform Issues in Sub-Saharan Africa. *Working Paper.* No.71 (Washington DC: World Bank).

World Bank (2005b), Brazil, Innovation increases land access and incomes of poor families. en breve. *Newsletter.* No.70, May 2005.

World Bank (2006), *World Development Report 2006 Equity and Development* (Washington: World Bank).

World Bank (2007), The Immoral Tactics of Vulture Fund Action: the Case of Zambia, February. Available at http://www.liberationafrique.org/IMG/pdf/ Vulture_Fund_and_Debt_Relief.pdf

World Commission on Environment and Development (WCED) (1987), *Our Common Future* (Oxford: Oxford University Press).

Yalcin-Heckmann, L. (1991), *Tribe and Kinship among the Kurds* (Frankfurt: Peter Lang).

Young, M. I. (1990), *Justice and the Politics of Difference* (New Jersey: Princeton Press).

Zupan, D. LTC (2004), On the Obligation to Conduct World Police Work. Available at http://www.usafa.af.mil/jscope/JSCOPE02/Zupan02.html

Index